CW01199492

Standard Catalogue of British Coins

COINS OF SCOTLAND IRELAND
AND THE ISLANDS
(Jersey, Guernsey, Man & Lundy)

PRE-DECIMAL ISSUES

Second Edition

SPINK
LONDON

A Catalogue of the Coins of Great Britain
and Ireland
first published 1929

Standard Catalogue of British Coins
Coins of Scotland, Ireland and the Islands
first published 1984
Updated and revised 2002

© Spink & Son Ltd
69 Southampton Row, Bloomsbury
London WC1B 4ET

The contents of this catalogue, including the numbering system and illustrations, are protected by copyright.

All rights reserved. No part of this publication may be reproduced, stored in a retrieval system, or transmitted, in any form or by any means, electronic, mechanical, photocopying, recording or otherwise, without the prior permission of Spink & Son Ltd.

ISBN 1 902040 47 3

Typeset by Columns Design Ltd, Reading
Printed by The University Press, Cambridge

CONTENTS

	Page
PREFACE TO FIRST EDITION	iv
PREFACE TO SECOND EDITION	v
THE VALUE OF A COIN	vi
CONDITION GRADING	vii
SOME NUMISMATIC TERMS AND ABBREVIATIONS	viii
SCOTLAND—Introduction	1
Latin legends	2
Some Scottish denominations	4
Select bibliography of Scottish coins	5
Map of Scottish mints	8
Catalogue of coins	9
IRELAND—Introduction	103
Latin and Erse legends on Irish coins	104
Select bibliography of Irish coins	105
Hiberno-Norse period	108
Map of Irish mints	110
Catalogue of coins	111
THE ISLANDS—Introduction	197
Latin and other legends	197
Select bibliography	198
Coins of Jersey	199
Coins of Guernsey	207
Coins of Man	213
Coins of Lundy	219

PREFACE TO FIRST EDITION (1983)

Seaby's first catalogue, *A Catalogue of the Coins of Great Britain and Ireland,* published in 1929 was a list of coins in stock offered for sale. Our *Standard Catalogue of the Coins of Great Britain and Ireland,* first published in 1945, was a general guide to values for the collector. In 1962 the first volume of a revised edition was published under the title *Standard Catalogue of British Coins*—Parts 1 and 2 being 'Coins of England and the United Kingdom', followed by Part 3, being 'Coins and Tokens of Ireland' by P.J. Seaby (1970), and Part 4, 'Coins and Tokens of Scotland' by P.F. Purvey (1972). A further major revision in 1978 saw 'Coins of England and the United Kingdom' issued in a larger format as 'Volume l' of the *Standard Catalogue of British Coins*.

Now we are pleased to be able to present 'Volume 2—Coins of Scotland, Ireland and the Islands'. This incorporates not only the previous Parts 3 and 4, suitably revised, but also the coinages of the Isle of Man, Guernsey, Jersey and Lundy Island. The catalogue has been compiled with the collector principally in mind, but it is hoped that the volume will also be a compact general handbook for the archaeologist, museum curator, history student and amateur coin finder, and, for that matter, any person who has a coin to identify and perhaps wishes to know its approximate value. We have endeavoured to incorporate new information that has come to our notice since the earlier catalogues were published and, of course, values have been amended in the light of current market conditions. If we omit all the personal acknowledgements made in the earlier editions it is no indication that the editors underestimate the value of the help they have received from many sources over the years. Collectors, students of numismatics and museum keepers have made a major contribution by their willingness to share their knowledge and expertise. However, they would like to record their thanks to Robert Sharman for his valuable advice in repricing the catalogue and to Alan Miles for providing the two new mint maps. All the photographs in this volume have been taken by Frank Purvey with the co-operation of the British Museum, the Ashmolean Museum, Oxford, the National Museum I of Ireland, Dublin, the Ulster Museum, Belfast, and the owners of several private collections.

We have appended to this preface notes on coin values and grades of condition, i.e., state of preservation, as this is a major factor in determining the value of a coin, and a list of numismatic terms. Under each of the three main sections of this catalogue we have given a brief introduction to the coinage, a list of Latin legends with their translations and a select bibliography. The arrangement of the list of coins is not completely uniform but generally, under each reign, it is divided into metals (gold, silver, copper, etc.), then into distinctive coinages or directly into denominations and varieties, every date of coin being listed. The token coinage of Scotland, Ireland and the Islands will be included in the forth- coming edition of Seaby's *British Token Coinage*. For the new collector we would recom- mend a reference to 'A Beginner's Guide to Coin Collecting', to be found on pages viii–xii in Volume 1.

PREFACE TO SECOND EDITION

This is the first edition since 1984 of *The Standard Catalogue of Coins of Scotland, Ireland and the Islands*. This new edition has been totally re-priced and brought up to date throughout. It incorporates recently published research, particularly in Alexander III, with a re-classification of the second coinage, Sterlings, based on the works of North and Stewart.

Many new varieties of Scottish Milled silver are now listed with prices, and the proof issues in the Irish section have been incorporated within the main body of the text. Many new varieties of Gunmoney have been discovered since 1984, and these have now been included. All the Free State and Republic issue proofs have been included and priced in the main body of the catalogue.

Mintage figures have been included in the Modern Irish and Channel Island sections, whilst many of the more unusual proofs are now included with prices in the Isle of Man section

We hope to publish revised editions of this catalogue on a more regular basis, and with this in mind, we would be grateful to hear from anyone with unpublished material with a view to including it in subsequent editions.

THE VALUE OF A COIN

Except in a very few instances this catalogue will not give the exact value of any coin. Its purpose is to give a general value for a particular class of coin in the states of preservation noted at the head of each column of prices, and also to give the collector an idea of the range and value of coins in the Irish series. The value of any particular piece depends on three things:

Its exact design, legend, mintmark or date.
Its exact state of preservation; this is of prime importance.
The demand for it in the market at any given time.

Some minor varieties are much scarcer than others, and, as the number of coins issued varies considerably from year to year, coins of certain dates and mintmarks are rarer and of more value than other pieces of similar type. The prices given for any type are for the commonest variety, mintmark or date of that type. Values given are our selling prices at the time of going to press and *not* the price we would pay.

NUMBERING USED. The numbering used in the Scottish section is the same as in *Scottish Coins and Tokens*. In the Irish section, however, the first digit 4 has been changed to a 6, thus retaining the essential reference number as used in *Irish Coins and Tokens*. The Islands section begins at 7000 and numerous gaps occur in order to facilitate the addition of new types, etc.

CONDITION GRADING

In order of merit as generally used in the British Isles.

Proof. See page viii.

FDC = *Fleur-de-coin*. Mint state, unused, flawless, without any wear, scratches or marks.

Unc. = *Uncirculated*. A coin in new condition as issued by the Royal Mint, but, owing to modern mass-production methods of manufacture, not necessarily perfect.

EF = *Extremely Fine*. A coin that shows little sign of having been in circulation, but which may exhibit slight surface marks on very close inspection.

VF = *Very Fine*. Only slight traces of wear on the raised surfaces; a coin that has had only slight circulation.

F = *Fine*. Considerable signs of wear on the raised surfaces, or design weak through faulty striking.

Fair. A coin that is worn, but which has the inscriptions and main features of the design still distinguishable, or a piece that is very weakly struck.

Poor. A very worn coin, of no value as a collector's piece unless extremely rare.

EXAMPLES OF CONDITION GRADING

George IV penny *Irish Free State florin*

EXTREMELY FINE

VERY FINE

FINE

FAIR

SOME NUMISMATIC TERMS AND ABBREVIATIONS

Blank	The coin as a blank piece of metal, i.e. before it is struck.
Cuirassed (cuir.)	Protected by armour on breast and shoulder.
Die	The block of metal, with design cut into it, which impresses the blank with the design.
Die variety	A coin of the same type but with a slight variation in the design through having been struck by another die.
Draped (dr.)	Drapery around bust.
Exergue (ex.)	That part of the coin below the main design, normally separated by a horizontal line, and frequently occupied by the date.
Field	That flat part of the coin between the main design and the inscription or edge of the coin.
Flan	The piece of metal as distinct from the design of the coin (one speaks of 'a cracked flan', 'a flaw in the flan', etc.). In U.S.A. 'planchet'.
Graining	The crenellations round the edge of the coin, commonly known as 'milling'.
Hammered	Refers to the old craft method of striking a coin between dies hammered by hand.
Laureate (laur.)	Head with laurel wreath.
Left, or Right (l., or r.)	Coin descriptions normally refer to the *viewer's* left or right.
Milled	Coins struck by dies worked in a coining press.
Mintmark (*Mm*.)	A special mark, usually at the beginning of the inscription, indicating period of issue.
Mule	A coin with the current type on one side and a previous (and sometimes obsolete) type on the other, or a piece struck from two dies not normally used together.
Obverse (O., *obv*.)	That side of the coin which normally shows the monarch's head, gives the name of the country or shows the main type.
Pattern	A number of pattern pieces exist for coins, the designs of which were not adopted for currency. These are not included in this catalogue.
Penny ('d', i.e., from *denarius*)	
Proof	A coin struck as a specimen of the coinage from specially prepared dies with polished surfaces that give the coin a high brilliance (though a few non-Irish proofs have a matt surface).
Reverse (R, *rev*.)	The opposite to the obverse.
Seated (std.)	
Shilling ('s.')	
Standing (stg.)	

SCOTLAND
INTRODUCTION TO SCOTTISH COINS

Scotland did not have a native coinage for well over a millenium after a coinage system had been adopted in Southern Britain and for over a century after the Norsemen first minted pennies in Ireland. This does not mean that coinage was unknown in ancient Alban: far from it, for the occasional Celtic coin from the South has been discovered north of the Border and, of course, many hoards and individual specimens of Roman coins have been found in the areas of Roman military occupation between the Hadrianic and Antonine fortification systems, and even north of these along the route to the North-East coast. But in the Celtic lands of Ireland, Wales, Strathclyde and Scotland, where the socio-economic system did not favour large urban settlements, there was not the same need for coin as there was in the more commercially developed South.

The few finds of 9th century Northumbrian *stycas* north of the Border are numismatic records of the Anglian hegemony imposed upon the natives of Lothian and the Strathclyde Britons, though there is insufficient evidence to warrant any assumption that there might have been a Northumbrian mint on Scottish soil. More spectacular are the substantial treasure hoards of the Viking period scattered along the western seaboard from Man to Islay, Iona, Tiree, Skye, N. Uist, Cromarty, Orkney and Shetland, reminding us that the Norsemen held the Western and Northern Isles, Caithness and other points on the mainland, and brought their own contribution to Scottish culture and character. These hoards represent both trade and plunder, comprising principally English silver pence but sometimes including *deniers* from continental Christian Europe and *dirhems* from the Moslem East. Though local tradition has it that the Vikings were the first to exploit the silver mines of Islay there has been no evidence presented for a Viking mint on the island.

Following the Norman conquest of England, after which many of the Anglo-Saxon aristocracy took refuge in Scotland and brought with them the techniques of a sophisticated central administration, the way was prepared for the first native Scottish coinage in the 12th century.

For over two centuries the Scottish coinage followed a course parallel to that of England both as regards general design and quality of metal. At one time in the reign of Alexander III at least sixteen separate mints were in operation. A distinctive Scots gold coinage appeared at the end of the 14th century, and the 15th century saw the first debasement of the silver coinage and the establishment of a base metal coinage. Two essays at genuine portraiture under James III ante-date the earliest English portrait pieces of Henry VII, and during the 16th and 17th century a great variety of interesting types were produced, especially under James VI. The Edinburgh mint was finally closed down shortly after the Act of Union in the reign of Queen Anne.

LATIN LEGENDS ON SCOTTISH COINS

CHRISTO AUSPICE REGNO (I reign under the auspices of Christ). Æ half-merk of Charles I.
CRUCIS ARMA SEQUAMUR (Let us follow the arms of the cross). N crowns of James V and Mary.
CRVX PELLIT OMNE CRIMEN (The cross drives away all sin). From a fourth-century hymn by Prudentius. Æ penny of Bp. Kennedy, c.1452–1480.
DA PACEM DOMINE (Give peace, O Lord). Æ testoons and half-testoons of Mary.
DAT GLORIA VIRES (Glory gives strength). Æ ryal, two-thirds ryal and one-third ryal of Mary and Henry Darnley and Mary alone.
DECUS ET TUTAMEN (An ornament and a safeguard: *Virg. Aen.* v. 262). Edge reading for William and Mary, William III, and Anne.
DEUS IUDICIUM TUUM REGI DA (Give the king Thy judgments, O God: *Psalm* lxxii. 1.). N lion noble, two-thirds lion noble and one-third lion noble of James VI.
DILICIÆ DOMINI COR HUMILE (An humble heart is the delight of the Lord). Æ testoons and half-testoons of Mary.
DILIGITE IUSTICIAM (Observe justice). N forty-four shillings of Mary.
DOMINUS PROTECTOR MEUS ET LIBERATOR MEUS (God is my Defender and my Redeemer: *comp. Psalm* lxx. 6). Æ groats and half-groats from David II; N lions and demis of Robert III.
ECCE ANCILLA DOMINI (Behold the handmaid of the Lord: *Luke* i. 38). N twenty shillings of Mary.
EXURGA T DEUS ET DISSIPENTUR INIMICI EIUS (Let God arise and let His enemies be scattered: *Psalm* lxviii. 1). N unicorns and half unicorns from James III; N crown of Mary, dated 1561; Æ ryal, two-thirds ryal and one-third ryal of Mary and Henry and Mary alone. N ducat of James VI.
FACIAM EOS IN GENTEM UNAM (I will make them one nation: *Ezek*. xxxvii. 22). N unit of James VI.
FECIT UTRAQUE UNUM (He has made both one). Æ testoon of Mary and Francis.
FLORENT SCEPTRA PIIS REGNA HIS IOVA DAT NUMERATQUE (Sceptres flourish with the pious, Jehovah gives them kingdoms and numbers them). N thistle noble of James VI.
HENRICUS ROSAS REGNA IACOBUS (Henry (united) the roses, James the kingdoms). N double crown and Britain crown of James VI.
HIS DIFFERT REGE TYRANNUS (In these a tyrant differs from a king). Æ balance half merk and quarter merk of James VI.
HIS PRÆSUM UT PROSIM (I am set over them, that I may be profitable to them). N unit of Charles I.
HONOR REGIS IUDICIUM DILIGIT (The King's power loveth judgment: *Psalm* xcix. 4). N ducat, two-thirds ducat and one-third ducat of James V; Æ 40s., 30s., 20s., and 10s. of James VI.
HORUM TUTA FIDES (The faith of these is whole). N ducat of Mary.
IN IUSTITIA TUA LIBERA NOS DOMINE (Deliver us, O Lord, in Thy righteousness: *comp. Psalm* xxxi. 1). Æ pattern half testoon of Mary and Francis.
IN UTRUNQUE PARATUS (Prepared for either, *i.e.* peace or war). N twenty pound piece of James VI.
IN VIRTUTE TUA LIBERA ME (In Thy strength deliver me). Æ testoons and half testoons of Mary.
IAM NON SUNT DUO SED UNA CARO (They are no more twain, but one flesh: *Matt*. xix. 6). Billon groat or 'non sunt' of Mary and Francis.
IESUS AUTEM TRANSIENS PER MEDIUM ILLORUM IBAT (But Jesus, passing through the midst of them, went His way: *Luke* iv. 30). N noble of David II.
IUSTITIA THRONUM FIRMAT (Justice strengthens the throne). Æ twenty pence and two shillings of Charles I.

IUSTUS FIDE VIVIT (The just man lives by faith: *comp. Rom.* i. 17). N three pounds and thirty shillings of Mary.

MONETA PAUPERUM (Money of the poor). Æ farthing of *c*.1452–1480.

NEMO ME IMPUNE LACESSET (No one shall hurt me with impunity): R two merk and one merk; 16s., 8s., 4s., 2s.; 10s., 5s., 30d., and 10d. of James VI. Æ 2d. of Charles I, 60s. and Æ of William and Mary.

PARCERE SUBJECTIS ET DEBELLARE SUPERBOS (To spare the humbled and subdue the proud: *Virg. Aen.* vi. 854). N twenty pound piece of James VI.

PER LIGNUM CRUCIS SALVI SUMUS (By the wood of the Cross are we saved). N crown of James V.

POST 5 & 100 PROAVOS INVICTA MANENT HÆC (After one hundred and five ancestors these remain unconquered). N lion noble, two-thirds lion noble and one-third lion noble of James VI.

PRO ME SI MEREOR IN ME (For me; but against me, if I deserve). R ryal, two-thirds ryal and one-third ryal of James VI.

PROTEGIT ET ORNAT (It protects and adorns). R 60s. and 40s. of William and Mary.

QUÆ DEUS CONIUNXIT NEMO SEPARET (What God hath joined together, let no man put asunder: *Matt.* xix. 6). R 60s., 30s., 12s., and 6s. of James VI and Charles I, and R half merk of Charles I.

QUOS DEUS CONIUNXIT HOMO NON SEPARET (Those whom God hath joined together, let not man put asunder). R ryal of Mary and Henry.

REGEM IOVA PROTEGIT (Jehovah protects the king). R thistle merk, half thistle merk, quarter thistle merk, and one-eighth thistle merk of James VI.

SALUS POPULI SUPREMA LEX (The safety of the People is the supreme law). N sword and sceptre and half sword and sceptre pieces of James VI.

SALUS REIPUBLICÆ SUPREMA LEX (The safety of the State is the supreme law). R. forty pence and 3s. of Charles I.

SALVATOR IN HOC SIGNO VICISTI (O Saviour, in this sign hast Thou conquered). N pattern angel of James III.

SALVUM FAC POPULUM TUUM DOMINE (O Lord, save Thy people: *Psalm* xxviii. 10). N demy and half demy of James I; lions and half lions from James II; rider, half rider and quarter rider of James III; R groat, 2d. and 1d. of James IV; testoon and half testoon of Mary; noble and half merk of James VI.

SERVIO ET USU TEROR (I serve and am worn by use). Billon plack of Mary.

SPERO MELIORA (I hope for better things). N rider and half rider of James VI.

TE SOLUM VEREOR (Thee alone do I fear). N hat-piece of James VI.

TUEATUR UNITA DEUS (May God guard these united, *i.e.* kingdoms). N half-crown and thistle crown of James VI; R 2s. and 1s. of James VI.

UNITA TUEMUR (These united we guard). N half-unit; Britain crown and halfcrown of Charles I.

VICIT LEO DE TRIBU IUDA (The Lion of the tribe of Judah hath prevailed: *Rev.* v. 5). R testoon of Mary and Francis.

VICIT VERITAS (Truth has conquered). Æ lion or hardhead of Mary, Francis and Mary, and James VI.

VINCIT VERITAS (Truth conquers). Æ hardhead of James VI.

XPC. REGNAT XPC. VINCIT XPC. IMPERAT (Christ reigns, Christ conquers, Christ commands). N lions and demies from Robert III.

SOME SCOTTISH DENOMINATIONS

Not all multiples and fractions are included in this list.

Gold
Crown (or écu). 20 shillings Scots, James V; 22s. Mary.
Britain Crown. £3 Scots, James I and Charles I.
Thistle Crown. 48s. Scots, James VI.
Demy. 9s., James I and II.
Ducat. 40s., James V; 60s., Mary; 80s., James VI.
Hat piece. 80s., James VI 1591–3.
Lion. 5s., Robert III; 10s., James II; 13s. 4d., James IV.
Lion Noble. 75s., James VI 1584–8.
Noble (half merk). 6s. 8d., David II.
Thistle Noble. 146s. 8d. (11 merks), James VI.
Pistole. £12 Scots, William II (III), 1701.
Twenty Pounds. James VI, 1575–6.
Three Pounds. Mary, 1555–8.
Rider. 23s. James III; £5 Scots, James VI.
Sword-and-Sceptre piece. £6 Scots, James VI.
Unicorn. 18s., James III & IV; 20s., James V.
Unit. £12 Scots, James VI and Charles I.

Silver
Penny. Standard unit of currency from *c.*1136 until 1513.
Halfpenny. From 1280 to *c.*1406.
Farthing. From 1280 to *c.*1333.
Groat. Fourpence from 1357; later rated at 6d., 12d., 14d. and 18d. Scots.
One-third groat. James V, 1526–39.
Testoon. Mary, 4 shillings Scots in 1553; 5s. from 1555.
Ryal. 30s. Scots, 1565–71.
Merk (i.e., mark). 13s. 4d. Scots, 1579–1675.
Noble (half merk). 6s. 8d. Scots, 1572–1675.
Sixty Shillings. James VI, from 1603, Charles I and William & Mary, 1691–2.
Forty Shillings. 1582 and 1687–1700. 30, 20, 16, 12, 10, 6, 5, 3, 2 and 1 shilling (equivalent to English penny) were also issued.
Dollar. Charles II, 1676–82.

Billon
Penny. James I–IV & Mary.
Halfpenny. James I, III & IV.
Plack. 4d. Scots, James III–V & Mary; 8d., James VI.
Bawbee. 6d., James V.
Lion ('hardhead'). 1½d., Mary, 1558–60; 2d., James VI.
Groat ('Nonsunt'). 4d., Mary & Francis, 1558–9.
Saltire Plack. 4d., James VI.

Copper
Farthing. James III.
Penny. James III & VI, Charles I.
Turner ('bodle'). 2d., James VI to William III.
Bawbee. 6d., Charles II to William & Mary.

SELECT BIBLIOGRAPHY OF SCOTTISH COINS

Included in this list are books which although not specifically on Scottish coins or tokens contain useful information.

ANDERSON, J. *Diplomatum et Numismatum Scotiae Thesaurus*. 1739.

RUDDIMAN, T. *An Introduction to Mr. James Anderson's Diplomata Scotiae*. 1773.

SNELLING, T. *A View of the Silver Coin and Coinage of Scotland*. 1774.

CARDONNEL, A. DE. *Numismata Scotiae*. 1786.

LINDSAY, J. *View of the Coinage of Scotland* (Supplements in 1859 and 1868). 1845.

WINGATE. *Illustrations of the Coinage of Scotland*. 1868.

COCHRAN-PATRICK, R.W. *Records of the Scottish Coinage*. 1876.

ROBERTSON. *Handbook to the Coinage of Scotland*. 1878.

BURNS, E. *The Coinage of Scotland. 1887* The standard work of reference.

GRUEBER, H.A. *Handbook of the Coinage of Great Britain and Ireland in the British Museum*. 1899.

RICHARDSON, A.B. *Catalogue of the Scottish Coins in the National Museum, Edinburgh*. 1901.
A useful catalogue in the style of Burns.

DAVIS, W.J. *The Nineteenth Century Token Coinage* (Reprinted with Addenda 1969). 1904.
One of the principal sources of reference to the countermarked Spanish dollars used in Scotland.

STEWART, I.H. *The Scottish Coinage*. 2nd Edition with Supplement. 1967. The best and most up-to-date synopsis of the coinage.

STEWART, I.H. ('Scottish Mints' in *Mints, Dies and Currency*, the memorial volume of essays for Albert Baldwin edited by R.A.G. Carson). A masterly treatise on the medieval coinage.

BATESON, J.D. AND MAYHEW, N.J. *Scottish coins in the Ashmolean, Oxford and the Hunterian Museum, Glasgow*. SCBI 35, 1987.

BATESON, J.D. *Coinage in Scotland*. 1997.

N.M. McQ. HOLMES AND LORD STEWARTBY. *Scottish Coinage in the first half of the Fourteenth Century*. BNJ Vol. 70, 2000.

In addition to the foregoing the following list of articles on specific subjects may be of use.

DAVID I and PRINCE HENRY

L.A. LAWRENCE. 'A Silver Coin of the time of Stephen, bearing the mint name Eden'. *BNJ* 1925–6.

G. ASKEW. 'The Mint of Bamburgh Castle'. *NC* 1940.

F.A. WATERS. 'A Coin of Prince Henry of Scotland as Earl of Carlisle, in the reign of Stephen'. *BNJ* XII, 1915.

IAN STEWART. 'An eighteenth century Manx find of early Scottish sterlings'. *BNJ* XXXIII, 1964.

— 'An uncertain mint of David I'. *BNJ* XXIX, 1959.

R.P. MACK. 'Stephen and the anarchy, 1135–54'. *BNJ* XXXV, 1966.

ALEXANDER III

IAN STEWART AND J.J. NORTH. 'Classification of the Single-Cross sterlings of Alexander III.' *BNJ* LX, 1990.

DAVID II

C.H. DAKERS. 'The Rex Scottorum pennies of David II'. *PSAS* LXXII.
H.J. DAKERS. 'The first issue of David II'. *BNJ* XXXII, 1941.
JAMES DAVIDSON. 'Some distinguishing marks on the later issues of David II'. *BNJ* XXVI, 1950.
N.M. McQ. HOLMES. 'An unrecorded farthing type of David II of Scotland', *BNJ* LXVI, 1996.

ROBERT III

C.H. DAKERS. 'Edinburgh light groats of Robert III'. *PSAS* LXXII.

JAMES I

C.H. DAKERS. 'Two unpublished groats of James I'. *PSAS* LXXI.

JAMES III

SIR G. MACDONALD. 'The Mint of Crossraguel Abbey'. *NC* 1919.
R.B.K. STEVENSON. 'Crossraguel Pennies—Re-attribution to Bishop Kennedy'. *PSAS* LXXXIV.
IAN STEWART. 'The attribution of the Thistle-Head and Mullet Groats'. *BNJ* XXVII, 1952.
— 'The heavy silver coinage of James III and IV'. *BNJ* XXVII, 1953.
MRS J.E.L. MURRAY and IAN STEWART. 'Unpublished Scottish coins'. Part IV, *NC*, 1967 and part V, 1970.
IAN STEWART. 'The Glenluce and Rhoneston Hoards of 15th century coins'. *PSAS* XCIII, 1959–60.

JAMES IV

IAN STEWART. 'The Maundy Groat of 1512'. *PSAS* XCVII.
MRS J.E.L. MURRAY. 'The early unicorns and the heavy groats of James III & IV'. *BNJ* 1971.

JAMES V

P. GRIERSON. 'The Eagle Crown'. *BNJ* XXVIII, 1957.
R.B.K. STEVENSON. 'The groat coinage of James V, 1526–38', *BNJ* LXI, 1991.
R.B.K. STEVENSON. 'The bawbee issues of James V and Mary', *BNJ* LIX, 1989.

MARY

J.K.R. MURRAY. 'The Stirling bawbees of Mary, Queen of Scots'. *Num. Circ.*, Dec. 1966 and Sept. 1968.
— 'The Scottish Coinage of 1560–1561'. *Num. Circ.*, April 1967.
— 'The Scottish coinage of 1553'. *BNJ* XXXVII, 1968.
MRS J.E.L. MURRAY. 'The First Gold Coinage of Mary Queen of Scots'. *BNJ* XLIX, 1979.
J.E.L. & J.K.R. MURRAY. 'Notes on the VICIT LEO Testoons of Mary, Queen of Scots'. *BNJ* L, 1980.

JAMES VI

R. KERR. 'The Forty shilling piece of James VI of Scotland'. NC 1948.
J.K.R. MURRAY. 'The gold forty shilling piece of James VI'. *BNJ* XXXVIII, 1969. See also *NC* 1968.
— 'Some notes on the small silver money of James I and VI'. *NC* 1968.

CHARLES I
R.B.K. STEVENSON. 'The "Stirling" turners of Charles I, 1632–9'. *BNJ* XXIX, 1959.
J.K.R. MURRAY. 'The Scottish gold and silver coinage of Charles I'. *BNJ* XXXIX, 1970.
J.K.R. MURRAY & B.H.I.H. STEWART. 'The Scottish Copper Coinages, 1642–1697'. *BNJ* XLI, 1972, and XLVIII, 1978.

CHARLES II
J.K.R. MURRAY. 'The Scottish Silver Coinage of Charles II'. *BNJ* XXXVIII, 1969.

JAMES VIII
HELEN FARQUHAR. 'Patterns and medals bearing the legend IACOBVS III or VIII.'. *BNJ* III, 1906.

ANNE
R.A. HOBLYN. 'The Edinburgh coinage of Queen Anne, 1707–1709'. *NC* new series XIX.

There are however, numerous other notes on Scottish coins and these will be chiefly found in the following publications:

Numismatic Chronicle (NC).

British Numismatic Journal (BNJ).

Proceedings of the Society of Antiquaries of Scotland (PSAS).

Spink's Numismatic Circular.

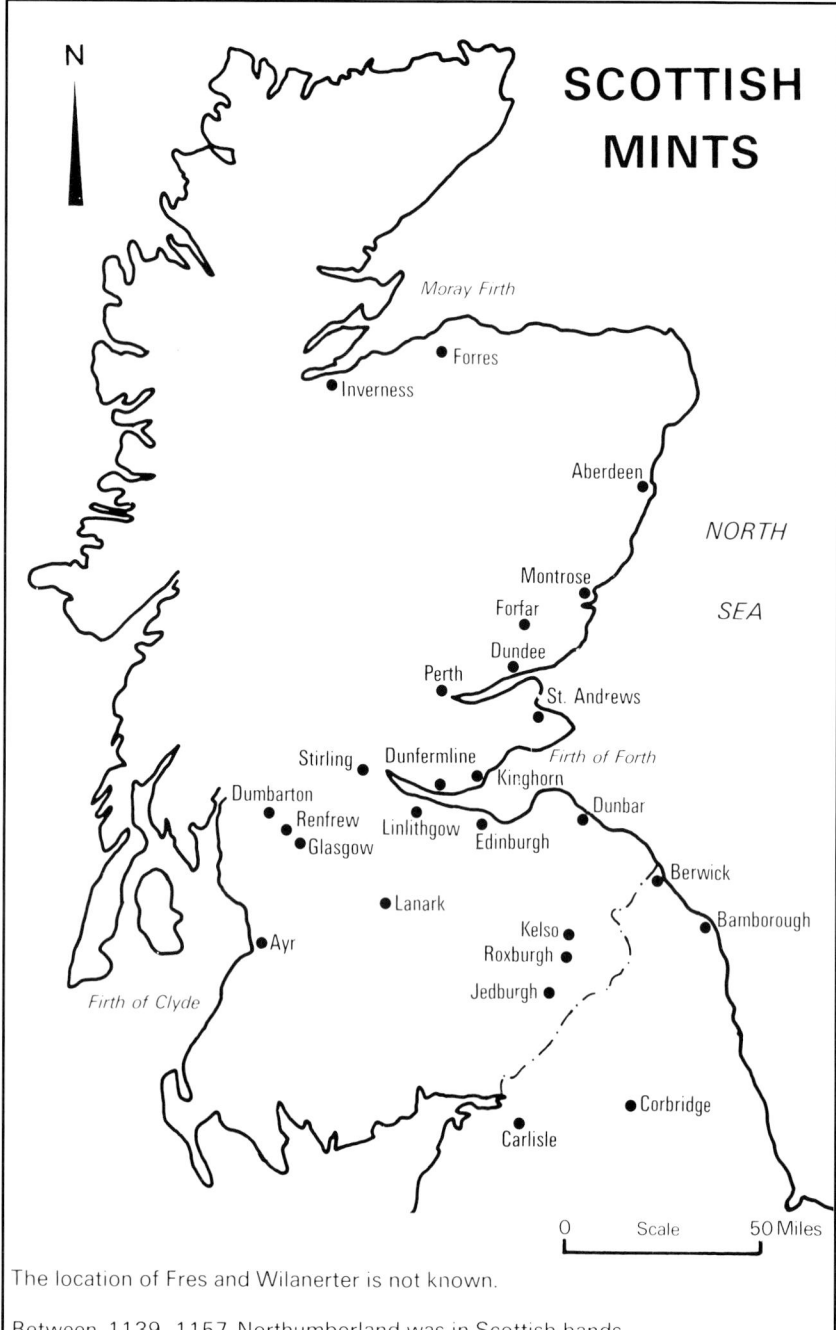

DAVID I 1124–1153

David I appears to have been the first independent Scottish king to issue coins, an event no doubt allied to the capture of Carlisle by the Scots under David and his son Prince Henry in 1136, which gave them an established mint and nearby silver mines. The moneyer of Henry I's last type at Carlisle (Erebald) is the moneyer on a unique coin of similar type but in David's name.

David was the ninth and youngest son of Malcolm 'Ceanmor', and he succeeded his brother Alexander I. His mother was an Anglo-Saxon princess, Margaret, the daughter of Eadward Aethling, so David was the great-grandson of Aethelred II of England. He received Cumbria and Lothian from his uncle King Eadgar in 1107 and the earldom of Northumberland on his marriage to the heiress of Earl Waltheof, thus making him an English baron in his own right.

Although the Scots under David were defeated at the battle of the Standard near Northallerton he concluded a peace treaty with Stephen in 1139 which gave to Prince Henry, his son, the Earldom of Northumberland. For the remainder of his reign Northumberland, Cumberland and Westmorland were in Scottish hands.

Approximate chronology of the early pennies, 1136–65:

Period A.   1136 to the beginning of the 1140s
Period B.   The middle and later 1140s
Period C.   Later civil war years to 1153 and David's death
Period D.   After death of David and Earl Henry.

Pennies only: Weight 22.5 grains; 0.925 silver.

Mints: *Carlisle, Edinburgh, Berwick, Roxburgh.*

		F £	VF £

Period A

		F	VF
5001	As Henry I (type XV), but **DAVIT REX**. Bust I. R. Cross moline-fleury. *Carlisle.* (*Stewart*, fig. 6)	2250	5500
5002	As Stephen (type I) in Stephen's name. Bust r., with sceptre. R. Cross moline, lis in angles. *Carlisle.* (*Stewart*, fig. 290)	525	1350

5003

		F	VF
5003	As last, but in David's name. *Edinburgh*	1350	4000

Period B

		F	VF
5004	Derivative coins of Stephen's type. Blundered legends, sometimes retrograde. Mint names often illegible. *Edinburgh, Roxburgh.* (*Stewart*, fig. 5)	550	1250

5005

		F £	VF £
5005	Copies of English pence. Rev., somewhat as Henry I (type XII) in David's name. Bust r. R. Cross pattée; a crescent or annulet enclosing a pellet in each angle. *Carlisle, Berwick, Edinburgh, Perth, Roxburgh*	750	2250
5006	Bishop of Carlisle (?). Crowned bust r., branch instead of sceptre. R. Cross fleury, three annulets in each angle. *Carlisle.* (*Stewart*, fig. 291)	*Extremely rare*	

5007

Period C

5007	Coins of good workmanship, **DAVIT REX**, etc. Crowned bust r., with sceptre. R. Cross fleury, single pellet in angles. *Carlisle* (moneyer Ricard); *Roxburgh* (moneyer Hugo); *Berwick* (moneyer Folpalt); *St Andrews* (Meinard)	575	1400
5008	Similar, but with other symbols in angles. *Berwick, Roxburgh*	625	1500

5009

Period D

5009	Coins of lesser workmanship, legends blundered, sometimes retrograde, **AVIT**, etc. R. Blundered legends. (*Stewart*, fig. 3)	475	1250
5010	Better workmanship, legends meaningless but composed of properly formed letters. R. Cross fleury and pellets. (*Stewart*, fig. 4)..................	500	1350

PRINCE HENRY 1139–1152
Earl of Northumberland and Huntingdon

Mints: *Bamborough* (?), *Carlisle*, *Corbridge*.
Pennies only. (*Struck during lifetime of David I.*)

Period A

	F £	VF £

5011

5011 I. Crowned bust r. with sceptre (as Stephen, type I). hENRICVS, hENRIC F RE, or NENCON. R. Cross moline and lis in angles. *Corbridge* (moneyer Erebald). (*Stewart*, fig. 8) 1350 4000

Period B or C

5012 II. Similar to last but N : ENCI : CON, etc. R. Cross fleury without pellets in angles. *Carlisle* (moneyer Wilelm). (*Stewart*, fig. 9) 1250 3750

Period D

5013

5013 III. Similar to last. R. Cross-crosslet with a cross in each angle. *Bamborough* (?) (moneyer Wilelm) 1400 4250
5014 Style of *obv.* as last but reading **STIFENE REX**. R. Similar die 950 2750

MALCOLM IV 1153–1165

Prince Henry's premature death in 1152 and David's the following year placed the latter's twelve year old grandson on the throne. He was known as the 'Maiden' on account of his tender years.

The coins of this reign are all extremely rare and it is likely that blundered coins in David's name continued to be struck (see Period D above).

In 1157 Northumberland and Cumberland were surrendered to the English and a stable Anglo-Scottish relationship was maintained until the end of the reign, although several rebellions in Scotland were suppressed in 1160–64.

Mints: *Roxburgh and Berwick.*
Pennies only.

5015

		F £	VF £

5015 I. As David I (5006). Bust r. with sceptre, **MALCOLM REX**. R. Cross fleury, pellets, or pellets and rosettes in alternate angles. *Roxburgh*. (*Stewart*, fig. 11).. 3250 7500
5016 IIa. Facing bust with two sceptres. R. As last. *Roxburgh*. (*Stewart*, fig. 12) .... *Extremely rare*
5017 IIb. As last. R. Cross fleury over lozenge fleury. *Roxburgh* .... *Extremely rare*
5018 III. Bust r. R. Cross fleury, pellets in angles, two with stalks. *Roxburgh* (?), *Berwick* (?). (*Stewart*, fig. 13) 3000 7250

5019

5019 IV. Bust l. R. Cross fleury, pellet in each angle. *Roxburgh* (?) 3250 7500

WILLIAM I 'The Lion' 1165–1214

William I, the younger brother of Malcolm, succeeded to the throne in 1165, the title 'Lion' being given him not for his valour, but for replacing the dragon on the arms of Scotland by the lion rampant. In July 1174 he was captured by the English and under the terms of the Treaty of Falaise in December, he was forced to do homage for the whole of Scotland and also to hand over the castles of Roxburgh, Berwick and Edinburgh. The latter, however, was restored as part of the dowry of Ermengarde, a cousin of Henry II, whom he married in 1186.

Richard Coeur de Lion, in need of funds for the Crusades, eventually sold back the independence of Scotland to William for 10,000 merks, an amount equivalent to 1,600,000 silver pence. Probably most of this sum was paid in bullion.

Mints: *Roxburgh, Berwick, Edinburgh, Dun* (*Dunfermline?*), *Perth*.
Pennies only.

Early issues, *c*.1165–74
5021 As David I (5007), but **+WILELMVS**. R. Cross pattée, lis in angles. Folpold of *Roxburgh*. (*Stewart*, fig. 16) 750 2250
5022 Bust l. or r. R. Cross pattée, crosslet of pellets in angles. *Berwick, Roxburgh* (*Stewart*, fig. 17) 700 2000

WILLIAM I

Crescent and Pellet coinage, *c.*1174–95

[The distinctive sceptres on the two groups correspond to those on the English 'Tealby' coinage (1158–80) and the 'Short Cross' coinage from 1180]

		F £	VF £
5023	I. (*c.*1174–80). Crowned bust l., with cross pattée sceptre-head. R. Cross pattée, pellet in crescent in angles, colons between the letters. No mint name	140	350

5024   5025

5024	With mint name: *Berwick, Edinburgh, Perth, Roxburgh, Dun* (? *Dunfermline*)	125	300
5025	II. (*c.*1180–95). Similar, but cross pommée sceptre-head. *Berwick, Edinburgh, Roxburgh, Eter* (?*Perth*)	110	275

5026

5026	Without mint name, moneyer Raul Derli(n)g. (Probably mostly *Berwick and Roxburgh*)	100	250

Short Cross and Stars coinage, 1195–1214

5027

Phase A (1195–*c.*1205)

5027	Head l. with sceptre, crown of pellets, **WILLELMVS REX**. R. Voided short cross, stars in angles; large coins. *Edinburgh, Perth, Roxburgh*	75	175
5028	— Similar, but head r. *Roxburgh*	125	300

Late William I and posthumous issue

Short Cross, Phase B, *c*.1205(?)–*c*.1230

5029

		F £	VF £
5029	Coins without mint name (legends sometimes retrograde). As previous, head l. or r., LE REI WILAM. R. HVE WALTER (The Edinburgh and Perth moneyers working jointly)	65	150
5030	— R. WALTER ADAM. (Adam replacing Hue at Edinburgh)	110	275
5031	— hENRI LE RVS or retrograde SVRELIRNEh. Coins with mint name	85	200
5032	— R. hVE WALTER ON RO (*Roxburgh*)	135	350
5033	— hENRI LE RVS (DE) PERT (*Perth*)	150	400

ALEXANDER II 1214–1249

Alexander II was sixteen years old on the death of his father, William the Lion. He joined the barons against John in 1214 and much of his reign is one of insurrection, invasion and intrigue. He repelled the Norse invasion of 1230 and died from a fever while trying to regain the Hebrides from Norway.

His first marriage in 1221, was to Joan, elder daughter of King John, and his second in 1239 was to Mary, daughter of Ingelram de Courci.

It would appear that for some twenty years after William's death coins were still being struck in his name. These are divided into two groups. The first is a continuation of the last substantive type of William with double moneyer's names and, rarely, a mint name (see 5029–33). The second group is allied to the style of coins in the name of Alexander, the issue being apparently confined almost entirely to the mint of Roxburgh.

It was not until quite late in the reign that coins were struck in the name of Alexander.

Alexander II in the name of William, issue commencing *c*.1230
(Short Cross Phase C)

5034

		F	VF
5034	Bearded portraits similar to Alexander II. R. Moneyers: Adam, Aimer and Peris either singly or in combination. *Roxburgh*	175	500

	F £	VF £

Alexander II in his own name from *c.***1235**
(Short Cross Phase D)

Mints: *Berwick* (v. rare) and *Roxburgh*.

| 5035 | Crowned head r. with sceptre .... | 650 | 1650 |

5036

5036	Crowned head l. with sceptre	600	1500
5037	Uncrowned head l. without sceptre	675	1750
5038	Uncrowned head r. with sceptre	675	1750

ALEXANDER III 1249–1286

Alexander III succeeded his father at the age of seven. His reign produced the most extensive of all Scottish medieval issues and included the introduction of the round half-penny and farthing. The first coinage, so largely represented in the Brussels hoard, shows a profusion of mints bursting into life during the substantive class III which is represented in all the eighteen mints. A curious feature (although not unknown in previous reigns) is the interlinking of certain mints through obverse dies and it is likely that some moneyers coined at more than one mint. The identity of some mints is open to speculation.

Closely following the 1279 English recoinage of Edward I, a new style long cross coinage was introduced *c*.1280 but without mint names.

This was a prosperous reign, cut short by Alexander riding his horse over a cliff during darkness at the age of forty-four. With all his children dead, his only heir was his granddaughter Margaret, known as the Maid of Norway.

Transitional Coinage (Short Cross Phase E, 1249–50)
| 5039 | **Penny.** Iᴀ. Beardless head l. or r. R. Short voided cross as previous reign. *Berwick, Roxburgh* (unique) .... | 750 | 2000 |

5040

| 5040 | — Iʙ. Similar. R. Voided long cross with large hooked ends. *Berwick* .... | 275 | 750 |

		F £	VF £
5041	— Ic. — R. Normal voided long cross with stars................... (IB and IC are mules between IA and II).	250	650

First coinage. Long Cross and Stars, 1250–*c*.1280
Obv. ALEXANDER REX. R. Mint and moneyer

5042	**Penny.** Type II. Youthful filleted hd. usually to r.	75	175
5043	— Type III. Small hd. l. with neat crown...............................	40	100

5044	— Type IV. Similar, but moulded bust and tall fleured crown with large jewels............................	70	200
5045	— TypeV. Tall thin hd. l.	45	125

5046	— Type VI. Tall crowned hd. r..	75	225
5047	— Type VII. Similar to last, but zig-zag profile, thick jewelled crown, hd. to r. or l.	60	160

| 5048 | Type VIII. Usually a squarish face with low crown, bust to r. or l. .... | 55 | 150 |

ALEXANDER III

The prices of nos. 5042–5048 are for the commonest mint of each type. A complete list of mints and moneyers with a value for the commonest type of each mint is given below.

Lists of mints, moneyers and types

	F £	VF £
Aberdeen: Alexander, II, III; Andreas, — II, III; Ion, II, III; Rainald VII ......*from*	65	175
Ayr: Simon, II, III, IV, VII ......*from*	110	275
Berwick: Arnald, VII, VIII; Iohan, VII, VIII; Robert, II, III, VI, VII; Wales, I, II, III; Robert and Wales jointly, II; Walter, III, VII, VIII; Willem, III, VII, VIII ......*from*	40	100
'Dun': Walter, III, IV; Wilam, III ......*from*	110	275
Edinburgh: Alexander, III, IV, V, VII; Nicol, III, VI; Wilam, III, V ......*from*	45	120
Forfar: Simond, III; Wilam, III ......*from*	125	300
'Fres': Walter, III, VII, VIII; Wilam(?), III ......*from*	135	325
Glasgow: Walter, II, III, IV, VIII ......*from*	110	275
Inverness: Gefrai, III ......*from*	135	325
Kinghorn: Wilam, III, VI ......*from*	150	350
Lanark: Wilam, II, III, V ......*from*	110	275
Montrose: Walter, III ......*from*	275	650
Perth: Ion Cokin, II, III, VII; Ion or Iohan, III, VII, VIII; Rainald, VII, VIII ......*from*	45	120
Renfrew: Walter, III, VI ......*from*	250	600
Roxburgh: Adam, III, VII, VIII; Andrew, II, III, VI, VII, VIII; Michel, II, III, VI; Wilam, II ......*from*	45	120
St Andrews: Thomas, III, IV ......*from*	125	300
Stirling: Henri, III, IV ......*from*	110	275
'Wilanerter': III, VI ......*from*	175	450

Second coinage, *c*.1280–

5049 **Penny.** A. Crowned hd. l. of new style, small neat portrait, ALEXSANDER DEI GRA (G'SIA, G'CIA or G'RA). R. ESCOSSIE REX, four mullets of 6 points each (24 points). Small lettering with closed C and E, thick waisted S, A usually unbarred .... | 100 | 275

5050
5052

5050	— Similar, but REX SCOTTORVM	35	90
5051	B. Varied portraits, with ALEXANDER DEI GRA (or G'RA). R. ESCOSSIE REX, 24 points. Larger lettering with open C and E, thin-waisted composite S, A usually barred	100	275
5052	— Similar, but REX SCOTORVM	30	70

ALEXANDER III

5053   5054

	F £	VF £
5053 Ma. Portrait as class A, ALEXANDER DEI GRA, composite crown. R. REX SCOTORVM, 24 points. Straight-sided lettering, open C and E, thick-waisted S, A usually unbarred	25	60
5054 Mb. Similar bur larger face with wider hair. R. 24–25 points	25	55

5055   5056

5055 Mc. Similar, but crown from single punch. R. 21, 23, 24, 26, 28 points	20	50
5055A R. Similar, unusual letter R with circular loop and curved tail, A barred. R. 24 points	100	250
5056 E. New lettering with incurved uprights. Wedge-tailed R, thin-waisted S, A unbarred. R. 20, 22–28 points	20	50

5057

5057 D. Straight-sided letters, usually with serifs, A barred, C with peaked waist and fishtail wedges, usually, mm. cross potent R. 24–26 points	25	55

5058   5059

5058 H. Obverse of cruder style, gaunt face and crude crown, A unbarred R. 24–26 points, (mules only, with reverses of other classes)	40	100
5059 J. Rough surface as John Balliol's first issue, crude plain lettering, reads GR. R. reads RE/XSC, 24 points	75	225

ALEXANDER III, MARGARET AND JOHN BALIOL

        5061   5063

		F £	VF £
5060	**Halfpenny.** Crowned bust l. with sceptre, ALEXANDER DEI GRA. R. Two mullets of 5 points each in alternate angles of reverse, REX SCOTORVM	100	250
5061	— Similar, but two mullets of six points	85	200
5062	— As last, but one is a star	125	350
5063	**Farthing.** Similar, reads ALEXANDER REX. R. SCOTORVM, four mullets of 6 points	125	350
5064	— Similar, but mullets in two quarters only and erased mullets showing in the other two	150	450

In the absence of mint names on the new style long cross pennies of *c.*1280, mint identity may be linked to the number of points to the mullets and stars on the reverse. Coins with a total of 24 points (Berwick?) account for around 56% of the total output and represent every class including the entire output classes A, B, Ma and early Mb. Those with 26 (Perth?) points account for 23% of output spanning late class Mb through to class H, those with 25 points for 9%, 23 points for 5.5%, 20 points for 4% and 28 points for 1.5%, with trace outputs of 21, 22 and 27 points. A value for each combination of points and the classes for which they are known is given below.

	F	VF
20 points; class E	30	70
21 points; classes Mc, E	100	250
22 points; classes E, D	100	250
23 points; classes Mc, E	30	70
24 points; classes A, B, Ma, Mb, Mc, R, E, D, H, J	20	50
25 points; classes Mb, Mc, E, D, H	25	60
26 points; classes Mb, Mc, E, D, H	20	55
27 points; class E	100	250
28 points; classes Mc, E, D	50	125

MARGARET 1286–1290

Margaret, the 'Maid of Norway', daughter of King Eric II of Norway, succeeded to the throne of Scotland at the age of three following the death of her grandfather in 1286.

Her projected marriage to the future Edward II would supposedly achieve a union of England and Scotland and a cessation of all antagonism between the two countries. Margaret sailed for Scotland in 1290 but unfortunately died in the Orkneys never having set foot in her kingdom.

No coins are known bearing her name, but it is likely that coins in Alexander's name continued to be struck during her reign and in all probability during the Interregnum and for the first few years following the placing of John Baliol on the throne by Edward I.

JOHN BALIOL 1292–1296

John Baliol, a descendant of David I, was chosen as king from the thirteen 'Competitors' for the Scottish throne who agreed to abide by the arbitration of Edward I of England in 1291.

His coins are of the same type as Alexander's but of coarser workmanship at first. Apart from the pence and halfpence of the St Andrews mint no mint name is given, but Berwick is likely to have been the main mint as it was under Alexander.

JOHN BALIOL

In all likelihood the system of mint-identity based on the number of points to the mullets on the reverse had broken down by this time, although the principal mint is again likely to be Berwick.

The loss to the Scots of Berwick, Edinburgh, Perth, Roxburgh and Stirling in 1296 was followed by John's abdication in July of that year. He was a prisoner of the English for three years before being allowed to return to his estates in France, where he died in 1313.

5065

		F £	VF £
First coinage, Rough surface issue			
5065	**Penny.** As issue I (5059) of Alexander III, but reading IOhANNES DEI GRA. R. Cross with four mullets, or stars, of 6 points, +REX SCOTORVM. ?*Berwick*	95	250
5066	— Similar, but two mullets of 6 points and two of 5. ?*St Andrews*	135	350
5067	— — R. CIVITAS SANDRE. *St Andrews*	125	300
5068	— — — As last but three mullets of 6 points and one of 5	150	375
5069	**Halfpenny.** As 5065. ?*Berwick.*	275	625
5069A	— As last, but only two mullets of 6 points	400	950
5070	— As 5065, but CIVITAS SANDRE. *St Andrews*	*Extremely rare*	

Second coinage, Smooth surface issue

5071

5071	**Penny.** As 5065 above, but smoother, neater style. R. four mullets of 5 points REX SCOTORVM+	100	275
5072	— Similar, but CIVITAS SANDREE. *St Andrews*	175	450
5073	—As last, but *obv.* reads I : DI : GRA : SCOTORVM : RX	350	850

5074

5074	**Halfpenny.** As 5071, but mullets in two quarters only	175	400
5075	— Similar, CIVITAS SANDREE	525	1250

5075A

| 5075A | **Farthing.** As 5071, mullets in four quarters | 650 | 1500 |

ROBERT BRUCE 1306–1329

After ten turbulent years with armies moving backwards and forwards across Scotland, Robert Bruce, another descendant of David I, was crowned king at Scone in 1306. Edinburgh was not recaptured by the Scots until 1313, the year before victory over Edward at Bannockburn. Hoard evidence would seem to indicate that no coins were issued until shortly before 1320 and may have been connected with the recovery of Berwick.

In 1318, Bruce's reign saw the gradual repossession of the kingdom partly from the English and partly from Scottish rivals. In 1328, Bruce's infant son David was married to the English princess Joanna, sister of Edward III.

All Robert's coins are rare, the halfpence and farthings particularly so. The weight of the penny was reduced to $21\frac{3}{7}$ grains.

5076

		F	VF
		£	£
5076	**Penny.** As 5071 above, but ROBERTVS DEI GRA. R. Mullets of five points	275	650
5077	**Halfpenny.** Similar. R. Two mullets of five points	525	1250

5078

| 5078 | **Farthing.** Similar. R. Mullets of five points in four quarters .... | 750 | 1750 |

EDWARD BALIOL 1332–1338

Son of John Baliol and a claimant to the Scottish throne backed by Edward III of England, Edward Baliol landed in Scotland supported by an English army and was crowned at Scone in September 1332. In 1334 he was forced to flee the country by the barons loyal to Robert Bruce's infant son David, and though later restored by Edward III he finally retired again to England in 1338, surrendering his titles to Edward in 1356 in return for a pension.

No coins are known bearing his name.

DAVID II 1329–1371

In 1329, David Bruce succeeded his father at the age of five, and was crowned in 1331. He had been married to Joanna, sister of Edward III, when he was four and she was six. Following the invasion of Edward Baliol he took refuge with his child bride in France and for seven years various guardians governed in his name. He returned to Scotland in 1341 to take the administration into his own hands, invaded England in 1346 and was captured at the Battle of Neville's Cross near Durham, remaining a prisoner of Edward III's for eleven years. His release in 1357 was on promise of payment of 100,000 marks over ten years.

His earliest coins have the unusual inscription MONETA REGIS DAVID SCOTOR (Money of King David of the Scots) and were probably struck at the same weight standard as those of his father (21¾ grs.) although a reduction in weight took place c.1351.

The influence of Edward III's new gold and silver coins on David is clearly seen as on his release he instituted Scotland's first, though shortlived gold coinage, a noble, closely resembling those of Edward III, also a silver groat (4d.) and halfgroat all struck to the size and weight of the English coins. It is interesting to note that on the new silver coins David used the inscription DEVS PROTECTOR MEVS ET LIBERATOR MEVS (God is my Protector and Liberator) which matches POSVI DEVM ADIVTOREM MEVM (I have made God my Helper) on the English coinage.

The Aberdeen mint was re-opened for a time and as on the contemporary English coins extensive 'privy' marking was used to differentiate the various issues and act as a security control. In 1367 a new coinage of silver was issued at a lighter weight with Edinburgh as the sole mint.

Mint master's initials: I = James Mulekin; D = Donatus Mulekin.

Mints: *Aberdeen, Berwick (?), Edinburgh.*

GOLD

5079

	F £	VF £
5079 Noble, or half-merk (= 6s. 8d., wt. 120 grs.), c.1357. King in ship holding sword and shield charged with the lion rampant, five or six lions on ship. R. Ornate floriate cross with crowns and lions, saltire crosses or trefoils in tressure, IhC AVTEM TRANCIENS P MEDIVM ILLORVM IBAT	27500	75000

SILVER

First coinage
Mint: *Berwick* (?)
First issue (?early 1330s), wt. per penny (?) 21¾ grs.

		F	VF
5080	**Halfpenny.** Crowned head l., MONETA REGIS D. R. +AVID SCOTOR, mullets of five points in two quarters	325	800
5081	— Similar, but legend reads DAVID DEI GRA REX. R. As last	350	850
5082	— — R. REX SCOTORVM	375	900
5083	— DAVID DEI GRACIA. R. REX SCOTORVM	375	900
5084	**Farthing.** As 5080 above, but mullets of five points in four quarters ..	425	1100
5085	— DAVID DEI GRACIA. R. AVID SCOTTOR	400	1000
5086	— As last. R. REX SCOTORVM	400	1000

DAVID II

	F £	VF £

Second issue (after *c*.1333)
Mint: *Edinburgh* (?)

5087	**Penny.** Wt. 18 grs. Crowned hd. 1., DAVID DEI GRA REX (or GRACIA) R. REX SCOTORVM, large lettering, four mullets of six points	30	85

5088

5088	— Similar, REX SCOTTORVM, small letters	25	65
5089	**Halfpenny.** As last, but DAVID DEI GRACIA. R. REX SCOTORVM, mullets of six points in three quarters	225	600
5090	As 5089, but I behind bust. R. I and mullets of six points in alternate angles	275	850
5090A	**Farthing.** Crowned head l., DAVID REX GRACIA. R REX SCOTORVM, mullets of six points in two (?) quarters..........................	525	1250

Second Coinage, 1357–67

5091   5092

5091	**Groat** (72 grains). *Edinburgh.* A. Small young bust l. breaking plain tressure. R. Cross and mullets, DNS PTECTOR MS, etc. in outer circle, VILLA EDINBVRGh in inner circle	65	140
5092	— — Trefoils in arcs of tressure, rosette or saltire stops	85	200
5093	— — Rosettes in arcs of tressure	125	325
5094	— — Pellets in arcs of tressure	100	250

5095

5095	— B. Large young bust l. R. Mullets only in quarters of cross	75	175
5096	— — Cross added in one quarter	90	225
5097	— — D added in one quarter	110	275

DAVID II

5098

		F £	VF £
5098	— C. Older head l. with aquiline nose, pierced pellet eyes	75	180
5099	— — D added in one quarter	110	275

5100

5100	— D. Similar to Robert II, hd. large and ugly, pellet eyes	70	170
5101	— — Pellet behind crown and in one quarter	85	200
5102	— — Pellet on sceptre handle	90	225
5103	*Aberdeen*. A. Small young bust. R. As 5091 but VILLA ABERDON	225	650
5104	— B. Large young bust	250	750
5105	**Halfgroat.** *Edinburgh*. A. Small young bust	75	200
5106	— B. large young bust. R. No extra marks	90	250
5107	— — Cross added in one quarter of *rev.*	125	300
5108	— — D added in one quarter	135	350
5109	— C. Older head. R. No extra marks	90	250
5110	— — D added in one quarter	125	325
5111	— — Pellet behind crown and in first quarter of *rev.*	135	350
5112	*Aberdeen*. A. Small young bust	300	750
5113	— B. Large young bust	325	825
5114	**Penny.** *Edinburgh*. A. Small young bust	50	125
5115	— B. Large young bust. R. No extra marks	60	150
5116	— — Cross added in one quarter	70	175
5117	— — D added in one quarter	90	225
5118	— C. Older head	75	180
5119	— D. 'Robert II' style head	65	160
5120	— — Pellet behind crown and in first quarter	85	225
5121	*Aberdeen*. A. Small young bust	175	500
5122	— B. Large young bust	225	650
5122A	**Halfpenny.** *Edinburgh*. As 5144	*Extremely rare*	

Third (Light) Coinage, 1367–71

The distinguishing mark of this coinage is the star behind the king's head or at the base of the king's sceptre

		F £	VF £
5123	**Groat** (61½ grs.). *Edinburgh*. As class C, 5098 above, star behind head	200	525
5124	— As class D, 5100 above, star on sceptre handle	70	150
5125	— As last, trefoils within tressure	80	175
5126	**Halfgroat.** *Edinburgh*. As 5098 above, star behind head	175	450

5127

5127	— — Star on sceptre handle	85	225
5128	— 'Robert II' style head, star on sceptre handle	90	250
5129	**Penny.** *Edinburgh*. 'Robert II' style head, star behind	135	375
5130	— — Star on sceptre handle	65	175

ROBERT II 1371–1390

Robert, the first Scottish king of the Stewart line, was the son of Walter, the sixth hereditary High Steward of Scotland, and of Marjorie Bruce, daughter of Robert Bruce.

He acted as regent during part of the period of imprisonment in England of David II and was himself imprisoned in England with his three sons for security reasons following the recognition of Edward III as David's successor. He was released in 1370 and peacefully succeeded to the throne on David's death.

The coinage was maintained at the same standard and in the same general style as that of David's last issue, but with coins being issued at Perth and Dundee in addition to those of the Edinburgh mint.

Moneyer's initial: B = Bonagius.

Mints: *Dundee, Edinburgh, Perth.*

SILVER

5131	**Groat.** *Edinburgh*. Crowned bust l., usually star at base of sceptre, trefoils within tressure. R Cross and mullets	75	175

5132   5143

		F £	VF £
5132	— Similar, but B behind head	150	375
5133	— Saltire behind head	175	450
5134	— Saltires within tressure	175	450
5135	*Dundee.* As 5132.R. VILLA DVNDE	325	750
5136	*Perth.* As 5131.R. VILLA DE PERTh	85	200
5137	— Similar but with B behind head	175	450
5138	**Halfgroat.** *Edinburgh.* As 5131	100	250
5139	— Similar, but B behind head	150	375
5140	— Saltire behind head, usually nothing in spandrils	125	300
5141	*Dundee.* As groat, B behind hd., saltire on sceptre handle	325	800
5142	— Similar, but saltire behind hd., sceptre handle plain	300	725
5143	*Perth.* As groat, 5136	85	200
5144	— B behind head, nothing in spandrils, cross on sceptre handle	225	525
5145	**Penny.** *Edinburgh.* Crowned bust l., star on sceptre handle	75	225

5146   5152

5146	— Similar, no star on sceptre handle	80	235
5147	— B behind head	175	450
5148	— Trefoil behind head	135	350
5149	*Dundee.* As 5147, but VILLA DVNDE	375	950
5150	*Perth.* As 5145–6. Star, saltire or nothing on sceptre handle. R. VILLA DE PERTh	85	250
5151	— — B behind hd., saltire on sceptre handle	150	400
5152	**Halfpenny.** *Edinburgh.* As penny. VILA EDINRVR, EIDINBVG, etc.	135	350
5153	*Dundee.* As last, but VILLA DVNDE	375	850

ROBERT III 1390–1406

John, Earl of Carrick, eldest son of Robert II, changed his name to Robert on succeeding to the throne. He was almost totally disabled by an accident which occurred before his father's death, and throughout his reign the administration was in the hands of his younger brother Robert Stewart, Duke of Albany.

During his reign a regular gold coinage was instituted, the lion and its half, the 'demy', being at first roughly equivalent to the English half and quarter noble.

The majority of the coins of this reign follow the regulations laid down in the Act of Parliament of 1393, but the coinage is divided by a reduction in the weights towards the end of the reign, the groat being reduced from $46\frac{1}{2}$ grains to between 28 and 30 grains.

Most of the surviving coins of Robert III are of the heavy issue, although lack of silver being brought to the mint for recoinage (a current problem at the English mints) is not the only reason why the light coins are so scarce. The number of dies employed would indicate a considerable issue, their rarity, perhaps, due to lack of finds of the period.

Pennies and halfpennies were only struck in substantially debased silver.

Mints: *Edinburgh, Aberdeen, Perth, Dumbarton.*

Heavy coinage, 1390–c.1403

5154

		F £	VF £
5154	**Lion** (= 5s., wt. $61\frac{1}{2}$ grains). First issue. Large crowned shield. R. St Andrew crucified on long saltire cross, lis at sides, XPC REGNAT XPC VINCIT XPC IMPERAT	550	1350

5155

| 5155 | Second issue. Small crowned shield. R. St Andrew on short cross .... | 600 | 1500 |
| 5156 | **Demy-Lion** (= 2s. 6d.). First issue. Shield in tressure. R. Long saltire cross, lys either side, large open trefoil above and below .... | 650 | 1600 |

		F £	VF £
5157	— Similar, but without tressure	425	975
5158	Second issue. Similar to last, but small closed trefoils	525	1250

Light coinage, *c*.1403–1406

5159	**Lion** (wt. *c*.38 grs.). I. Crowned arms. R. St Andrew, XPC legend	750	1750
5160	II. St Andrew, often without cross visible, D N S PTECTOR M S legend	625	1500
5161	**Demy-Lion** (wt. *c*.20 grs.). Ia. As 5158, but smaller	600	1350
5162	Ib. King's name and titles both sides ....*Extremely rare*		
5163	II. R. DNS PTECTOR legend	625	1450

SILVER

Heavy coinage, 1390–*c*.1403

5164	**Groat** (wt. 46 grs.). *Edinburgh*. First issue. Rough tall facing bust, three large pellets at cusps of tressure of seven arcs. R. Long cross, pellets in angles	65	150
5164A	— — Fleur de lis in legend	70	165
5164B	— — Nine arcs to tressure	200	525
5165	— — As 5164, but no pellets at cusps, bust breaks tressure	135	350
5166	— Second issue. Neat bust, with or without trefoils at cusps	70	165
5167	— — Similar, but annulets in spandrils	75	175
5168	*Aberdeen*. Second issue. As 5166	275	600
5169	— As 5167	300	650
5170	*Perth*. Second issue. As 5166	75	180
5171	— As 5167	100	250
5172	**Halfgroat**. *Edinburgh*. First issue. As 5164	100	250
5173	— — As 5165	150	350
5174	— Second issue. As 5166	125	275
5175	*Perth*. As 5166	135	325

		F £	VF £

Light coinage, *c*.1403–1406

| 5176 | **Groat** (wt. *c*.28 grs.). *Edinburgh*. Smaller portrait, not well defined, single pellets on cusps of tressure .... | 165 | 450 |
| 5177 | — Multiple pellets on cusps, or four pellets on head .... | 165 | 450 |

5178   5180

5178	*Dumbarton*. Busts varied, three pellets, one pellet or nothing on cusps. R. VILLA DVNBERTAN	650	1500
5178A	— — five arcs to tressure	725	1650
5179	*Aberdeen*. Bust with small head (as James I coins), with or without pellets on cusps	325	800

DEBASED SILVER

5180	**Penny** (wt. $17\frac{1}{4}$ grs.). *Edinburgh*. First issue. Rough facing bust with tall neck. R. Cross and pellets	250	525
5181	— Second issue, neater bust, larger crown	250	525
5182	— — R. Omitting mint, REX SCOTORVM	275	600
5183	— King's name repeated on *rev.*	325	725
5184	*Perth*. Second issue. As 5181	350	750
5185	*Aberdeen*. Similar	525	1250
5186	**Halfpenny.** *Edinburgh*. First issue. As 5180	210	500
5187	— Second issue. As 5181	225	525
5188	*Perth*. Second issue. Similar	325	750

JAMES I 1406–1437

At Robert III's death, his son James was a prisoner of the English. A regency was formed first under Robert, Duke of Albany, and on his death in 1420, under his son Murdoch. In 1424 James married Janet Beaufort and returned to Scotland against a ransom of £40,000. James was murdered in 1437.

The practice of debasing the smaller denominations begun during the previous reign continued through the fifteenth century. As their intrinsic value became less, so the nominal value of the silver groat increased. Gold coins were reduced to a fineness of 22 cts.

Probably the billon pence and halfpenny of group A were struck during the period of the Regency. The fleur-de-lis groats (so called from the reverse which has fleurs-de-lis and three pellets in alternate angles) were the first substantial issue of James and probably resulted from the Act of Parliament of Perth in May 1424, just six weeks after his return to Scotland.

For the second and last time, Inverness is operative as a mint.

Mints: *Aberdeen, Edinburgh, Inverness, Linlithgow, Perth, Stirling*.

JAMES I

GOLD

5189   5192

	F £	VF £
5189 **Demy** (= 9s., wt. 54 grs.). I. Lion rampant on lozenge, *mm.* crown. R. Saltire cross flanked by two lis in fleured tressure of six arcs. Small quatrefoils in arcs, **SALVVM FAC POPVLVM TVVM ONE**, or similar ..	525	1200
5190 II. Similar, but large quatrefoils with open centre	475	1050
5191 — As above, but chain pattern inner and outer circles	600	1500
5192 III. Large quatrefoils with small pellet centres, normal circles	425	950
5193 **Half demy.** II. Similar to 5190	625	1450

5194

5194 — Tressure of seven arcs	550	1350

SILVER

5195

5195 **Groat** (= 6d., wt. *c*.36 grs.). First fleur-de-lis issue *Edinburgh*. Small neat bust, often with various ornaments, sceptre to l. R. Long cross, fleur-de-lis and three pellets in alternative angles, many varieties	110	275
5196 — Similar, sceptre to r.	175	475
5197 — Similar, but with chain circles	225	625
5198 — *Perth*. As 5195. R. **VILLA DE PERTH**	225	550
5199 — *Linlithgow*. Similar. R. **VILLA DE LINLITHGO**	350	825

5200

		F £	VF £
5200	Second fleur-de-lis issue. *Edinburgh*. Bust of rougher work, large crown with tall central fleur	135	325
5201	— *Perth*. Similar	275	650
5202	— *Linlithgow*. Similar	375	850

5203

		F	VF
5203	— *Stirling*. Similar. R. VILLA STREVELIN etc.	425	925
5204	**Penny** (wt. *c*.16 grs.). A. (Probably struck prior to 1424, during the period of the Regency). *Edinburgh*. Bust as Robert III coins, IACOBI etc. R. Cross and pellets, no initial cross	125	325
5205	— — Similar, but lis by neck	135	375
5206	— — Large head with neck, IACOBVS. R As above	135	375
5207	— *Aberdeen*. R. No initial cross	375	950
5208	— *Inverness*. R. Similar, VILLA INVERNIS	625	1350
5209	B. *Edinburgh*. Bust as 1st issue groats, but without sceptre. R. Initial cross before VILLA	150	350
5210	— — Similar, but saltires by neck or crown	150	350
5211	— *Inverness*. As 5209	650	1500
5212	C. *Edinburgh*. As 5209, but annulet stops and annulets and saltires by crown	175	500
5213	— Bust from halfpenny punch	225	675
5214	— *Aberdeen*. Bust as on 2nd issue groats, but without sceptre, annulet stops, sometimes annulets by bust	375	950
5215	**Halfpenny.** A. *Edinburgh*. R. No initial cross	375	950
5216	C. *Edinburgh*. Bust as on 2nd issue groats	450	1250

JAMES II 1437–1460

The murder of James I in 1437 left the Scottish throne to his seven year old son James.

No immediate changes were made to the coins, the first coinage of James II being merely a continuation of that of his father. For the sake of clarity the first and second issues of 'Fleur-de-Lis' groats are usually ascribed to James I and the third and fourth issues to James II, although the change of reign may well have occurred just prior to the end of the second issue.

The second coinage which began in 1451, in an attempt to bring it more into line with the English issues, sees the reappearance of the lion and half-lion, and also a heavier groat worth 12d. A revaluation making the groat 8d. was proposed but apparently never carried out. This coinage was continued in the next reign, until *c.*1467, but all varieties are listed under this reign.

James was crowned at Holyrood in 1437 and married Mary of Gueldres in 1449. Much of his reign was marred by his quarrel with the Douglas family, and in 1455/6 he proposed joint action with the French against England. The substantial support he sought never materialised and after ravaging Northumberland he concluded a peace treaty with Henry VI in 1457. James established annual circuits of the justiciary court and made other beneficial changes in the judicial system.

James was killed by the accidental bursting of a cannon during the siege of Roxburgh castle in 1460.

GOLD

Mints: *Aberdeen, Edinburgh, Linlithgow, Perth, Roxburgh, Stirling.*

First coinage, 1437–51

5217

		F	VF
		£	£
5217	**Demy.** IVa. As James I (5189), but quatrefoils on *rev.* with large central pellets, annulet stops	525	1250
5218	— Similar, but annulet in centre of *rev.*	650	1600
5219	IVb. As 5217, but saltire stops	525	1250

Second coinage, 1451–60

| 5220 | Lion (10s., wt 54 grs.). First issue. Crowned shield between two small crowns. R. St Andrew on cross between two lis, **SALVVM FAC** etc. ... | 750 | 2000 |

		F £	VF £
5221	Second issue (10s.). I. As 5220, but *mm*. crown on *obv*., cross (*rev*.). R. Crowned lis by saint, **XPC REGNAT** etc.	725	1800
5222	— II. Crowned shield between two lis. R. Crowned lis by Saint, *mm*. crown both sides	675	1650
5223	**Half lion** (5s.). II. Uncrowned shield. R. Crown either side of Saint	1000	2500
5224	— Similar, but small crown over shield	1250	2750

SILVER

First coinage, 1437–51

		F	VF
5225	**Groat** (= 6d.). Third fleur-de-lis issue. *Edinburgh*. As 5200, but tall, thinner crown, bushy hair, no extra ornaments	175	375
5226	— Similar, but king's name both sides	350	825
5227	— As 5225, but sceptre to r.	210	525
5228	*Linlithgow*. Similar to 5225	425	950
5229	— *Stirling*. Similar to 5225	375	850

JAMES II

5230

	F £	VF £
5230 Fourth fleur-de-lis issue. *Edinburgh*. As 5225, but bust in mantle and hair more wavy. Spreading ornate crown with tall central lis	200	475

Second coinage, 1451–60

5231

5231 **Groat** (= 12d., wt. 59 grs.). First issue. *Edinburgh*. Bust in mantle as last. R. Crowns and three pellets in alternate angles of cross	275	650
5232 Second issue (= 12d, same wt.). I. *Edinburgh*. Large crowned bust of English style, pellet pointed spikes in crown, annulets by neck, *mm.* cross. R. As last	275	650

5233

5233 II. *Edinburgh*. Similar, but different lettering without annulets by neck, *mm.* crown or cross *(rare)*	165	400
5234 — — — Similar, but saltires by neck	200	475
5235 III. *Edinburgh*. As 5233, but crown with trefoil pointed spikes	185	450
5236 — — — Crosses or saltires by neck	175	425

5237

		F £	VF £
5237	— — — Trefoils by neck	185	450
5238	— — — *Aberdeen*. Saltires or nothing by neck, VILLA ABIRDEN	750	1750
5239	— — *Perth*. Saltires by neck	425	1000
5240	— — *Roxburgh*. Saltires by neck, VILLA ROXBVRGh	850	2250
5241	— — *Stirling*. Lis or saltires by neck, VILLA STERLING	525	1250
5242	IV. *Edinburgh*. New unjewelled crown without trefoils, beaded circles, lettering partly similar to light groats and placks of James III, *mm.* crown or cross	550	1350

5243

5243	**Half groat** (= 6d.). *Edinburgh*. As 2nd issue groats, but crown with small plain spikes and usually mm. cross (*obv.*), crown (*rev.*)	600	1250
5244	— *Aberdeen*	750	2000
5245	— *Perth*	675	1650

BILLON

First coinage, 1437–51

5246	**Penny** (*c*.16 grs.). *Edinburgh*. Group D. Bust and lettering as 5225. R. Cross and pellets	275	750
5247	— *Stirling*. Similar	525	1250

Second coinage, 1451–60

5248

5248	**Penny** (10–12 grs.). First issue. *Edinburgh*. Thin neat bust. R. Cross with pellets in two angles only	300	800
5249	— — R. Crown in one quarter and trefoil of pellets joined by a central annulet in three quarters	350	950

5250

		F £	VF £
5250	Second issue. *Edinburgh*. Bust of English style, mm. crown. R. Trefoil of pellets in each angle	200	550
5251	— — Saltires by neck	225	650
5252	— — Lis by neck	250	700
5253	— *Aberdeen*. Saltires by neck.	*Extremely rare*	
5254	— *Perth*	450	1000
5255	— *Roxburgh*. Lis by neck. R. **VILLA ROXBV**	*Extremely rare*	

JAMES III 1460–88

James III was crowned at Kelso in 1460 at the age of 9. During his minority Henry VI was received at the Scottish court, Berwick was acquired and the truce with England prolonged. The Boyds, in whose custody he had been since 1456, arranged a marriage in 1469 with Margaret of Denmark, part of whose dowry was the Orkney and Shetland islands.

James' extravagance and partiality to favourites alienated him from the loyalty of his nobles who eventually placed his eldest son at their head. He was murdered following his defeat at Sauchieburn and buried at Cambuskenneth.

During this reign new denominations were introduced; in gold, the rider with its half and quarter, and the unicorn (issued at a baser standard of 21 cts.), although the half-unicorn may not have been issued until the next reign, and in billon, the plack and half plack. The thistle head makes its first appearance as a Scottish emblem, and the numeral '3' occurs on some coins to denote the third king bearing the names of James.

An innovation during this reign was a coinage bearing the likeness of the monarch in the new renaissance style, thus pre-dating English coins of similar style by several years.

All the silver issues are of sterling silver (.925 fineness) except for the base silver issue of c.1471 which is of 0.770 fineness only.

Mints: *Edinburgh, Berwick, Aberdeen.*

Mint-master's initials:
A or L = Alexander Livingston. R = Thomas Tod.

GOLD

5256

Issue of 1475–83

5256   **Rider** (= 23s., wt. $78\frac{1}{2}$ grs.). I. King in armour holding sword, galloping r. R. Crowned shield over long cross, **SALVVM**, etc.   950   2250

JAMES III

		F £	VF £
5257	— Similar, but A below king, small lis in front	1000	2500
5258	II. King riding l., inscriptions reversed	1250	3250
5259	**Half-rider.** II. As last	1350	3500
5260	— Similar, but lis below sword arm	1250	3250

5261

5261	**Quarter-rider.** II. As 5260	1500	4250

Issue of 1484–88

5262

5262	**Unicorn** (= 18s., wt. 59 grs.). Unicorn, l. with shield. R. Large wavy star over cross fleury, **EXVRGAT** legend both sides, Roman N's, *mm.* cross fleury	825	2000

SILVER

1. Light issue, *c*.1467

5263

5263	**Groat** (= 12d., wt. $39\frac{1}{4}$ grs.). *Edinburgh*. Facing bust, saltires by neck, *mm.* cross pattée. R. Trefoil of pellets and mullets of six points in alternate angles	225	525
5264	— Similar, but 'heavy' facing bust without saltires by neck.	200	500

5265

	F £	VF £
5265 — T and L by neck	275	700
5266 *Berwick*. As above, T and L by neck	425	1000
5267 **Halfgroat** (= 6d.). *Edinburgh*. As groat, crosses by neck, numeral '3' after king's name	*Extremely rare*	
5268 — Similar, but no numeral	*Extremely rare*	
5269 *Berwick*. As 5267	750	1500

II. Base silver issue of 1471 to *c*.1483 (.770 fineness)

5270

5270 **Groat** (= 6d., wt. *c*. 33½ grs.). *Edinburgh*. Bust half-right in surcoat and armour. R. Floriate cross, with thistleheads and mullets in alternate angles	225	700
5271 — Similar, but T to l. of king's head	400	1100
5272 **Halfgroat**. *Edinburgh*. As 5270	525	1450

III. Light issue of 1475

5273　　　　　　　5274

5273 **Groat** (12d.). *Edinburgh*. Small facing bust with crown of five tall fleurs, *mm*. cross pattée. R. Mullets of six points, and three pellets, in alternate angles, ЄDIПBVRGh	165	450
5274 — Similar, but crown of three tall fleurs	150	425

JAMES III

		F £	VF £
5275	— Similar, but saltires by bust	225	575

5276

5276	*Berwick.* As 5273, VILLA BERWICIh	375	950
5277	— As 5274	400	1000

5278

| 5278 | **Halfgroat**. *Berwick.* As groat (5274) with crown of three tall fleurs .... | 575 | 1350 |

5279

| 5279 | **Penny** (= current for 3d.). *Edinburgh.* Neat round face with low crown. R. Mullets of six points and pellets as groat, no outer circles .... | 225 | 675 |

IV. Light issue, *c.*1482

5280

| 5280 | **Groat** (= 12d.). *Edinburgh.* Small facing bust with low crown of five fleurs, *mm.* cross fleury. R. Alternately pellets and mullets of five points, EDENBEOVRGE .... | 150 | 400 |

		F £	VF £
5281	— Similar, but reverse as 5273	275	750
5282	**Halfgroat**. *Edinburgh*. Crown of four fleurs, I above, A and T by neck. R. I in centre of cross	425	1000
5283	**Penny**. *Edinburgh*. As 5279, but mullets of five points	175	500

V. Heavy issue of 1484–1488 (Rough issue)

5284	**Groat** (= 1s. 2d., wt. $47\frac{1}{8}$ grs.). *Edinburgh*. Draped bust with crown of five fleurs (double punched to show ten fleurs), *mm*. cross fleury. R. Pellets and crowns in alternate angles, ЄDINBVRG	475	1250

This may be an irregular civil war issue, struck in 1488

VI. Main issue, 1484–1488

5285	**Groat** (= 1s. 2d.). *Edinburgh*. Bust half-left with arched crown. R. Pellets with annulet, and crowns in alternate angles, *mm*. cross fleury	175	600
5286	— Similar, but crown and saltire before bust, lis behind	425	1250
5287	— As 5285, but annulet on inner circle before face	135	500

5288

5288	— As 5285, but annulet before bust	150	525
5289	— As 5285, but annulet behind head	165	575
5290	*Aberdeen*. As 5285, but *mm*. mullet on *obv*.	425	1250
5291	— As 5287	375	1050
5292	**Halfgroat**. *Edinburgh*. As groat 5285, but *mm*. plain cross on *rev*.	325	950

BILLON

5293

5293	**Plack** (= 4d., wt. $31\frac{1}{2}$ grs., 0.500 fineness). *Edinburgh*. Shield in tressure of three arcs, crown above, cross pattée either side. R. Floreate cross fourchée, saltire in central panel, crowns in angles	85	250

		F £	VF £
5294	— Similar, but star in centre of *rev*	100	300
5295	— As 5293, but I in place of saltire in centre of *rev*.	125	350
5296	**Half plack**. *Edinburgh*. As 5293	90	275
5297	— Similar, but no marks by shield	125	350
5298	— As 5295, with I in place of saltire on *rev*.	135	375

Billon and copper

5299	**Penny**. *Edinburgh*. A. Bust as on first issue light silver, *mm*. cross fourchée. R. Long cross and pellets	160	325
5300	— B. Facing bust, *mm*. as last. R. Short cross as on base silver coins, slipped trefoils or quatrefoils in angles	175	400

5301

5301	— C. Facing bust with five fleurs (as on later light coins), *mm*, plain cross. R. Cross and pellets	150	300
5302	— Similar, but with three fleurs in crown	165	350
5303	— D. Bust nearly facing, with annulets by crown (sometimes above) and with pellets in angles of *rev*., *mm*. cinquefoil	275	650
5304	**Halfpenny**. As C, but three fleurs in crown	*Extremely rare*	

COPPER (or BRASS)

Regal issues (known as 'Black Money')

5305	**Farthing**. I. (*c*.1466). *Edinburgh*. Large crown, I REX SCOTORVM. R. Saltire cross, small saltire either side	275	750
5306	II. (*c*.1470). Crown of five fleurs, IR below, IACOBVS etc. R. Crown over saltire cross, small saltires in angles, VILLA EDINBVR	250	700

Other issues (perhaps Ecclesiastical)

5307	**Penny**. Issued by (?) Bishop James Kennedy of St Andrews (Previously known as 'Crosraguel' pennies). I. IACOBVS DEI GRA REX, orb tilted downwards. R. CRVX PELLIT OIE CRIM etc. Latin cross in quatrefoil	70	250
5308	— CRVX legend both sides	110	350
5309	IIa. Orb tilted upwards		
5310	IIb. A jewel in each section of orb	150	475

		F	VF
		£	£
5311	III. Rosette in centre of orb	65	250
5312	**Farthing.** I. IACOBVS D G R, crown over IR. R. MONEPAVP, cross with crowns and mullets alternately	225	525
5313	II. Large trefoil containing mullet and three lis, crowns in top angles, no legend. R. As last	175	475
5314	— Similar, but MO PAVPER	200	500

JAMES IV 1488–1513

James IV was crowned at Scone in 1488 at the age of 15. In 1495 he received Perkin Warbeck at the Scottish court and arranged his marriage to Lady Katherine Gordon. For two years he carried out border raids in Warbeck's favour but later made a truce with Henry VII, whose daughter, Margaret Tudor, he married in 1503. Well educated and an able administrator, he instigated numerous legislative reforms. He patronised learning and was interested in astrology and surgery.

Despite rising national opposition to the treaty with England he preferred the alliance to continue while Henry VII was still alive, although closer ties with France were being formed. With the accession of Henry VIII relations between the two countries deteriorated, culminating in James assisting Louis XII of France against Henry. At the head of a large army he invaded Northumberland and was killed at the slaughter of Flodden Field in 1513.

The unicorn continued to be struck at a fineness of 21 carats or worse, while the crown (or lion) was apparently even baser. All the silver was struck at 11.1 deniers (.925) but the billon plack was very base indeed, some having the appearance of pure copper.

All the coins were struck at Edinburgh.

GOLD

5315	**Unicorn** (= 18s., wt. 59 grs., 21 cts. or less). I. As James III, except royal title on *obv.*, Lombardic N, *mm.* lis, crown of three lis around neck of unicorn. Six-pointed star stops	700	1750
5316	— 'V' or broken star stops, *mm.* sometimes cross pommée	800	2000

5317	II. Crown of five lis, *mm.* cross pattée, lis or pellet stops	750	1850

		F £	VF £
5318	III. *Obv.* as last. R. Roman lettering	900	2500
5319	— 4 after king's name, Roman letters both sides, *mm.* crown, pellet and star stops	1250	3250
5320	**Half unicorn.** I. As unicorn 5315, star stops	650	1450
5321	— Similar, but Roman N, star stops or none	675	1500

5322

5322	— As 5316, but *mm.* also lis or two stars	600	1350
5323	— II. Similar, *mm.* cross potent, QR at end of *obv.* legend. R. I in centre of sun of 14 wavy rays	2500	7500
5324	— III (possibly James V). Similar, *mm.* crown, small star in centre of *rev.*	1250	500
5325	**Lion or crown** (= 13s. 4d., wt. $52\frac{1}{4}$ grs.). I. St Andrew standing l., holding saltire cross. R. Lis either side of crowned shield	*Extremely rare*	

5326

| 5326 | II. Crowned shield, lis either side, IIII at end of legend, *mm.* crown. R. St Andrew on long saltire cross | 1350 | 3250 |

5327

5327	**Half lion.** I. Crowned shield between crowned lis. R. St Andrew on cross between crowned lis	1500	4000
5328	II. As 5326 within IIII at end of legend, no *mm.* on *rev.*	1650	4500

5328A

	F	VF
	£	£

5328A Pattern angel, on heavy flan, wt. 491 grs. IACOBVS 4 etc., St Michael spearing dragon. R. Shield on ship, I 4 above, SALVATOR IN HOC SIGNO VICISTI .... *Extremely rare*

SILVER

Heavy coinage, 1489–*c.***1496**

5329 Groat (= 1s. 2d., wt. $47\frac{1}{8}$ grs.). Ia. Neat unclothed bust with crown of five fleurs. R. Crown and pellets in alternate angles of cross, lis in centre 425 1050

This is a reverse die of James III with a lis added.

5330

| 5330 | — Ib. Taller bust. R. As above, but no lis on cross .... | 375 | 900 |
| 5331 | — Ic. Similar, but medieval 4 after king's name .... | 500 | 1250 |

5332

5332 — IIa. (= 1s. 2d., wt. $47\frac{1}{2}$ grs.). *Edinburgh*. Facing bust with thin cheeks, crown of five fleurs, annulet on breast. R. Pellets and annulet in two angles, crown opposite lis in other angles, EDINBRVG 400 950

5333

		F £	VF £

5333	— IIb. Larger bust with heavy eyelids, crown of three fleurs, low spikes between, no annulet	350	850
5334	— IIc. Similar, but tall spikes In crown	375	900
5335	**Halfgroat**. Ia. Facing bust with crown of four fleurs, Ω or 4 at end of legend. R. As 5330	425	1000
5336	— Ib. No numeral at end of inscription. R. As 5330	950	400

Light coinage, *c*.1496–1513

5337	**Groat** (= 12d., wt. $39\frac{1}{4}$ grs.). III. Neat facing bust, *mm*. crown. R. Pellets and mullets in alternate angles, **SALVVM** legend	275	750
5338	— Similar, but medieval 4 at end of *obv*. legend	275	750
5339	— — Also star by neck	300	850

5340   5342

5340	— ΩRA or ΩT (*quartus*) at end of *obv*. legend	250	675
5341	— — Also stars by neck	265	700
5342	— As above, but IIII at end of *obv*. legend	225	650
5343	IV (approx. 33 grs.). Bearded bust, jewels in band of crown, 4 after king's name. R. As above, but with **EXVRGAT** legend	575	1600

Struck as Maundy money from 11 lbs. $1\frac{1}{2}$ ozs. of silver ordered by the king to be coined into twelvepenny groats for distribution in *Cena Domini* in 1512.

5344

		F £	VF £
5344	**Halfgroat**. III. As groat, no numeral, **SALVVM** legend	325	800
5345	— — With stars by neck	375	950
5346	— As 5344, but *obv.* legend ends IIII	350	900

5347

5347	**Penny** (= 3d.). Facing bust, no numeral, *mm.* crown. R. Cross with mullets and pellets..	525	1350

BILLON

5348	**Plack** (= 4d.). I. Shield in tressure, crowns above and at sides, legend ends QRA. Lombardic lettering	75	225

5349   5351

5349	II. No QRA	20	65
5350	III. Similar, but Roman lettering on one side	30	80
5351	IV. Similar, but 4 after king's name, pellet and trefoil stops, Roman lettering both sides	25	75
5352	— Similar, star stops	30	80
5353	**Half plack**. I. Lombardic lettering, QR at end of *obv.* legend	140	375
5354	II. Similar, but without QR	125	325
5355	— Similar, but omitting crowns by shield	135	350
5356	— Similar, but lis by shield	135	350

5357   5360

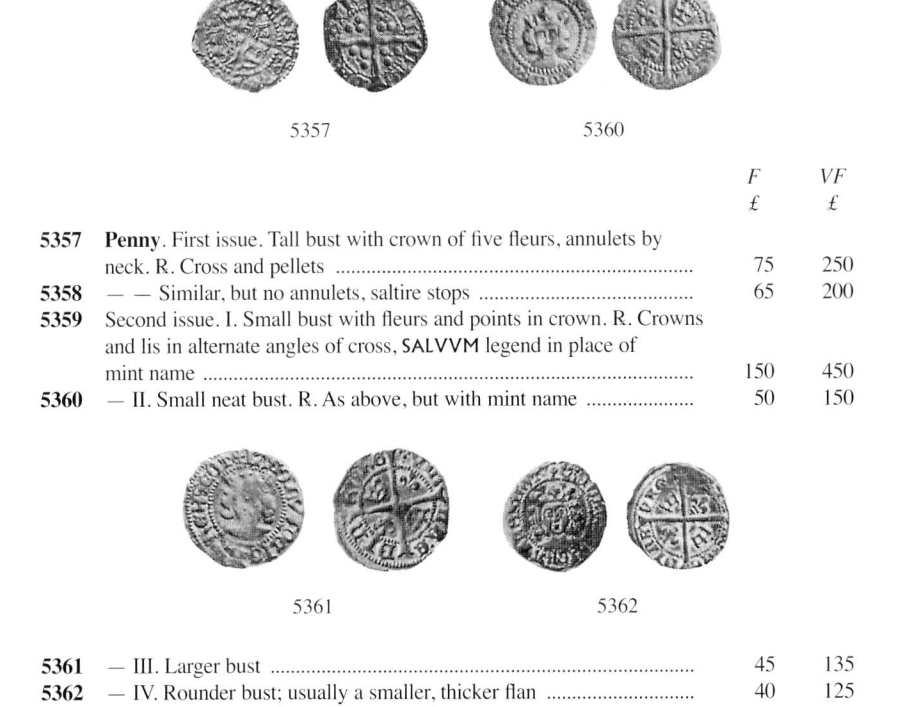

		F £	VF £
5357	**Penny**. First issue. Tall bust with crown of five fleurs, annulets by neck. R. Cross and pellets	75	250
5358	— — Similar, but no annulets, saltire stops	65	200
5359	Second issue. I. Small bust with fleurs and points in crown. R. Crowns and lis in alternate angles of cross, **SALVVM** legend in place of mint name	150	450
5360	— II. Small neat bust. R. As above, but with mint name	50	150

5361   5362

5361	— III. Larger bust	45	135
5362	— IV. Rounder bust; usually a smaller, thicker flan	40	125

JAMES V 1513–1542

James V was a little over one year old at his father's death. Taken by his mother to Stirling, she was later forced to hand him over to the Regent Albany to be educated. He was declared competent to rule in 1524 although he did not rule absolutely until 1528 after his escape from Edinburgh and the clutches of Angus, who had held him in close confinement since 1526. He married Madeleine, daughter of Francis I of France in 1537 and on her early death married Mary of Guise (mother of Mary Queen of Scots) the following year.

He refused to support the English reformation and was given the title 'defender of the Faith' by Pope Paul III. His quarrel with the Douglases and other prominent nobles eventually led to the annexation to the Crown of all the Western Isles. He died at Falkland in 1542, being succeeded by his only legitimate daughter, Mary, then only one week old.

The unicorn continued to be struck in 21 ct. gold although now current for 20s., and was later to be raised to 22s. An 'eagle crown' current for 17s and possibly struck from $22\frac{1}{2}$ ct. gold may belong to this period, although no specimens are now known to exist.

A gold crown current at 20s., was struck to a $21\frac{1}{2}$ ct. standard and the introduction of the ducat or 'bonnet piece' of 40s. dated 1539 provides the first example of a dated Scottish coin.

Silver groats were not struck until late in the reign, all of which are scarce. The commonest coin in circulation continued to be the billon plack which was joined by a new coin in 1538, the bawbee, current for 6d.

The coinage continued to be struck in Edinburgh but gold crowns were struck at Holyrood and are often referred to in contemporary documents as 'Abbey crowns'. Those gold coins countermarked with a cinquefoil were probably struck for James, Earl of Arran, who supplied the gold, this being a family device.

GOLD

	F £	VF £

First coinage, *c*.1518–1526

5363 **Unicorn** (20s., wt. 59 grs.). Similar to James IV, but no numeral, and with trefoil and pellet stops; **X** or **XC** below unicorn. R. James IV die, with cinquefoil countermark, *mm*. lis 1250   3000

5364   5365

5364 R. Mullet or pellet in centre of wavy star, cinquefoil countermark, *mm*. crown 900   2250
5365 — — Similar, but without countermark 1000   2500
5366 **Half unicorn**. As last 1350   3500
5367 **'Eagle crown'** (17s., wt. 53.5 grs.). Crowned shield, saltires beside. R. Dove with halo (Holy Spirit) facing, **IOHANNIS ALBANIE DVCIS GVBERNA** .... *No extant specimens*

Second coinage 1526–39

5368 **Crown** (20s., wt. $52\frac{1}{4}$ grs.). I. Pointed shield with saltire each side, arched crown above. R. Cross fleury, thistles in angles, **PER LIGNV CRVCIS SALVI SVMVS** 1350   3250

5369

5369 II. Shield with smaller open crown. R. As above but **CRVCIS ARMA SEQVAMVR**, annult stops 625   1750

5370

		F £	VF £
5370	III. Similar, but shield with rounded base, trefoil stops	475	1100
5371	IV. Similar, but pellet stops	525	1250
5372	V. Similar, but very small crown above shield	*Extremely rare*	

Third coinage, 1539–42

5373

5373 **Ducat,** or 'Bonnet piece' (= 40s., wt. $88\frac{1}{3}$ grs.). Bearded bust of king r., wearing bonnet. R. Crowned shield over cross fleury

1539	2500	6000
1540	2000	4500

Gold and silver
5374 **Two-third ducat** (= 26s. 8d.). 1540. Similar. R. Crowned shield dividing I 5 .... 1750 3750

5375

5375 **One-third ducat** (= 13s. 4d.). 1540. As above 2750 6500

SILVER

Second coinage, 1526–39

	F £	VF £

5376

	F	VF
5376 **Groat** (= 1s. 6d., wt. 42 grs., 0.833 fineness). I. Bust r., mantled; double-arched crown. R. Pointed shield over cross fourchée, VILLA EDINBRVGH	225	600

5377   5378   5379

	F	VF
5377 II. Similar bust, but single arched crown. R. As last, but OPPIDVM EDINBVRGI	150	425
5378 III. Similar, but with open mantle, sometimes trefoil of pellets in field. R. Rounded shield, OPPIDV, trefoil stops	110	300
5379 IV. Similar, head with pointed nose. R. Similar to last, but mainly colon stops	120	325

5380

	F	VF
5380 **One-third groat** (= 6d.). IV. As groat	135	375

BILLON

First coinage, 1513–1526

	F £	VF £

5381

		F £	VF £
5381	**Plack** (= 4d., wt. 31½ grs). As James IV, but no numeral. R. Crowns and saltires in alternate angles of cross, mullet in centre	20	65
5382	— (1532/3). Similar, but ornamental Roman letters, annulets in spandrills, crowns in all four quarters of cross, **VILLA DE EDINBVRG**	*Extremely rare*	

Third coinage, 1538–1542

5383	**Bawbee** (= 6d., wt. 29 grs., 0.250 fineness). Crowned thistle dividing I 5. R. Crown on saltire cross, lis each side	20	60

5384   5387

5384	— Similar, but annulet over I or on inner circle	20	60
5384A	— — annulet over 5	35	95
5385	— — Annulet over I and 5	35	95
5386	**Half bawbee**. As 5383, but without lis on *rev.*	80	225
5387	— Annulet over I	75	210
5388	— Annulet over 5	70	200
5389	**Quarter bawbee** (wt. 8.2 grs.). *Obverse* type doubtful. R. Crown on saltire cross, *mm.* crown	*Extremely rare*	

MARY 1542–67

One of the most romantic, and tragic figures in Scottish history, Mary, became Queen when only seven days old. Educated in France with the French royal children and brought up in the Catholic faith, she married the Dauphin, Francis, in 1558 and was prostrated on his death two years later. In 1565 she married Henry Stewart, Lord Darnley and the following year bore him a son, who later became James I of England.

Suspicion implicated her and her favourite, the Earl of Bothwell, in Darnley's death by explosion in a house at Kirk o'Field, Edinburgh, in 1567. That same year she married Bothwell with Protestant rites and agreed to her abdication.

She escaped to England in 1568 after the battle of Langside and was imprisoned by Elizabeth. After numerous intrigues and plots she was beheaded at Fotheringhay Castle in 1587. Few historical periods are mirrored so closely in the coinage as that of Mary.

In the first period, before her marriage, the 1553 gold coinage, still being struck to a 22 ct. standard, bears the initials **IG** Jacobus Gubernator (James, Earl of Arran, Regent and Governor of Scotland), while some of the testoons and half testoons have the letter **A** (Acheson the mint master) by the shield.

The second period sees the transition in the royal titles and arms after the Dauphin became Francis I of France.

The first widowhood of 1560–5 is represented by a unique piece in gold, and in silver by a testoon and its half bearing a superb portrait of Mary said to have been inspired by the portrait by the French painter, François Clouet, also known as Janet.

No gold was struck after the first widowhood. Of the last two periods, her marriage to Darnley is noted with the change of titles to Henry and Mary etc. and on a unique ryal the couple are shown face to face although the commonest coins of this and the final period after Darnley's death are the non-portrait ryals and their parts.

Among the billon coins, the bawbee continues to be prolific, and is joined by a 12d groat commonly called a 'Nonsunt' and a 1½d piece known as a lion or 'hardhead' which at its worst was 23/24 alloy.

The mint of Stirling was used for an issue of bawbees and is the last occasion that coining took place outside Edinburgh.

NB The testoons and ryals (and their parts) are often found countermarked with a crowned thistle (see page 62) and the billon placks and hardheads with a heart and star (see James VI, p. 77).

GOLD

First period, 1542-58. Before marriage

5390

	F £	VF £
5390 **Abbey Crown** or écu (Issued at 20s. in 1542, raised to 22s. 10d. in 1543. wt. 52¼ grs.). Crowned shield, cinquefoil each side. R. Cross fleury with thistles in angles, **CRVCIS ARMA SEQVAMVR**	1100	2500

MARY

5391

		F £	VF £

5391 Twenty shillings (44⅙ grs.). 1543. Crowned shield. R. Crowned MR
monogram, cinquefoil below, ECCE ANCILLA DOMINI 2000 4500
5392 Forty-four shillings (78½ grs.). 1553. First issue. Crowned shield
dividing I G. R. Crowned monogram of MARIA REGINA dividing
I. G., DILIGITE IVSTICAM 1350 3500
5393 — Similar, but cinquefoil in place of I G on both sides, 1553 .... 1350 3500

5394   5396

5394 — Similar, but I G on *obv.*, cinquefoils on *rev.*, 1553 .... 1000 2500
5395 Second issue. Crowned arms dividing MR. Crowned monogram of
MARIA with crowned cross potent each side, 1557 .... *Extremely rare*
5396 Twenty-two shillings. As 5394, but crown on *obv.* divides legend.
R. MR, cinquefoil each side. 1553 .... 850 2000

5397

5397 Three pound piece or portrait ryal. (117¾ grs.). Bust l. R. Crowned
arms, IVSTVS FIDE VIVIT ....
1555 .... 2250 5500
1557 .... 3000 6500
1558 .... 3250 7000
5398 Thirty shilling piece or half ryal. Similar
1555 .... 3250 6500
1557 .... *Extremely rare*
1558 .... 3750 7500

	F	VF
	£	£

Second period, 1558–60. Francis and Mary

5399

5399 **Ducat** (= 60s., 117¾ grs.). 1558. Busts of Francis and Mary face to face, crown above. R. Cross of eight interlinked dolphins, Lorraine crosses in angles, HORVM TVTA FIDES 42500   90000

Third period, 1560–65. First widowhood

5400

5400 **Crown** (50½ grs.). 1561. Crowned arms. R. Four crowned M's crosswise, thistle heads in angles, EXVRGAT legend. *Possibly a pattern* .... *Extremely rare*

SILVER

First period, 1542–58. Before marriage

5401

5401 **Testoon**. Type I (= 4s., wt. 78½ grs., 0.916 fineness). 1553. Crowned bust r. R. Crowned shield, cinquefoil each side, DA PACEM DOMINE 1350   4000

5402

		F £	VF £
5402	Type II (= 5s., wt. $117\frac{3}{4}$ grs., 0.725 fineness). 1555. Large M crowned, crowned thistle each side. R. Shield over cross potent, DILICIE DNI COR HVMILE	125	425
5403	— Similar, but annulet over left thistle	135	450

5404

5404 Type IIIa (= 5s., wt. $94\frac{1}{4}$ grs., 0.916 fineness). Small high-arched crown over shield dividing MR, annulets below. R. Cross potent, cross (rarely cross-crosslet) in each angle, IN VIRTVTE TVA LIBERA ME
1556 .... 100 375
1557 .... 110 400
5405 — Similar, but no annulets
1556 .... 110 400
1557 .... 125 425

5406

5406 IIIb. Similar, but low-arched crown, without annulets below M and R
1557 .... 125 425
1558 .... 100 350

5407   5408

	F £	VF £
5407 — — With annulets		
1557	125	425
1558	125	425
5408 — Similar, but A (Acheson) by shield below the R, 1558	250	750
5409 **Half testoon**. Type I. Uncrowned bust l. R. Crowned shield between MR, IN IVSTICIA TVA LIBERA NOS DNE, 1553. *Probably a pattern*	*Extremely rare*	
5410 Type II. 1555. Large M as 5402	225	650
5411 Type IIIa. As 5404, high arched crown with annulets below M and R		
1556	165	525
1557	150	500
5412 — Annulet also above R, 1556	175	600

5413

5413 — Similar without annulets below M and R		
1556	125	425
1557	150	500
1558	135	475
5414 — Similar, but date on reverse only, 1558	175	575
5415 — Similar, A by shield below the M, 1558	275	800

Second period, 1558–60. Francis and Mary

5416   5417

	F £	VF £
5416 Testoon (= 5s., wt. 94¼ grs., 0.916 fineness). I. Crowned arms of Francis (as Dauphin) and Mary over cross potent. R. Large **FM** monogram crowned, Lorraine cross each side, **FECIT VTRAQVE VNVM**		
1558	135	400
1559	135	400
5417 II. 1560. Arms of Francis (as King of France) and Mary, Scottish crown above, cross on left, saltire on r., **VICIT LEO DE TRIBV IVDA**	150	450
5417A — Similar, but no crowns on reverse	200	525

5418

	F £	VF £
5418 — Similar, but crown of five lis over arms		
1560	135	425
1561	250	650
1565, a die sinker's error for 1560	275	750
5418A — Transitional issue (?), as illustration but obverse legend as 5416, ending **D D VIEN**		
1560	650	1350
5419 **Half testoon.** I. As 5416		
1558	175	525
1559	200	575
5420 II. 1560. As 5417, with Scottish crown	150	475
5421 — — As 5418, with crown of five lis	150	475

Third period, 1560–65. First widowhood

5422

	F	VF
	£	£

5422 Testoon (= 5s., wt. 94¼ grs. Bust l. in contemporary costume, date below in tablet. R. Crowned arms of France and Scotland, crowned M each side, SALVM legend

    1561 .... 950 2750
    1562 .... 1200 3250

5423 Half testoon. Similar
    1561 .... 1350 4250
    1562 .... 1750 5250

Fourth period, 1565–67. Mary and Henry Darnley

5424 Ryal (= 30s., wt. 471¼ grs.). I. Busts of Henry and Mary face to face, date below, HENRICVS & MARIA, etc. R. Crowned shield, thistle each side, QVOS DEVS COIVNXIT HOMO NON SEPARET, 1565 .... 32500 80000

5425

5425 II. Crowned shield, thistle each side, MARIA & HENRIC, etc. R. Tortoise climbing a palm tree, DAT GLORIA VIRES on scroll, EXVRGAT legend. Sometimes called a 'Crookeston' dollar.
    1565 .... 275 725
    1566 .... 250 650
    1567 .... 300 750

MARY

		F £	VF £
5426	**Two-thirds ryal.** As above		
	Undated	750	1750
	1565	225	575
	1566	235	600
	1567	500	1250
5427	**One-third ryal.** As above		
	1565	200	525
	1566	275	750

Fifth period, 1567. Second widowhood

5429

5429	**Ryal.** 1567. As 5425, but name of Mary only	300	750
5430	**Two-thirds ryal.** 1567. As 5426	250	625
5431	**One-third ryal.** As 5427		
	1566	450	1050
	1567	350	825

BILLON

First period, 1542–58. Before marriage. Issue of 3/4 alloy

5432   5434

5432	**Bawbee** (= 6d., wt. 29½ grs.). *Edinburgh*. Crowned thistle dividing MR. R. Plain saltire cross through crown, cinquefoil each side, OPPIDVM EDINBVRGI	30	60

		F £	VF £
5433	— Similar, but voided saltire cross	30	65
5434	*Stirling* (Struck for Mary of Guise in 1544). *Obv.* As above. R. Cross potent with cross in each angle, OPPIDVM STIRLINGI	100	325

5435

5435	**Half bawbee.** *Edinburgh.* As 5432, but only one cinquefoil, below crown	65	200
5436	— Similar, but voided saltire cross	65	200

Issue of 11/12ths alloy

5437

5437	**Plack** (= 4d., wt. 29½ grs.). 1557. Crowned shield dividing MR. R. Ornate cross with plain cross in centre and crowns in angles, SERVIO ET VSV TEROR	35	100

5438 5439

5438	**Lion** or 'hardhead' (= 1½d., wt. 14¾ grs.). Large M crowned, annulets beside. R. Crowned lion rampant, VICIT VERITAS 1556	75	225
5439	— Similar, but without annulets		
	1555	30	95
	1556	60	175
5440	**Penny** (wt. 11¼ grs.). I. (1547). Facing infant head, arched crown. R. Cross fourchée with cinquefoils and crowns in angles, OPIDVM EDNBVR	135	400

5441　　　　　　　　5443

		F £	VF £
5441	— Similar, but open crown	145	450
5442	II. Similar, but older face. R. OPIDV EDINBVRGI	150	500
5443	III. (1554). Crowned facing bust with no inner circles. R. Cross fourchee with lis and crowns in angles, OPPIDVM EDINBVRG	200	650

Issue of 45/48ths alloy

5444　　　　　　　　5445

5444	**Penny.** Cross potent with four small crosses potent in angles. R. Crown over **VICIT / VERITAS / 1556**	125	375

Issue of 23/24ths alloy

5445	**Lion** (= 1½d.). As 5439, but dated 1558	30	90

Second period, 1558–60. Francis and Mary

Issue of half alloy

5447　　　　　　　　5449

5447	**Twelvepenny Groat** or 'Nonsunt' (wt. 26¼ grs.). Crowned **FM** monogram, to l. a crowned heraldic dolphin looking right, crowned thistle on r. R. **IAM NON / SVNT DVO / SED VNA / CARO** in panel, date below		
	1558	75	175
	1559	65	150
5448	— Similar, but dolphin looking left, 1559	70	165

Issue of 23/24ths alloy

5449	**Lion,** or 'hardhead' (= 1½d.). 1559. Crowned **FM** monogram, dolphin each side looking r. R. Crowned lion rampant	30	85

		F £	VF £
5450	— Similar, but dolphins looking l., 1558 ('58' only on coins are all probably contemporary forgeries)	25	65
	1559 (genuine)	25	70
	1560 (genuine)	45	125

JAMES VI 1567–1625

James VI acceded to the throne of Scotland on his mother's abdication in 1567, aged one year. A council of regency was established and his excellent education was largely due to George Buchanan. He married Anne of Denmark in 1589. The death of Elizabeth I left James as her nearest heir and he therefore ruled both kingdoms from 1603.

Following the gunpowder plot of 1605 he ordered severe sanctions against Romanist priests and during his reign the King James, or 'Authorised' version, of the Bible was published.

The frequent calling-in and changes of design has left us with a legacy of the most beautiful designs and varied legends, especially the gold coins, of any reign in the Scottish series. The half-length figure of the young king in armour and holding a sword must rank among the very finest of portraits on a British coin.

Billon and copper coins were issued in much reduced quantities, none at all being struck during the first sixteen years of the reign. Scottish documents of 1585 refer to the striking of coins at Dundee and Perth because of the pestilence in Edinburgh, but no coins are known with other than an Edinburgh mint-signature. Due to the number of forgeries in circulation hardheads and placks of Mary were called in in March 1575 and the genuine coins re-issued with a heart and star countermark, the arms of the Earl of Morton, Regent at that time.

By 1578 the value of silver had risen so much that the silver coins of both Mary and James were called in and countermarked with a crowned thistle. The ryals were re-issued at 36s 9d and the testoons of Mary at 7s. 4d. In 1611 the value of the gold unit and its fractions were raised by 10%.

After his accession to the English throne, James established a currency of similar weight and fineness in both realms although a 12:1 ratio between the Scottish and English denomination was still maintained.

GOLD

Before Accession to English Throne

Note. There is no gold corresponding to the First Coinage.

Second coinage

5451

	F £	VF £

5451 **Twenty pound piece** ($471\frac{1}{4}$ grs., 22 ct.). Half length bust of young king in armour. R. Crowned shield, **PARCERE SVBIECTIS & DEBELLARE SVPERBOS**

1575 .... 15000 36500
1576 .... 14500 35000

Third coinage

5452

5452 **Ducat** (= 80s., wt. $94\frac{1}{2}$ grs., 21 ct.). 1580. Bust in ruff l. R. Crowned shield dividing date, **EXVRGAT** legend 2500 5500

JAMES VI

Fourth coinage

5453

	F £	VF £
5453 **Lion noble** (= 75s., wt. 78½ grs., 21½ ct.). Crowned lion sejant with sword and sceptre, POST 5 & 100 etc. R. Four crowned IR cyphers crosswise, S in centre, DEVS IVDICIVM TVVM REGI DA		
1584	2750	6000
1585	3000	7000
1586	2850	6500
1588	3250	7500
5454 **Two third noble** (= 50s.). Similar		
1584	3000	6500
1585	3250	7500
1587	3250	7500
5455 **One third noble** (25s.). Similar, 1584	3500	8250

Fifth coinage (1588)

5456

5456 **Thistle noble** (= 146s. 8d. or 11 merks, wt. 117¾ grs., 23⅓ ct.). Crowned shield on ship, thistle below. R. Thistle plant with crossed sceptres and lions rampant in panel surrounded by eight thistles, undated FLORENT SCEPT PIIS REGNA HIS IOVA DAT NVMERATO 1250 2750

5457

	F £	VF £

Sixth coinage

5457 Hat piece (= 80s., wt. $69\frac{3}{4}$ grs., 22 ct.). Bust in tall hat r., thistle behind. R. Crowned lion seated 1. holding sceptre, cloud and 'Jehovah' in Hebrew above, TE SOLVM VEREOR

1591	2650	6250
1592	2350	5500
1593	2500	6000

Seventh coinage

5458

5458 Rider (= 100s., wt. $78\frac{1}{2}$ grs., 22 ct.). King in armour with sword, on horse galloping r. R. Crowned shield SPERO MELIORA

1593	525	1350
1594	475	1200
1595	525	1350
1598	550	1400
1599	500	1300
1601	675	1750

5459 Half-rider. Similar

1593	475	1250
1594	350	900
1595	600	1500
1598	600	1500
1599	400	1000
1601	425	1050

Eighth coinage

		F £	VF £
5460	**Sword and sceptre piece** (= 120s., wt. 78½ grs., 22 ct.). Crowned arms. R. Crossed sword and sceptre, crown above, thistles at sides, **SALVS POPVLI SVPREMA LEX**		
	1601	235	625
	1602	225	600
	1603	250	700
	1604	275	725
5462	**Half-sword and sceptre piece.** Similar		
	1601	185	450
	1602	200	525
	1603	675	1650
	1604	225	650

AFTER ACCESSION TO ENGLISH THRONE

I. Ninth coinage, 1604–9, and II. Tenth coinage, 1609–25

5463	**Unit or sceptre piece.** (= £12 Scots or £1 sterling, wt. 154⅚ grs., 22 ct.). I. King half-length r. wearing Scottish crown and holding orb and sceptre. R. Crowned shield dividing IR. English arms in 1st and 4th quarter, **FACIAM EOS** etc.	375	850
5464	II. Similar, but Scottish arms in 1st and 4th quarters	325	750
5465	**Double crown** (= £6 Scots, wt. 77⅖ grs.). I. As 5463 but without sword and orb; king's name abbreviated and *rev.* legend **HENRICVS ROSAS REGNA IACOBVS**	650	1650

		F £	VF £
5466	II. Similar, but Scottish arms in 1st and 4th quarters	525	1250

5467

| **5467** | **Britain crown** (= £3 Scots, wt. 38.7 grs.) I. As 5465 .... | 725 | 1850 |
| **5468** | II. Similar but Scottish arms in 1st and 4th quarters .... | 250 | 650 |

5469

| **5469** | **Halfcrown** (= 30s. Scots, wt. $23\frac{2}{3}$ grs.) I. As 5465 but I D G ROSA SINE SPINA. R. TVEATVR etc. .... | 350 | 900 |
| **5470** | II. Similar, but Scottish arms in 1st and 4th quarters .... | 250 | 650 |

5471

| **5471** | **Thistle crown** (= 48s. Scots). I. crowned rose. R. Crowned thistle, TVEATVR legend .... | 325 | 700 |

SILVER

BEFORE ACCESSION TO ENGLISH THRONE

First coinage. See p. 70 for countermarked coins

5472	**Ryal,** or 'Sword dollar' (= 30s.). Crowned shield dividing I R. R. Crowned sword, pointing hand on l., XXX on r., PRO ME SI MEREOR IN ME		
	1567	250	550
	1568	275	625
	1569	265	600
	1570	250	550
	1571	250	575

5474

	F	VF
	£	£

5474 Two-thirds ryal. Similar, but XX on *rev.*
1567	175	475
1568	200	525
1569	250	600
1570	250	600
1571	200	525

[Varieties are known dated 1561 in error, also 1571 exists without the crowns above I R]

5476

5476 One-third ryal. Similar but X on *rev.*
1567	165	475
1568	275	750
1569	325	850
1570	175	500
1571	200	575

Second coinage

5478

		F £	VF £
5478	**Half merk**, or 'noble' (= 6s. 8d., wt. $104\frac{3}{4}$ grs., $\frac{2}{3}$rds fine). Crowned shield between 6 and 8. R. Ornate cross with crowns and thistles in alternate angles, **SALVVM FAC** etc.		
	1572	70	175
	1573	75	200
	1574	75	200
	1575	85	225
	1576	90	250
	1577	75	200
	1580	75	200
5479	**Quarter merk** or 'half-noble' (= 3s. 4d.). As above but 3 and 4 by shield		
	1572	85	250
	1573	75	225
	1574	75	225
	1576	110	325
	1577	85	250
	1580	100	300

5480

5480	**Two merks**, or 'thistle dollar' (= 26s. 8d., wt. $342\frac{2}{3}$ grs., 0.916 fine). Crowned shield. R. Leaved thistle between I and R, **NEMO ME IMPVNE LACESSET**		
	1578	1650	3250
	1579	1250	2500
	1580	1750	3500

	F £	VF £

5481 **Merk** (= 13s. 4d.). As above
1579	2000	4500
1580	1750	4000

Revaluation of 1578. Countermark crowned thistle

Testoon of Mary. As 5402–3. (Value 7s. 4d.)	150	475

As 5404–8   As 5416

— — As 5404–8 (Value 7s. 4d.)	135	450
— of Francis and Mary. As 5416. (Value 7s. 4d.)	135	425
— — As 5417–18. (Value 7s. 4d.)	135	425

As 5422

— of Mary alone. As 5422. (Value 7s. 4d.)	950	3000
Half-testoons, similar. (Value 3s. 8d.)	1350	4500
Ryal of Mary and Darnley. As 5425. (Value 36s. 9d.)	235	575
Two-thirds ryal. As 5426. (Value 24s. 6d.)	225	550
One-third ryal. As 5427. (Value 12s. 3d.)	175	475
Ryal of Mary alone. As 5429. (Value 36s. 9d.)	275	650
Two-thirds ryal. As 5430. (Value 24s. 6d.)	275	650

JAMES VI

As 5431

	F £	VF £
One-third ryal. As 5431. (Value 12s. 3d.)	325	750
Ryal or 'Sword dollar' of James VI. As 5472. (Value 36s. 9d.)	235	525
Two-thirds ryal. As 5474. (Value 24s. 6d.)	165	450
One-third ryal. As 5476. (Value 12s. 3d.)	150	450

Third coinage

5482

5482	Sixteen shillings (wt. 171⅓ grs., 0.916 fine). 1581. Crowned shield. R. Crowned thistle dividing I R, NEMO legend	1350	2750
5483	**Eight shillings.** 1581. Similar	900	2000
5484	**Four shillings.** 1581. Similar	950	2250
5485	**Two shillings.** 1581. Similar	*Extremely rare*	

Fourth coinage

5486

5486	**Forty shillings** (471⅙ grs., 0.916 fine). 1582. Half-length figure l. in armour, holding sword. R. Crowned shield between I R, and XL S HONOR REGIS IVDICIVM DILIGIT	2250	5250

		F £	VF £

5487 Thirty shillings. Similar, but X^XXS

1581	650	1500
1582	225	600
1583	250	625
1584	300	775
1585	425	950
1586	450	1000

5488 — XXX on one line 1582 .... 475 1100

5489 Twenty shillings. Similar, but XX S

1582	210	700
1583	225	725
1584	575	1650
1585	650	1750

5490

5490 Ten shillings. Similar, but X S

1582	175	650
1583	325	1000
1584	265	850

Sixth coinage

5491

5491 Balance half merk (= 6s. 8d., $71\frac{1}{3}$ grs., 0.875 fine). Crowned shield between two thistles. R. Balance with sword behind, HIS DIFFERT REGE TYRANNVS

1591	165	450
1592	175	525
1593	200	625

5492 Balance quarter-merk. 1591. Similar, but without thistles on *obv*. ... 425 1000

JAMES VI

Seventh coinage

5493

		F £	VF £
5493	**Ten shillings** (wt. 92¼ grs., 0.916 fine). Bare headed bust in armour r. R. Crowned, triple-headed thistle, **NEMO** legend		
	1593	85	275
	1594	75	250
	1595	85	275
	1598	85	275
	1599	85	275
	1600	375	850
	1601	450	950
5494	**Five shillings.** Similar		
	1593	225	600
	1594	65	275
	1595	85	325
	1598/6	85	325
	1599	85	325
	1600	450	950
	1601	475	1050
5495	**Thirty pence.** Similar		
	1594	110	250
	1595	135	325
	1596	150	425
	1598/6	150	425
	1599	135	325
	1601	200	475

5496

5496	**Twelve pence.** Similar, but single pellet behind head		
	1594	175	450
	1595	75	225
	1596	200	525

Eighth coinage

5497

		F £	VF £
5497	**Thistle merk** (= 13s. 4d., wt. 104¾ grs., 0.916 fine). Crowned shield. R. Crowned thistle, REGEM IOVA PROTEGIT		
	1601	75	210
	1602	70	200
	1603	75	210
	1604	85	275
5498	**Half thistle-merk.** Similar		
	1601	50	135
	1602	45	125
	1603	60	150
	1604	125	300
5499	**Quarter thistle-merk.** Similar		
	1601	50	145
	1602	35	100
	1603	90	250
	1604	100	275
5500	**Eighth thistle-merk.** Similar		
	1601	45	125
	1602	25	75
	1603	100	250

AFTER ACCESSION TO ENGLISH THRONE

5501

JAMES VI

		F £	VF £
5501	**Sixty shillings** (= 5s. English). I. King on horseback r. wearing Scottish crown, thistle on housings. R. Shield with arms of England in 1st and 4th quarters, QVAE DEVS legend.	225	750
5502	II. Similar, but Scottish arms in 1st and 4th quarters	250	825

5503

5503	**Thirty shillings.** I. Similar to 5501	75	225
5504	II. Similar to 5502	85	250
5505	**Twelve shillings.** I. Bust r., XII behind. As 5501	100	300
5506	II. As last. R. Similar to 5502	110	325
5507	**Six shillings.** I. As 5505 but VI; date over shield		
	1605	425	1250
	1606	350	850
	1609/7	400	1000

5508   5509

5508	II. As last, but shield as 5502		
	1610	325	675
	1611	325	675
	1612	325	675
	1613	350	725
	1614	350	725
	1615	325	675
	1616	375	800
	1617	375	800
	1618	375	800
	1619	275	650
	1622	275	650
5509	**Two shillings.** I. Crowned rose, I D G ROSA SINE SPINA. R. Crowned thistle with angular scales, TVEATVR legend. *Mm.* thistle	25	85
5510	**One shilling.** I. Similar, but uncrowned rose and thistle. *Mm.* thistle	45	135

BILLON and COPPER

Before Accession to English Throne

5511

	F £	VF £

| 5511 | **Eightpenny Groat** (wt. 28 grs., 0.250 fine). Crowned shield. R. Crowned thistle, no inner circles, **OPPIDVM EDINBVRGI** (1583–90) .... | 20 | 65 |
| 5512 | — — OPPID EDINB, hairline or no inner circles .... | 20 | 65 |

5513   5515

5513	— Similar, but beaded inner circles	25	70
5514	**Twopenny plack.** As 5511	125	300
5515	As 5512	70	200
5516	As 5513	75	225
5517	**Hardhead** (= 2d., $23\frac{1}{2}$ grs., $\frac{23}{24}$ths alloy). I. (Issued August 1588) I R crowned. R. Crowned shield, **VINCIT VERITAS** (1588)	80	250

5518   5519

| 5518 | II. (Issued November 1588). Similar, but lion rampant on *rev.*, two pellets behind .... | 25 | 85 |
| 5519 | **One Penny plack.** As last but no pellets .... | 75 | 225 |

5520

| 5520 | **Fourpenny plack** ($23\frac{1}{2}$ grs., $\frac{23}{24}$ths alloy). Thistle over two sceptres in saltire. R. Lozenge with thistle-head at each point (1594) .... | 100 | 350 |

5521

	F £	VF £
5521 Æ **Two-pence** or 'Turner'. Bare headed bust r., IACOBVS 6 etc. R. Three thistle heads, OPPIDVM EDINBVRGI (1597)	75	325
5522 Æ **Penny.** As 5521, but single pellet added behind head (1597)	125	450

Countermarking of 1575. (Genuine coins countermarked with a heart and star.)

As 5437

Placks of Mary. As 5437	50	125
Lion, or hardhead of Mary. As 5438, 5439	30	95

Lion, or hardhead of Mary and Francis. As 5445, 5449, 5450	35	85

AFTER ACCESSION TO ENGLISH THRONE

5523

5523 Æ **Twopence**, or Turner. I. Issue of 1614. Triple thistle. R. Lion rampant, two pellets behind, FRANCIE ET HIBERNIE REX	20	65
5524 II. Issue of 1623. Similar, but FRAN & HIB REX	15	50
5525 Æ **Penny.** I. As 5523, but single pellet	50	150
5526 II. As 5524, but single pellet	65	175

CHARLES I 1625-1649

Charles I, second son of James VI and Anne of Denmark, became heir apparent to the throne in 1612 and king in March 1625 at the age of 25. He was married by proxy to the Princess Henrietta Maria of France in June the same year. His Scottish coronation did not take place until 1633.

The history of this unfortunate King's reign culminating in civil war and his execution is well known, but numismatically it is of the highest interest, and the English and Scottish issues together represent the largest number of coins and types of any British monarch.

Although coining ceased on the death of James VI, a directive was made authorising the use of the old dies until new irons could be prepared by Charles Dickieson. Apart from the change in title and a slight difference in the style of the beard the first silver issues of Charles I bearing his name are similar in type of James's last issue.

Nicholas Briot, a Frenchman, previously employed at the French and English mints received an appointment as master of the Scottish mint in August 1635 and was later joined by his son-in-law John Falconer, who eventually succeeded him in 1646.

Briot's work is of the highest calibre, and his introduction of the use of the mill and screw press (albeit no more popular with fellow mint workers in Scotland than in England) has given both the English and the Scottish series coins of a technical excellence previously unknown.

It should be noted that on some coins Charles is shown wearing the English crown, with central cross, rather than the Scottish crown, with central lis. The only coins made in Scotland during the Civil War years, 1642–60 were copper *turners,* which were struck in 1642, 1644, 1648 and 1650.

GOLD

First coinage, 1625-1634

5527

	F	VF
	£	£
5527 Unit. As James I, last coinage but for king's name and CR at shield....	750	1800

CHARLES I

5528

		F £	VF £
5528	**Double crown.** Similar	1250	3000
5529	**Britain crown.** Similar	1750	4500
5530	**Milled angel** (= 10s., wt. $64\frac{2}{3}$ grs., 23 ct., $3\frac{1}{2}$ grs. fine). 1633. Coronation issue. St Michael spearing dragon, X to r. R. Ship with English arms on sail, B before bowsprit, AMOR POPVLI PRÆSIDIVM REGIS	2500	6500

Third coinage, 1637–1642

5531

5531	**Unit.** I. (Briot's coinage). Similar to 5527, thistle and B after *obv.* legend. R. Crowned CR at shield, HIS PRÆSVM VT PROSIM	625	1500
5532	Similar, but *obv.* legend begins with B and ends with thistle head	900	2250
5533	II. (Falconer's coinage). Similar, but thistle and F after *obv.* and *rev.* legend	2250	6000

5534

| 5534 | **Half unit.** I. Bust l., B below, UNITA TVEMVR .... | 700 | 1750 |
| 5535 | II. Similar, but F after *obv.* legend .... | 2000 | 5500 |

5536   5539

		F £	VF £
5536	**Britain crown.** Crowned bust l. breaking legend which ends with B, CR crowned	1000	2500
5537	Similar, but B before *obv.* legend	1100	2650
5538	**Britain halfcrown.** As crown, B below bust, CR uncrowned	400	950
5539	Similar, B over crown on *rev.*	425	1000

SILVER

First coinage, 1625–1634

5540	**Sixty shillings.** As last coinage James I	375	1250
5541	**Thirty shillings.** Similar	100	275

5542

5542	**Twelve shillings.** Similar	125	300
5543	**Six shillings.** Similar date over shield on *rev.*	300	750
	1625	325	800
	1626	350	900
	1627	325	800
	1628	350	900
	1630	325	800
	1631	300	750
	1632	300	750
	1633	350	850
	1634	350	850

5544

5544	**Two shillings.** As James I last coinage	45	135
5545	**Shilling.** Similar, C struck over I	75	225

Second coinage (Briot's hammered issue, 1636)

5546   5548

	F £	VF £
5546 **Half merk.** browned bust l. to edge of coin, VI/8 behind. R. Crowned arms, CHRISTO AVSPICE REGNO	60	175
5547 — **Milled pattern.** Similar, but crowned CR added to *rev.*, dated 1636 above crown	*Extremely rare*	
5548 **Forty pence.** Similar, but XL, SALVS REIP SVPR(EM) LEX around large crowned and leaved thistle	65	175
5549 — **Milled pattern.** Similar, but crowned CR added to *rev.* (undated)	*Extremely rare*	
5550 **Twenty pence.** Similar, but XX, IVST THRONVM FIRMAT	60	150
5551 — **Milled pattern.** Similar, but crowned CR added to *rev.* (undated)	450	1350

Third, coinage, 1637–1642

I. Briot's issue.
II. Intermediate issue.
III. Falconer's first issue with F.
IV. Falconer's second issue with F.
V. Falconer's anonymous issue.

5552

| 5552 | **Sixty shillings.** I. King riding l. R. Crowned arms, QVAE DEVS legend, *mm*. B over thistle and B after *rev.* legend | 250 | 750 |

	F £	VF £
5553 **Thirty shillings.** I. Similar to last, B and flower on *obv.*, B and thistle on *rev.* (i.e. a London *obv.* die)	100	300
5554 II. As last, but without B	90	275

5555

5555	IV. As last, but F by horse's hoof, smooth ground below horse. R. Lozenges, stars, or nothing over crown	80	250
5556	Similar, but rough ground below horse	80	250
5556A	— F over crown on *rev.*	100	300
5557	V. Similar, but no F	80	250

5558

5558	**Twelve shillings.** I. Bust to edge of coin, B at ends of legends	65	175
5559	II. As last but thistle over crown on *rev.*	85	225

5560

| 5560 | III. As last, but F over crown on *rev.* | 70 | 185 |

CHARLES I

5561

		F £	VF £
5561	IV. Bust of new style slightly breaking inner circle, F after *obv.* legend	65	175
5562	— R. Thistle before legend and F over crown	70	185
5563	— Bust wholly within inner circle. R. As last	75	200
5564	V. As 5561, but without F, **MAG.BRIT**	70	185
5565	**Six shillings.** I. Bust to edge of coin, B at end of *obv.* legend	65	175
5566	— Similar, but B and lis at end of *obv.* legend	65	175
5567	— As last, but B over crown on *rev.*	70	200

5568   5571

5568	— As last, but B after *rev.* legend	70	200
5569	III. Bust to edge of coin, F over crown on *rev.*	60	165
5570	— Mule. Briot *obv.* of class I. R. As last	100	250
5571	IV. Bust within legend as 5563, *mm.* thistle	60	150
5572	V. Bust of new style within inner circle, but without F	65	175
5573	**Half merk.** I. Crowned bust l. to edge of coin. R. Crowned CR by shield, B under bust and above crown	45	135

5574

5574	Similar, but B after legend on *rev.*	50	150

5575

		F £	VF £
5575	**Forty pence.** I. Crowned bust l. to edge of coin, various combinations of lozenges by XL (or none), hair line inner circle, B below bust or after legend and over crown on *rev.*, **SALVS** legend	40	100
5576	— Similar, but B below thistle on *rev.*	50	120
5577	— As last, B after *rev.* legend	50	120
5578	III. As last, **SCOT ANG** or **M(AG) BR**. F at end of *rev.* legend	35	85

5579

5579	— F above crown on *rev.*	35	80
5580	— Mule. Briot *obv.* of class I. R. As last	65	150
5581	**Twenty pence.** I. Bust to edge of coin, numeral **XX**, lozenges above and below, usually B below bust and at end of *rev.* legend, **IVSTITIA** etc.	15	45

5582   5589

5582	— B over crown on *rev.*	15	50
5583	— B over crown on *obv.* R. As last	20	60
5584	— B before bust. R. As last	20	60
5585	— —R. B within crown	25	75
5586	— No lozenges by numeral, B after *rev.* legend	15	50
5587	III. As last, without lozenges, B at end of *obv.* legend F at end of *rev.* legend	50	125
5588	— F at end of *rev.* legend only	15	50
5588A	— — also with F above crown and with F omitted, **SCOT ANG** or **MAG BR** etc.	20	60
5589	IV. Bust of new style, slightly breaking inner circle, F over crown on *rev.*	15	50
5590	— Bust wholly within inner circle. R. As last	20	65
5591	V. As 5589, but no F	15	45
5591A	— Similar, but **MAG BRIT**	50	125

CHARLES I

Fourth coinage, 1642

5592   5593

		F £	VF £
5592	**Three shillings.** Crowned bust l., thistle behind. R. Crowned arms, **SALVS** legend	50	150
5593	**Two shillings.** Similar, but large II behind bust, **IVST THRONVM FIRMAT** legend	35	90
5594	Small II behind bust	40	100
5595	Without numerals, **B** below bust which extends to edge of coin	50	150

COPPER

Coinage of 1629

5596

5596	**Twopence,** or Turner. As James VI, but **CAROLVS**, etc.	10	35
5597	**Penny.** Similar	75	200

Earl of Stirling coinage, 1632–1639
Twopence, or Turner (wt. 13 grs.)

5598   5599

5598	**1.** 'English' crown, *mm*. lozenge (*obv*.), flower (*rev*.)	6	25
	a — *mm*. lozenge (both sides)	6	25
	b — *mm*. lozenge–rosette	5	20
	c — *mm*. flower (over lozenge)–flower	6	25
5599	**2.** 'Scottish' crown with jewelled band and arches, *mm*. lozenge (both sides)	5	20
	a — *mm*. lozenge (*obv*.), star (*rev*.)	6	25
	b — *mm*. lozenge–rosette	5	20
	c — *mm*. lozenge–flower	5	20
	d — *mm*. lozenge–stop and saltire	5	20
	e — *mm*. stop and saltire (both sides)	5	20
	f — *mm*. trefoil–lozenge. With trefoil stops, instead of lozenges, below **C II R**	15	50

5600

	F £	VF £

Copper
5600 **3.** 'Scottish' crown with plain band and arches, *mm*. flower 5 20
   a — *mm*. lozenge (*obv*.), flower (*rev*.) 6 25
   b — *mm*. flower–rosette 6 25
   c — *mm*. flower–lozenge 6 25
   d — *mm*. flower–star 6 25
5601 **4.** Crown with five crosses
   a — *mm*. saltire (both sides) 8 30
   b — *mm*. lozenge (*obv*.), flower (*rev*.) 8 30
   c — *mm*. lozenge–rosette 8 30
   NB There are many variations in the legends of these Turners and also many contemporary forgeries (including those with mintmarks lis and lion).

Penny

Known to have been struck, but none extant

Coinages of 1642, 1644, 1648 and 1650

5602

5602 **Twopence,** Turner or Bodle. Crowned CR. R. Thistle, no mark of value, *mm*. lozenge, LACESSET 10 30
5602A — LACESSIT 15 45
5602C **Pattern** (?). As 5602. With small neat letters .... *Extremely rare*
5603 **Pattern threepence.** Striking in silver for a copper threepence (26 grs.). Two interlinked C's, large thistle on *rev*., NEMO etc. .... *Extremely rare*
5603A — — Similar, but bust of Charles I on *obv*. .... *Extremely rare*

CHARLES II 1649–1685

Charles II, the eldest surviving son of Charles I and Henrietta Maria, was proclaimed King of Scotland in Edinburgh less than a month after his father's execution.

After being virtually a prisoner at the hands of Argyll he was crowned at Scone on 1 January 1651 following his acceptance of the Scottish Covenant.

Nearly ten years of exile passed before his return to London and coronation in April 1661 after the collapse of the Commonwealth, during which period no coins were struck, the mint being closed from about 1650 until 1663.

CHARLES II 87

For the first silver coinage the punches were made in London by Thomas Simon and for the second coinage by John, Joseph and Philip Roettiers. The actual dies were made at the Scottish mint under the direction of Sir John Falconer, the Master of the Mint. Both coinages were machine made, the second coinage with new machinery obtained from London in 1675.

No gold coins were struck for Scotland and the fineness of the silver at 11 deniers (0.916) fine is the same as those of Charles I.

In 1682 the Scottish Mint was closed on account of the illegal activities of certain mint officials and remained inactive until 1687.

SILVER

First coinage – The die axes of the first coinage is usually with inverted reverse though there does not seem to have been a strict quality control in this matter, and coins with en medaille (upright) die axis and with other angles are known. Examples of these 'unusual' die axis may be worth a 10–20% premium above the prices quoted.

5604

		F £	VF £	EF £
5604	**Four merks** (= 53s. 4d.). I. 1664. Bust r., thistle above. R. Cruciform shields, crowned interlinked C's in angles, value LIII/4 in centre			
	1664	600	1250	—
5605	II. Similar, but thistle below bust			
	1664	750	1500	—
	1665	Extremely rare		
	1670	500	1000	3000
	1673	500	1000	3000
	1673 4 of value on reverse over horizontal 1	750	1500	—

		F £	VF £
5606	III. Similar, but F below bust		
	1670	?Exists	
	1674	500 1000	4000
	1674/3	600 1200	4500
	1674 BR instead of BRI on reverse	750 1500	—
	1675	600 1250	4000

		F £	VF £	EF £
5607	**Two merks.** (= 26s. 8d.) Type I. 1664. As 5604, with thistle above head, but value **XXVI/8** in centre	250	750	2000
5608	Type II. As 5605, with thistle below bust			
	1664	300	900	3000
	1670	200	650	1850
	1673	200	650	1850
	1674	250	750	2000

5609

5609	Type III. As 5606, F below bust			
	1673		*Extremely rare*
	1674	175	600	1500
	1675	175	600	1500
	1675 **BR** instead of **BRI** on reverse	300	900	2000

5611

5611	**Merk.** (= 13s. 4d.) Type II. As 5605, thistle below bust and value **XIII/4** in centre of *rev.*			
	1664 small thistle below bust	100	280	800
	1664 large thistle below bust	120	300	850
	1665	120	300	850
	1666	180	500	1250
	1668	100	300	950
	1669 legend stops vary, some with colons	75	200	650
	1669 error with no stops on obverse	120	350	1200
	1669 Scottish Arms in 2nd and 4th quarters	150	400	1400
	1670 legend stops vary, some with colons	75	200	650
	1671 legend stops vary, some with colons	75	200	650
	1672 legend stops vary, some with colons	75	200	650
	1672 — reversed 2 in date	150	400	1250
	1673	75	200	650
	1673 error **BRA** for **BRI**	200	600	1500
	1674	90	250	750

		F £	VF £	EF £
5612	**Merk.** Type III. As 5606, F below bust			
	1674	150	400	1100
	1675	125	350	950
	1675 reverse error XII instead of XIII	140	375	1000
5613	Type IV. No thistle or F			
	1675	200	600	1500
5614	**Half merk.** (= 6s. 8d.). Type II. As 5605 but VI/8 in centre			
	1664	150	400	1100
	1664 — *cmk.* 1665 behind head (dated 1664 on *rev.*)	*Extremely rare*		
	1665	125	350	950
	1666	180	500	1250
	1667	150	400	1100
	1668	125	350	950
	1669 stops on both sides vary	80	220	700
	1669 error no stops on obverse	150	350	1000
	1669 Scottish Arms in 2nd and 4th quarters error	150	350	1000
	1670 stops on both sides vary	90	250	750
	1670 error no stops on obverse	150	350	1000
	1671 straight ribbon behind head	80	220	700
	1671 curly ribbon behind head	80	220	700
	1672	80	220	700
	1673	90	250	750

5615

5615	**Half-merk.** Error shields, England, France and Ireland transposed			
	1665	200	600	1500
	1666	300	700	1500
5616	Type III. 1675. As 5606, F below bust	125	350	950
5617	Type IV. 1675. No thistle or F below bust	90	250	750

Second coinage — This coinage was struck with a die axes of reverse inverted.

5618	**Dollar.** Bust 1., F before. R. Cruciform shields, interlinked C's in centre, thistles in angles			
	1676 legend stops vary both sides	350	1000	2500
	1679	300	900	2250
	1680	450	1500	3500
	1681	350	1000	2500
	1682	250	800	2000
5619	**Half dollar.** Similar			
	1675	250	600	1750
	1676	350	900	2250
	1681	200	500	1500

5620

		F £	VF £	EF £
5620	**Quarter dollar.** Similar			
	1675	100	250	600
	1676	100	250	600
	1676 error DRI for DEI	200	500	1200
	1677	100	250	600
	1677/6	110	275	650
	1678	150	400	900
	1679	100	250	600
	1680 CAROVLS error for CAROLVS	200	500	1250
	1681	100	250	600
	1682	100	250	600
	1682 CAROVLS error for CAROLVS	200	500	1250
	1682 Irish Arms below date due to 90° die rotation	180	450	1100
	1682 — with CAROVLS error	350	850	2000
5621	**Quarter dollar.** Error shields, 1682, Irish arms in first shield			
	1682	250	600	1500
5622	**Eighth dollar.** Similar			
	1676	80	200	500
	1676 Struck with reverse at 90° die axis	100	250	600
	1677	80	200	500
	1678/7		*Extremely rare*	
	1679	250	600	1500
	1680	100	250	600
	1680 error shields on reverse dies rotated by 180°	200	500	1250
	1682	250	600	1500
	1682 reversed 2 in date in error	350	750	2000
5623	**Eighth dollar.** Error shields, 1680, French arms in first shield	350	900	2000

5624

5624	**Sixteenth dollar.** Similar, but St Andrew's cross on *rev.*, emblems in angles			
	1677	75	200	500
	1678	100	300	750
	1678/7	75	200	500
	1679/7		*Extremely rare*	
	1680	250	600	1500
	1680/79	200	500	1250
	1681	100	250	600

COPPER

Coinage of 1663

		F £	VF £	EF £
5625	**Twopence**, Turner or Bodle. Crowned **CR** with small II to r. R. Thistle, **NEMO** etc., mm. usually rosette or cross of pellets, occasionally lion rampant or cinquefoil .... *from*	15	40	100

Coinage of 1677

5626	**Bawbee**, or sixpence Scots, 1677. Bust l., **ANG FR ET HIB REX**. R. Crowned thistle	80	200	500
	— with **AN G** instead of **ANG**	100	250	600
5627	Similar, **ANG FR ET HIB R** 1677	100	250	600

5628

5628	Similar, **AN FR ET HIB R**			
	1677	60	150	350
	1678	50	120	300
	1679	40	100	250
	1679 **CAR H** instead of **CAR II**	75	175	400
	1679 **SOC** instead of **SCO** error	100	300	750

5630

5629	Cruder head and irregular letters, 1679 (?forgery)		*fair*	25
5630	**Turner**, or Bodle. Crown over crossed sword and sceptre. R. Thistle, **NEMO**, etc.			
	1677	45	110	275
	1677 **FBA** for **FRA** error	75	175	400
	1677 **IIIB** for **HIB** error	75	175	400
	1677 **REXI** instead of **REX** error	85	200	500
	1678	60	150	350
	1678 **FRAN** instead of **FRA**	75	175	400
	1679		*Extremely rare*	
5631	Similar, but **NMEO** in error, 1677	85	200	500
5632	Similar, **LAESSET** error, 1677	85	200	500
	Similar, **LACSSET** error, 1677	85	200	500

JAMES VII (II of England) 1685–1689

James II, younger brother of Charles II, was created Duke of York in 1634 and Lord High Admiral in 1638. With the support of Samuel Pepys (the diarist) and Matthew Wren he greatly improved the organisation and efficiency of the Navy. In 1660, he married Anne Hyde, daughter of the Earl of Clarendon. His conversion to Catholicism and the possibility of a Catholic succession eventually led to William of Orange being assured of the support of the Army should he land in England. The defection of the army, and also that of his daughter Anne, caused James to order his Queen and infant son to France. James landed in Ireland in March 1689 to rally support, but was completely defeated by William of Orange at the Battle of the Boyne on 1 July 1690. James died at St Germain on 5 September 1701.

Only silver coins were issued during this reign, the largest of which, the forty shilling piece is the first Scottish coin to bear a lettered edge.

The so-called '60 Shilling' pieces were never issued and only late strikings of 1828 by Matthew Young are known.

A reduction in the weight of the coins made the proportions to English a little over 13 to 1 as against 12 to 1 from the accession of James VI.

5634

	F £	VF £	EF £

5634 **Sixty shillings.** 1688. Laureate bust r., 60 below. R. Crowned arms in the collar of the Order of the Thistle, edge plain (Matthew Young restrike) Struck in silver .... *FDC* 1500
5635 Similar, struck in gold .... 3 known *FDC* 12,500
5636 **Forty shillings.** 1687. Laureate bust r., IACOBVS etc., 40 below. Crowned arms. *Edge:* NEMO ME IMPVNE LACESSET ANNO REGNI TERTIO 1687 .... 125 500 1500

5637

5637 Similar, but IACOBUS, 1687. *Edge:* TERTIO 125 500 1500
— — LACESSIET error on edge 250 750 2000

		F	VF	EF
		£	£	£
5638	IACOBUS, 1687. *Edge:* QVARTO	125	500	1500
5639	IACOBVS, 1688. *Edge:* QVARTO	125	500	1500
5640	IACOBUS, 1688. *Edge:* QVARTO	125	500	1500

5641

5641 Ten shillings. Similar to 5637, but 10 below. R. St Andrew's cross and national emblems, stops vary both sides

1687	100	300	800
1688	150	500	1250
1688 error unbarred A in FRA on reverse	175	600	1400

WILLIAM AND MARY 1689–1694

William III was the son of William II Prince of Orange, and Mary, daughter of Charles I. Appointed Captain General of the Dutch Forces in 1672 and later proclaimed Stadholder, he married Mary, daughter of James II of England in 1677.

On account of James' Catholic leanings William became the chief hope of the Protestant cause and eventually accepted an invitation to lead an armed expedition to England and landed at Torbay in 1688. James II fled to Ireland and was defeated by William at the Battle of the Boyne.

He formed the Grand Alliance with the United Provinces and was responsible for the vigorous treatment of Scottish rebels culminating in the massacre of Glencoe in 1692.

Mary died in 1694 and the Act of Settlement secured the ultimate succession of the House of Hanover.

SILVER

5642 Sixty shillings. Conjoined busts, 60 below. R. Crowned arms. *Edge:* PROTEGIT ET ORNAT ANNO REGNI TERTIO

| 1691 | 300 | 900 | 2500 |
| 1692 | 300 | 900 | 2500 |

5643 *Trial striking in copper.* 1691. *Edge*: NEMO ME IMPVNE LACESS O REGNI QVARTO .... *Extremely rare*

Forty shillings. Similar, but 40 below busts, edge as 5642 – it is now thought the SEXTO edge does not exist

5644	1689. *Edge*: PRIMO	250	650	1500
5645	1689. *Edge*: SECVNDO	200	500	1250
5646	1690. *Edge*: PRIMO	120	375	900

		F £	VF £	EF £
5647	1690. *Edge*: SECVNDO	120	375	900
5648	1691. *Edge*: SECVNDO	150	425	1000
5649	1691. *Edge*: TERTIO	120	375	900
	1691. — error with no lozenges in Dutch shield	150	500	1250
5650	1692. *Edge*: TERTIO	140	400	950
5651	1692. *Edge*: QVARTO	120	375	900
5652	1693. *Edge*: QVARTO	120	375	900
5653	1693. *Edge*: QUINTO	120	375	900
5654	1693. *Edge*: SIXTO	150	500	1250
5655	1693. — error with no lozenges in Dutch shield	180	450	1100
5656	1694. *Edge*: SIXTO	150	425	1000
	1694. — error with no lozenges in Dutch shield	150	500	1250

5657

5657	**Twenty shillings.** Similar, but 20 below busts.			
	1693 obverse stops vary	250	750	1750
	1694	400	1250	3000
5658	**Ten shillings.** 1689. Similar, but 10 below busts, GRATIA, small shields, English crown, die axes can vary	*Extremely rare*		
5658A	— 1690	200	500	1250
	— 1690 with 0 over 9	250	600	1400
5659	Similar, but large shield, Scottish crown on *rev.* 1691, large 10 below bust with J type 1 in date	125	300	700
	1691, small 10 below bust with I type 1 in date	100	250	600
5660	— GRA. 1691, small numerals below bust	150	450	1100
5661	— GRATIA 1692, small 10 below bust, I type 1	125	300	700
5662	— — — larger 10 below bust, J type 1	100	250	600
5663	— GRA 1694, small 10 below bust, I type 1	180	475	1200
	— — 1694, large 10 below bust, J type 1	200	500	1400
5664	**Five shillings.** 1691. Similar, but V below crowned WM monogram on *rev.*			
	1691	125	350	750

5665

5665	Similar, but V below busts, 1694	80	200	500
	— 1694, inverted A for 2nd V in GVLIELMVS	125	300	750

	F £	VF £	EF £

5666 **Bawbee.** Conjoined busts l., *mm.* Cross of five pellets

	F	VF	EF
1691	50	100	300
1691 REX REGINA error, ET omitted between	100	200	600
1692 *mm.* five pellets	60	120	350
1692 — ET 1692 REGINA error	120	250	700

5667

	F	VF	EF
5667 1692, *mm.* rosette or small leaved thistle	70	150	400
5668 — *mm.* two small trefoils	70	150	400
5669 — *mm.* lis	80	200	500
5670 — *mm.* star	70	150	400
5671 1693, *mm.* star	50	100	300
1693, *mm.* star with 3 over 2 in date	75	100	400
5672 1694, *mm.* star	50	100	300
5673 1694. *mm.* lis	50	100	300

5674

5674 **Bodle,** or Turner. Crowned **WM** monogram. R. Crowned thistle

	F	VF	EF
1691	30	60	200
1692	30	60	200
1693	30	60	200
1694	30	60	200
5675 Similar, 1694, *obv.* legend ends REGIN	60	120	400
— 1694, IMPUNE instead of IMPVNE on *rev.*	70	150	500

WILLIAM II (III of England) 1694–1702

GOLD

5676

		F £	VF £	EF £
5676	Pistole (= £12 Scots., wt. 106 grs., 22 cts.). 1701. Bust l., sun rising from sea below. F. Crowned **WR** by arms	2750	6000	—
5677	**Half-pistole.** 1701. Similar	3500	7000	—

[These coins were struck from gold dust imported by the Darien Company trading with Africa. The company badge, a sun rising from the sea, appears on the coins.]

SILVER

5678 **Sixty shillings.** 1699. Bust l., 60 below. R. Crowned arms. Recorded in the 19th century but no physical specimens ever seen in living memory and with no records of it ever having been minted.

5679

Forty shillings. Similar, but 40 below bust, edge as William and Mary

5679	1695. *Edge*: SEPTIMO	150	350	900
	1695 — no stops on obverse	200	500	1250
	1695 — no lozenges in Dutch shield	175	400	1000
5680	1695. *Edge*: OCTAVO	150	350	900
5681	1696. *Edge*: OCTAVO	150	350	900
5682	1697. *Edge*: NONO	200	450	1100
5683	1698. *Edge*: DECIMO	150	350	900

WILLIAM II

97

		F £	VF £	EF £
5684	1699. *Edge*: VNDECIMO	250	500	1250
5685	1700. *Edge*: VNDECIMO	Extremely rare		
	1700. *Edge*: DUODECIMO	Extremely rare		

5686 Twenty shillings. Similar, but 20 below bust

1695	125	400	1000
1696 with or without stop after date	125	400	1000
1697	200	600	1250
1697 with inverted reverse die axis	300	750	1500
1698	125	400	1000
1698/7	150	500	1250
1699	125	400	1000

5687

5687 Ten shillings. Similar, but 10 below bust

1695	75	200	500
1696	75	200	500
1697	75	200	500
1697 with inverted reverse die axis	100	300	700
1698	85	225	550
1698/7	75	200	500
1699	200	600	1250

5688 Five shillings. Similar, but 5 below bust. R. Crowned thistle, GVL D G etc.

1695	75	225	500
1696	50	150	350
1697	75	225	500
1697 with inverted reverse die axis	100	300	700
1699	75	225	500
1700	75	225	500
1701	90	300	800

5689	1702. GVLIELMVS DEI GRATIA	100	350	950

COPPER

5690	**Bawbee.** 1695. Bust l., BR FR. R. Crowned thistle	60	275	750
5690A	— Similar, BRIT FRA	100	400	1000
5691	1696. Pellet stops both sides	60	275	750
5692	— — Pellet stops (*obv.*), annulets (*rev.*)	60	275	750

5693

	F £	VF £	EF £
5693 1697	90	375	950

5694 5698

		F	VF	EF
5694	**Bodle.** I. 1695. Flat sword and sceptre, crown above. R. Crowned thistle, **GVLIELMVS** and **HIB R**	40	150	400
5695	— **GVLIELMVS** and **HIB REX**	40	150	400
5696	— **GVL** and **HIB REX**	30	120	300
5696A	1696, **GVL** and **HIB REX**	60	200	500
5697	Type II. 1695. Sword and sceptres high, **GVL**, pellet stops on *rev.* 1695	30	120	300
5698	1696. No stops on *rev.* (A var. known with stops.)	40	150	400
5699	1697. No stops on *rev.*	50	175	500
	1697. — with reverse struck inverted	60	200	550

ANNE 1702–1714

Anne, second daughter of James II, was educated in the protestant faith and married George, Prince of Denmark in 1683. Her reign is dominated by the wars of the Spanish succession and the ascendancy of the first Duke of Marlborough, culminating in the Treaty of Utrecht.

The Act of Union uniting the realms of England and Scotland is an important numismatic landmark as it provided for a coinage of the same standard and value in both countries.

The purpose or function of the 5 or 6 pointed star mark on some coins is not known.

The After Union coins, although technically now British rather than Scottish coins, are included as they were the product of the Edinburgh mint.

The coins of 1709 are the last native coins to be struck in Scotland.

Before Union

5700   5702

		F £	VF £	EF £
5700	**Ten shillings.** Draped bust l., 10 below. R. Crowned arms, legend ends REG. 1705	100	300	750
	1706	100	300	750
5701	1706, legend ends REGINA	150	450	1000
5702	**Five shillings.** 1705. Similar, 5 below. ANNA DEI GRATIA			
	1705	40	100	250
5703	1705 ANNA D G M BR FR & HIB REG	40	100	250
	1705, — — with 5 over 4	35	85	200
5704	1705 AN D G M BR FR & HIB REG	40	100	250
	1705 — — with 5 over 4	40	100	250
	1705 — — no stops on reverse	40	100	250
5705	1705 AN D G MAG BR FR & HIB R	40	100	250
5706	1706 AN D G MAG BR FR & HIB R	50	150	350

After Union

5707	**Crown.** 1707. 'Second' bust l., E below. R. Four shields crowned, Garter star in centre. *Edge*: SEXTO	85	300	600
5708	1708. *Edge*: SEPTIMO	95	325	650
5708A	1708/7. *Edge*: SEPTIMO	100	375	700
5709	**Halfcrown.** 'Second' bust, E below. 1707. *Edge*: SEXTO	40	100	400
5710	— 1707. Edge: SEPTIMO	*Extremely rare*		

5710A

5710A	— 1708. *Edge*: SEPTIMO	40	100	400
5711	— 1709. *Edge*: OCTAVO	50	125	400
5712	**Shilling.** 'Second' bust. 1707 E below	35	100	300

		F £	VF £	EF £
5712A	— 1707 E no stops on reverse	*Extremely rare*		
5713	— 1707 E*	70	200	450
5714	— 1708 E	70	175	400
5714A	— 1708 E no rays to garter star	*Extremely rare*		
5715	— 1708 E*	45	120	325
5715A	— 1708/7 E*	*Extremely rare*		
5716	'Third' bust. 1707 E	35	75	250
5717	— 1708 E	55	150	350
5717A	— 1708/7 E	75	175	400
5718	'Edinburgh' bust, 1707 E	*Extremely rare*		
5718A	— 1708 E*	65	150	400
5718B	'Edinburgh' bust struck from cruder local dies with two very large top curls to hair, 1708 E*	800	—	—
5719	— 1709 E	200	500	—
5720	— 1709 E*	70	175	450
5721	**Sixpence.** 'Second' bust. 1707 E	25	50	125
5722	— 1708 E	35	75	175
5722A	— 1708/7 E	40	90	200

5723

5723	— 1708 E*	35	85	200
5723A	— 1708/7 E*	40	95	225
5724	— 'Edinburgh' bust. 1708 E*	40	95	225

[Proof strikings of the 1707 E shilling and sixpence with plain edges are known, all are very rare. Late strikings only of a fourpence and twopence are known from original dies dated 1711 which were never used.]

JAMES VIII 1688–1766
(The Old Pretender)

In 1708 James, Prince of Wales (son of James II of England) made a vain attempt to invade Scotland.

Dies were prepared by Norbert Roettiers for what was intended to be a British crown piece dated 1709, styling James as **IACOBVS III MAG BRIT FRAN ET HIB REX**. He was also responsible for the 'Restoration of the Kingdom' medal which was struck in silver and copper.

During a second invasion in 1715 James actually landed in Scotland and his Coronation was planned at Scone for 23 January 1716. This never took place and he was forced to return to France in February 1716.

Dies were again prepared by Roettiers, this time for a Scottish coinage, styling James as **IACOBVS VIII SCOT ANGL FRAN ET HIB REX** and bearing the arms of Scotland instead of those of Great Britain as on the crown of 1709. No contemporary strikings are known from the 1716 dies but a number of pieces were struck from the original dies in 1828 by Matthew Young, after which the dies were defaced, however, there are modern reproductions of this restrike.

5725	**Guinea.** 1716. Bust r. R. Cruciform shields, with sceptres in angles.	
	Struck in silver	*FDC* £1250
5726	Similar. *Struck in gold.*	*Extremely rare*
5727	Similar. *Struck in bronze.*	*Extremely rare*
5728	Bust l., **IACOBVS TERTIVS**. *Struck in silver*	*FDC* £1250
5729	Similar. *Struck in bronze*	*Extremely rare*
5730	**Crown.** 1709. Bust r., **IACOBVS III** etc. R. Crowned oval shield. Edge plain	*Unique*

5731

5731	1716. Bust r., **IACOBVS VIII** etc. R. Crowned square shield	*FDC* £850
5732	Similar. *Struck in gold*	*Extremely rare*
5733	Similar. *Struck in white metal*	*FDC* £600
5734	Similar. *Struck in bronze*	*Extremely* rare

CHARLES III 1720–1788
('Bonny Prince Charlie', the Young Pretender)

Charles Edward Stewart, titular heir to the Scottish throne, was the son of James VIII and Grandson of James II of England.

His French expedition to invade England in 1744 was foiled by the English fleet at Dunkirk, and he finally landed in Scotland at Glenfinnan in 1745. After several minor victories he was crushingly defeated at Culloden Moor in 1746 by forces under the command of the Duke of Cumberland, nicknamed the 'Butcher'. His months as a fugitive in the highlands and his escape to France are the source of much Scottish lore. He died in Rome at the age of 68.

Charles is said to have carried on the age-old superstition of 'touching' for the King's evil. The 'touch-piece' used was in silver with the *obv.* legend **CAR III D G M B F ET H R**. The *rev.* legend **SOLI DEO GLORIA** is the same as on the touch pieces of earlier British monarchs.

HENRY IX 1725–1807

The younger brother of Prince Charles, Henry IX, 1725–1807, Henry Benedict Maria Clement, Cardinal York, attempted to come to England to support the rising of 1745. On his brother's death in 1788 styled himself as Henry IX. He also touched for the King's evil and contemporary touch pieces in silver and pewter (or tin) are known, pierced for suspension. It is possible that unpierced specimens in gold, silver and bronze may be of somewhat later origin. On his death, in 1807, the Stewart jewels (carried off by James II) were left to George IV.

UNITED KINGDOM COINS BEARING SCOTTISH EMBLEMS

Shillings of George VI were struck bearing a Scottish lion seated on a Scottish crown, with a shield bearing the cross of St Andrew on the left and a thistle on the right. Shillings of Elizabeth II were struck bearing the Scottish Shield with lion rampant.

These coins were struck as a compliment to the Scottish ancestry of Queen Elizabeth, Queen Consort of George VI (died 30 March 2002), but it should be emphasised that these were part of the United Kingdom coinage and were not issued exclusively for use in Scotland.

For a detailed listing of these coins, see nos 4083, 4104, 4109, 4140 and 4148 in the *Spink Standard Catalogue of British Coins, Vol. I, Coins of England and the United Kingdom*.

IRELAND

INTRODUCTION TO IRISH COINS

In dealing with the coinage of Ireland there are three main groups to consider: the Hiberno-Norse issues of the Scandinavian kings of Dublin, the Anglo-Irish coinages of Ireland under the English monarchy, and the republican coins of the Irish Free State and Eire. If it is objected that the latter should not be included in a catalogue of 'British' coins the editors can only reply that they have been included for convenience and that it is not part of a plot to take over the South! Northern Ireland, of course, uses United Kingdom coinage (see Volume 1).

Currency is not necessarily *coin,* as coins by definition are objects (normally of metal) of definite weight and value, stamped with an officially authorized device. In ancient Ireland gold ornaments are likely to have circulated as a form of currency and some types of ornament are known as 'ring money', but cattle were probably used as the standard unit of wealth. Without large urban settlements the Irish did not require the complications of a coinage system until very late in their history and then it was imposed by foreigners.

Coinage began in Asia Minor in the seventh century BC, reached Western Europe at the end of the third century BC and coins of Gaulish type were circulating in S.E. Britain by the end of the second century BC. Roman coins have been found on the east coast of Ireland, brought from Britain by raiders or traders, but it was not until almost 1000 AD that coins are known to have been struck in Ireland and then they were issued by the Norsemen of Dublin, not by the Irish.

Many of the medieval coins are quite rare, especially the later Hiberno-Norse types, the earliest Anglo-Irish coinage of John and some of the issues of Henry VI and Edward IV, and unpublished varieties may well come to light with the discovery of new hoards. The early Tudor coins tend to be from poorly engraved dies, many being carelessly struck. The coinages of the Civil War period and of James II's abortive attempt to hold Ireland after his flight from England are particularly interesting. The coins of the Irish Free State have been particularly admired for their fine animal designs.

LATIN AND ERSE LEGENDS ON IRISH COINS

ANO DOM (In the year of the Lord). James II gunmoney crown.
CAPUT IONIS REGIS, etc. (The head of King John). Halfpence of John.
CHRISTO AVSPICE REGNO (I reign under the auspices of Christ). Charles I halfcrowns of the Confederated Catholics.
CHRISTO VICTORE TRIVMPHO (I exalt in the victory of Christ). James II gunmoney crown.
ECCE GREX (Behold, the flock!). Charles II, St Patrick's halfpenny.
EXVRGAT DEVS DISSIPENTVR INIMICI (Let God arise and let his enemies be scattered: *Psalm* 68, 1). Sliillings of James I.
FLOREAT REX (May the King flourish). St Patrick's halfpenny and farthing.
MELIORIS TESSERA FATI ANNO REGNI SEXTO (An improved token uttered in the sixth year of the reign). James II pewter crown.
POSVI DEVM ADIVTOREM MEVM (I have made the Lord my helper: *comp. Psalm* 54, 4). Groats and halfgroats, Edw. IV–Hen. VII, and on some later Tudor coins.
POSVIMVS DEVM ADIVTOREM NOSTRVM (We have made the Lord our helper). Shillings and groats of Mary & Philip of Spain.
PROVIDEBO ADIVTORIVM (I will provide help). On some groats of Henry VII.
QVIESCAT PLEBS (He calms the common people). Charles II, St Patrick's farthing.
TIMOR DOMINI FONS VITÆ (The fear of the Lord is the fountain of life: *Prov.* 14, 27). Base shillings of Edward VI.
TVEATVR VNITA DEVS (May God guard the united, i.e., the kingdoms). Sixpences of James I.
VERITAS TEMPORIS FILIA (Truth, the daughter of Time). Mary Tudor.

Saorstat Eireann (Irish Free State).
Eire (Ireland).
Eiri amac na Casca (The Easter Rising).
Coroin (crown), *Floirin* (florin), *Scilling* (shilling), *Reul* (sixpence), *Pingin* (penny), *Feorling* (farthing).
Leat (half).
Deic (ten).

SELECT BIBLIOGRAPHY OF IRISH COINS

The earliest accounts of Irish coinage occur in Sir James Ware's *De Hibernia & anti-quitatibus eius disquisitiones*, London, 1654 (Chap. XXV), followed by Bishop William Nicolson's *The Irish Historical Library*, London, 1724 (Chap. VIII). James Simon's work is the first book devoted solely to the coinage of Ireland:

SIMON, J. *Essay towards an Historical Account of Irish Coins*. 1749.
— Ditto, together with *Supplement to Mr. Simon's Essay on Irish Coins* (first pub. 1776). 1810.
LINDSAY, J. *A View of the Coinage of Ireland, from the Invasion of the Danes to the Reign of George IV*. 1839.
NELSON, DR P. *The Coinage of Ireland in Copper, Tin and Pewter*. 1905 (reprinted from *BNJ*).
COFFEY, G. *A Catalogue of the Anglo-Irish Coins in the Collection of the Royal Irish Academy*, 1911.
DOWLE, A. & FINN, P. *A Guide Book to the Coinage of Ireland, from 995 A.D. to the present day*. 1969.
YOUNG, D. *Coin Catalogue of Ireland 1722–1968*. 1969.
DOLLEY, M. *Medieval Anglo-Irish Coins*. 1972.

See also Herbert Grueber's *Handbook of the Coins of Great Britain and Ireland in the British Museum* (1899), and, for numerous statutes relating to Irish coinage, Rev. Rodger Ruding, *Annals of the Coinage of Great Britain, etc.* (3rd edn 1840). Various specialized papers on Irish numismatics have appeared in the following periodicals: *Transactions/Proceedings of the Royal Irish Academy* (*TRIA/PRIA*), *Proceedings of the Royal Society of Antiquaries of Ireland* (*PRSAI*), *Journal of the Royal Society of the Antiquaries of Ireland* (*JRSAI*), *Numismatic Society of Ireland, Occasional Papers* (*NSI*), *Irish Numismatics* (*IN*), *Numismatic Chronicle* (*NC*), *British Numismatic Journal* (*BNJ*), *Seaby's Coin & Medal Bulletin* (*SCMB*), and Spink's *Numismatic Circular* (*SNC*). In addition to 'Notes on Irish Coins' by Dr E.J. Harris (*SCMB* 1964–65), we note the following specialist works:

HIBERNO-NORSE COINAGE

ROTH, B. 'The Coins of the Danish Kings of Ireland'. *BNJ* VI, 1909.
O'SULLIVAN, W. 'The Earliest Irish Coinage'. *JRSAI* LXXIX, 1949.
DOLLEY, R.H.M. *The Hiberno-Norse Coins in the British Museum* (*SCBI* 8), 1966.
— 'Some New Light on the early Twelfth Century Coinage of Dublin'. *SCMB*, Oct. 1972.
HILDEBRAND, B.E. *Anglo-Saxon Coins in the Royal Swedish Cabinet of Medals at Stockholm, all found in Sweden*, 1881.
SEABY, W.A. *Hiberno-Norse Coins in the Ulster Museum (in preparation)*.

ANGLO-IRISH COINAGE: JOHN–EDWARD III

DOLLEY, M. & SEABY, W. *Sylloge of the Anglo-Irish Coins in the Ulster Museum, Belfast*, Part 1, John–Edward III, 1968.
O'SULLIVAN, W. *The Earliest Anglo-Irish Coinage*, 1964.
SMITH, A. 'On the Type of the first Anglo-Irish Coinage'. *NC*, 1864.
— 'Inedited Silver Farthings coined in Ireland', *NC*, 1863.
DOLLEY, M. & O'SULLIVAN, W. 'The Chronology of the First Anglo-Irish Coinage', in *North Munster Studies*, 1967.
DOLLEY, R.H.M. 'The Irish Mints of Edward I in the light of the coin-hoards from Ireland and Great Britain'. *PRIA* LXVI, 1968.
SEABY, W.A. 'A St Patrick Halfpenny of John de Courci'. *BNJ* XXIX, 1958.
DYKES, D.W. 'The Irish Coinage of Henry III'. *BNJ* XXXII, 1963.

— 'The Coinage of Richard Olof'. *BNJ* XXXIV, 1964.
— 'The Anglo-Irish Coinage of Edward III'. *BNJ* XLVI, 1976.
CLARKE, D.T.D., SEABY, W.A. & STEWART, I. 'The 1969 Colchester Hoard', The Anglo-Irish Portion. *BNJ* XLIV, 1974.
NORTH, J.J. 'The Anglo-Irish Halfpence, Farthings and post-1290 Pence of Edward I and Edward III'. *BNJ* 67, 1997.

HENRY VI–HENRY VII

SMITH, A. 'On the Irish coins of Edward the Fourth'. *TRIA* XIX, 1839.
SYMONDS, H. 'The Irish silver coinages of Edward IV'. *NC,* 1921,
— 'On the Irish coins of Henry the Seventh'. *TRIA* XIX, 1841.
DOLLEY, M. 'A note on the Attribution of the Regally Anonymous "Three Crowns" Coinage'. *SNC,* April 1968.
— 'The sequence and chronology of the "portrait" Anglo-Irish groats of Henry VII'. *SNC,* Nov. 1969.

HENRY VIII & EDWARD VI

SYMONDS, H. 'The Irish Coinages of Henry VIII and Edward VI'. *NC,* 1915.
CARLYON-BRITTON, R. 'Henry VIII Harp Groats and Half-Harp Groats and Edward VI Harp Groats'. *NC,* 1955.
DOLLEY, M. & HACKMANN, W.D. 'The Coinages for Ireland of Henry VIII'. *BNJ* XXXVIII, 1969.
POTTER, W.J.W. 'The Coinage of Edward VI in his own Name', Pt. I. *BNJ* XXXI, 1962.
DOLLEY, M. 'Was there an Anglo-Irish Coinage in the Name of Edward VI'. *SNC,* Sept. 1969.
CHALLIS, C.E. 'The Tudor Coinage for Ireland'. *BNJ* XL, 1971.

MARY TUDOR & ELIZABETH

SMITH, A. 'On the Irish Coins of Mary'. *PRSAI,* 1855.
SYMONDS, H. 'The Coinage of Mary Tudor'. *BNJ* VIII, 1911.
— 'The Elizabethan Coinages for Ireland'. *NC,* 1917.

JAMES I & CHARLES I

SMITH, A. 'Notes on the Irish Coins of James I'. *NC,* 1879.
— 'On the Ormonde Money'. *PRSAI,* 1854.
— 'Money of Necessity issued in Ireland in the reign of Charles I'. *JRSAI,* 1860.
NELSON, P. 'The Obsidional Money of the Great Rebellion'. *BNJ* XVI, 1919–20.
O'SULLIVAN, W. 'The only Gold Coins issued in Ireland'. *BNJ,* 1964.
DOLLEY, M. 'A note on the Weight and Fineness of the 1646 "Ormonde" Pistole'. *BNJ* XXXV, 1966.
SEABY, W.A. & BRADY, G. 'The Extant Ormonde Pistoles and Double Pistoles'. *BNJ* XLIII, 1973.

CHARLES II–GEORGE IV

SMITH, A. 'Money of Necessity issued in Ireland in the reign of James II'. *NC,* 1870.
STEVENSON, D. 'The Irish Emergency Coinages of James II 1689–1691'. *BNJ* XXXVI, 1967.
DOLLEY, M. 'Some Reflections on the Volume of the "Brass Money" of James II'. *SCMB,* Dec. 1974.
— 'A Provisional Note on the 1804 Bank of Ireland Token for Six Shillings Irish'. *IN* 35, Sept.–Oct. 1973.

— 'Some Preliminary Observations on the Pennies Irish of 1822 and 1823'. *IN* 36, Nov.–Dec. 1973.
— 'The Armstrong and Legge *(recte* "Knox"?) Halfpence Irish with dates 1680–4'. *SCMB,* April 1979.
TURNER, R. 'The Gun Money Crowns of James II'. *SCMB,* July 1975.
POWELL, J.S. 'The Irish Coinage of Armstrong and Legge'. *SCMB,* June 1978.
WARHURST, MRS M. 'New Evidence for the Date of the so-called "St Patrick's" Half-pence and Farthings'. *IN* 59, Sept.–Oct. 1972.
DAVIS, W.J. *The Nineteenth Century Token Coinage of Great Britain, Ireland* (etc.)), 1904.
FRAZER, W. 'On the Irish "St. Patrick" or "Floreat Rex" Coinage subsequently circulated in New Jersey by Mark Newbie'. *JRSAI* XXV, 1895.
BATEMAN, D. & DOLLEY, M. 'Some Remarks on the "Pewter" (Tin) Petty Coinage of March/April 1960'. *IN* 50, March–April 1976.

IRISH FREE STATE & EIRE

YEATS, W.B. *et al. The Coinage of Saorstát Éireann.* 1928.
REMICK, J.H. *The Coinage of the Republic of Ireland.* 1968.

HIBERNO-NORSE PERIOD

(Late 10th Century to early 12th Century)

The Vikings began raiding the British Isles towards the end of the eighth century and in the first half of the ninth century large groups of Norsemen were settling in Ireland under leaders such as Turgeis, Olaf the White and Ivar the Boneless. The main centres of occupation were around Dublin, Dundalk, Wexford, Waterford, Cork, Limerick and other areas, and the newcomers were soon raiding along the waterways to the very centre of Ireland. Many of these Norsemen were driven out by the Irish in 901, but others returned a decade later and a succession of Norse kings held Dublin: Sihtric, Raghnall, Guthfrith, and the most famous of them all, Olaf Sihtricsson, known as Anlaf Cuaran, who was defeated at Tara by Maelsechnaill in 980 and then made a pilgrimage to Iona where he ended his life. Where the Norse (and Danes) did settle they intermarried and were converted to Christianity, and eventually they became the allies and naval auxiliaries of the Irish kings. The Norse fortresses, then, grew into commercial centres and it was at the chief of them, Dublin (*O.Ir.* Dubh-linn, 'black pool'; *O. Norse,* Dyflinr), that the first Hiberno-Norse coins were issued by the 'Ostmen', as the Scandinavians came to be called.

The first pennies known to have been minted in Ireland were produced at Dublin before the end of the tenth century, and at first directly in imitation of contemporary Anglo-Saxon coins. Many of these early coins have been found in Viking hoards buried in Scandinavia and the Baltic countries. Basically the earlier coins bear the name and stylised effigies of Æthelred II (987–1016), Cnut (1016–35) and of the contemporary King of the Ostmen, Sihtric Anlafsson (Silkenbeard) who ruled over the Scandinavian settlers at Dublin and whose forces were defeated by the hosts of Brian Boru at the Battle of Clontarf in 1014. Some coins actually bear the names of English moneyers and English mints, e.g., **LVND** (London) **LEIG** (Chester), **EFOR** (York), **PECED** (Watchet), etc., but most of these seem to have been products of Norse imitators at Dublin.

As time went on the Hiberno-Norse coins became more and more debased in style, the inscriptions meaningless with the weight dropping considerably below that of contemporary Anglo-Saxon issues. After the Norman conquest of England in 1066, Hiberno-Norse coins show in the many changes of design on the reverse the influence of the sterling pennies issued during the late 11th Century, although the Irish coins being of such light weight did not circulate outside their country of origin. It is not known with certainty who were the authorities issuing these later coins, it is possible they were Hibernian as much as Hiberno-Norse. Later still, in the early 12th Century, the coins became so thin that they could not be struck between the hardened metal dies in the ordinary manner, but each design was impressed separately or else the coin was impressed on one side only. As such they are known as 'bracteates'.

It has been estimated that surviving examples of this large coinage total no more than 2,000 specimens of which 1,300 are contained in three major public collections. The largest and most important group is in the National Museum of Ireland at Dublin, and a summary of the types housed there has been published by Dr William O'Sullivan in *The Earliest Irish Coinage* (1949 revised 1961). A smaller but representative collection is in the British Museum, London, and this has been fully published by Mr Michael Dolley in a volume of the *Sylloge of Coins of the British Isles* – 'The Hiberno-Norse Coins in the British Museum' (1966). The third collection, also important, is that in the Ulster Museum made up chiefly from the Irish portion of the Carlyon-Britton collection.

A typical early coin reads **SIHTRIC RE+ DYFLIN** (Sihtric, King of Dublin), with the name of the moneyer and mint on the reverse, e.g., **FÆREMIN MO**[*netarius*] **DYFLIN** (Færemin, moneyer at Dublin).

All the coins of this period are silver pennies.

IRISH MINTS

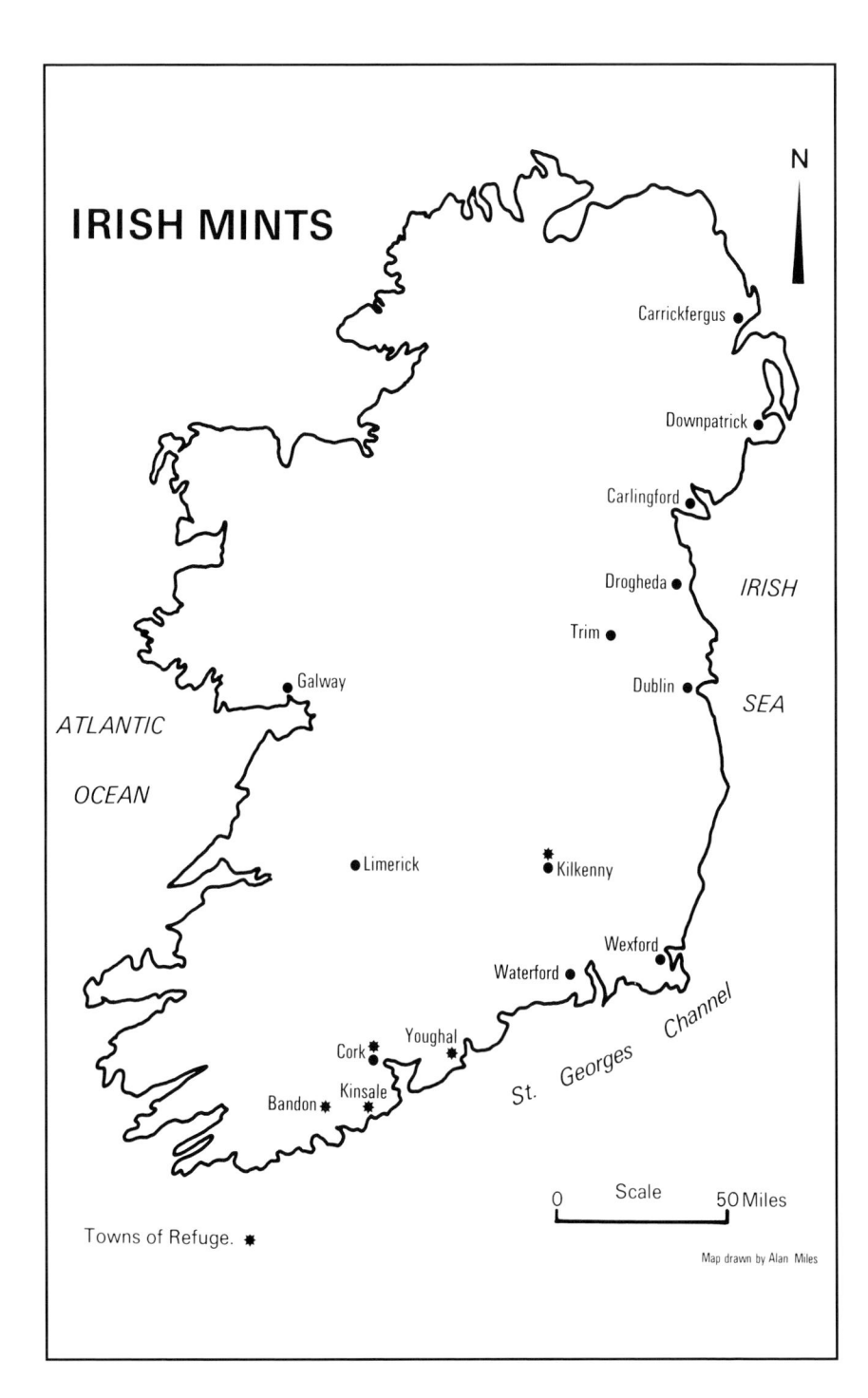

- Carrickfergus
- Downpatrick
- Carlingford
- Drogheda
- Trim
- Dublin
- Galway
- Limerick
- Kilkenny
- Wexford
- Waterford
- Cork
- Youghal
- Bandon
- Kinsale

ATLANTIC OCEAN

IRISH SEA

St. Georges Channel

Scale 0 – 50 Miles

Towns of Refuge. ✴

Map drawn by Alan Miles

I. Sihtric Anlafsson and Related Issues, *c*.995–1020

Coins exist of some of the types in this group which have somewhat crude engraving or blundered legends, and these may be worth rather less than the prices indicated. Some close copies appear to have been minted in Scandinavia.

6100   6103

		F £	VF £
6100	Imitation of Æthelred II of England, **CRVX** type, *c*.995–1000. With name 'Sihtric'. R. Voided cross, **CRVX** in angles. *Dublin*. *O'S* 1	750	1500
6101	— — Similar, but with other mint name. *O'S* 2	600	1350
6102	— With name 'Æthelred'. *Dublin*. *O'S* 3	500	1250
6103	Imitation of Æthelred's *Long Cross* type, *c*.1000–1010. With name **SIHTRIC RE+DYFLIN**, etc. *Dublin*. *O'S* 6	350	800
6104	— — Similar, but with other mint name. *O'S* 7	500	1250
6105	— — — With name **SIHTRIC CVNVNC**. *BM* 28	800	2000

6106

		F £	VF £
6106	— With name 'Æthelred'. *Dublin*. *O'S* 8	250	525
6107	— — Similar, but with other mint name. *BM* 37–42	350	850
6108	— With inscription **DYMN ROE+ MNEGNI**, etc., on *obv*. *Dublin*. *O'S* 9	450	1000
6109	— — Similar, but with other mint name. *BM* 30	500	1200
6110	— With name **OGSEN HEA MELNEM**. *O'S* 11	600	1350

Hiberno-Norse Issues, *c*.995–1020

6113　　　　　　　　6118

		F £	VF £
6113	Imitation of Æthelred's *Helmet* type, *c*.1004–1010. With name of Sihtric. *Dublin O'S* 5	950	2500
6115	— With name of 'Æthelred'. *Dublin BM* 45–6	750	2000
6116	— — Similar, but with other mint name. *BM* 46A & B	1000	2500
6117	Imitation of Æthelred's *Last Small Cross* type, *c*.1010–16. With name of Sihtric. *Dublin. O'S* 24	525	1250
6118	— —Similar, but with other mint name. *BM* 53–8	450	1000
6119	— With name of 'Æthelred'. *Dublin. BM* 59	650	1500
6120	— — Similar, but with other mint name. *H*.3358	750	1750

6121

6121	Imitation of Cnut of England, *Quatrefoil* type, *c*.1016–20. With name of Sihtric. *Dublin. O'S* 25	1000	2500
6121A	— With name of 'Cnut'. *Dublin. H*.280–3.	850	2000

II. Later Variants of Long Cross Coins, *c*.1015–35

Distinguished from earlier *Long Cross* pence by the addition of pellets in angles of cross.

6122

Coins with unblundered legends (mostly 23–20 grs. weight)

6122	With name of Sihtric, as 6103. *Dublin. O'S* 10	200	450
6123	— —Similar, but with other mint name. *S*.1	450	1000
6124	With name of 'Æthelred'. *Dublin*. S.7	300	650

Hiberno-Norse Issues, c.1015–35

Coins with blundered legends on one or both sides (mostly 20–12 grs.)

		F £	VF £
6125	As 6122, but generally cruder style	135	300
6125A	As 6122, inverted crozier behind head. *O'S* 12	140	325

6125   6126

Coins with blundered legends and symbol in one or more quarters of reverse (mostly 12–9 grs.)

6126	As 6125, but ⨆ on neck and in one angle of *rev. O'S* 14	150	350
6127	As 6125, but triquetra in one angle. *BM* 102	175	400
6128	As 6125, with spiral and millrind symbols. *BM* 110	225	500
6128B	As 6125, but with hand behind neck	300	650

6129

6129	*Obv.* as 6125. Hand of good style in one angle of cross exhibiting Stigma. *BM* 62	450	1000

See Isle of Man section for the Manx imitations of Hiberno-Norse Long Cross Coins.

III. Long Cross and Hand Coinage, c.1035–60

6130   6132

Usually blundered legends (mostly 16–12 grs. weight)

6130	Bust with hand before face, thumb to nose. R. One or two crude hands in angles of cross. *O'S* 18	300	650
6131	Bust with hand on neck. R. As above. *O'S* 19	125	275
6132	— Similar, but without hand on neck (sometimes other marks on, before or behind bust). Many varieties. *O'S* 16	80	175
6133	— — R. One crude hand, and sometimes S or other symbol. *O'S* 20	120	250

IV. 'Scratched-Die' Coins, c.1060–1065

Reverse dies appear to have been part punched, part engraved.

6134   6136

		F £	VF £
6134	Bust l. R. Crude hand and cross in angles of long cross. *BM* 145–7 ...	175	375
6135	Bust r. R. As above. *BM* 148	325	750
6136	Helmeted facing bust with triple-strand moustache. R. As above. *O'S* 47	350	825
6136A	— As 6136 R. Uncertain symbols in inner circle	375	850

V. Mainly Imitations of Late Anglo-Saxon, Norman and North European Coins, c.1065–c.1095

Not arranged in chronological order.

6137   6139

6137	Bust l. R. CRVX in angle of cross. S.14	750	1750
6138	Bust l., sometimes with symbol on neck. R. Long cross with pellets, annulet and anchor (?) in angles. *BM* 157–67	350	750
6139	Bust l., crozier to l. R. Comb (?), pellets and annulet in angles of cross. *BM* 169–74	350	750
6140	As 6132, but with cruder bust. R. Crude hands in angles of cross. *BM* 207	275	600
6140A	— Similar. R. Crosses in two angles	250	550
6141	Bust r. R. Long cross with two anchors (?). *BM* 177	425	1000
6142	Bust l. R. As *rev.* of Cnut *Short Cross*. *O'S* 26	525	1200
6143	Bust r. R. As last. *BM* 178–80	550	1250
6144	Bust l. or r. R. As *rev.* of Harthacnut *Jewel Cross*. *S.* 8	575	1350
6145	Bust l. R. As *rev.* of Edward the Confessor *Expanding Cross*. *BM* 176	650	1500
6146	Bust l. R. As *rev.* of Edward the Confessor *Helmet* type. *BM* 218	650	1500

Hiberno-Norse Issues, *c*.1065–95

6147   6151

		F £	VF £
6147	As 6139. R. As *rev.* of Edward the Confessor *Small Cross*. BM 205 ..	450	1000
6148	Bust l. R. Cross pattée over cross with triple pellet ends. *BM* 219	525	1200
6149	Bust l. R. As *rev.* of Edward's *Small Cross*. *O'S* 31	550	1250
6150	Bust r. R. Derived from Edward's *Cross and Piles* type. BM p.166.....	600	1350
6150A	Bust l., cross on neck. R. Short voided cross, small crosses at ends, no inscription	600	1350
6151	Bust l. R. Derivative of rev. of Harold II **PAX** type. *O'S* 33	725	1600

6151A   6154

6151A	— — Similar, but bird above and below centre band of *rev.* *O'S* 35 ..	850	2000
6152	Bust r. of different style. R. Similar to 6151. *O'S* 34	800	1750
6153	Bust l. or r. R. As *rev.* of William I *Profile left* type. R. 200, 202	800	1750
6154	Bust l. R. As *rev.* of William I *Bonnet* type. *BM* 222	900	2000
6154A	Bust l. R. 'Bow' cross, cross and pellets at centre	675	1500

6155   6157

6155	Bust l., with various symbols on neck. R. Cross crosslet over celtic cross. *O'S* 39	850	1850
6156	— Similar, but *rev.* as William I *Two Stars* type. *O'S* 40	900	2000
6157	Bust l. R. As *rev.* of William I **PAX** type. *O'S* 27	1000	2500

Hiberno-Norse Issues, c.1065–95

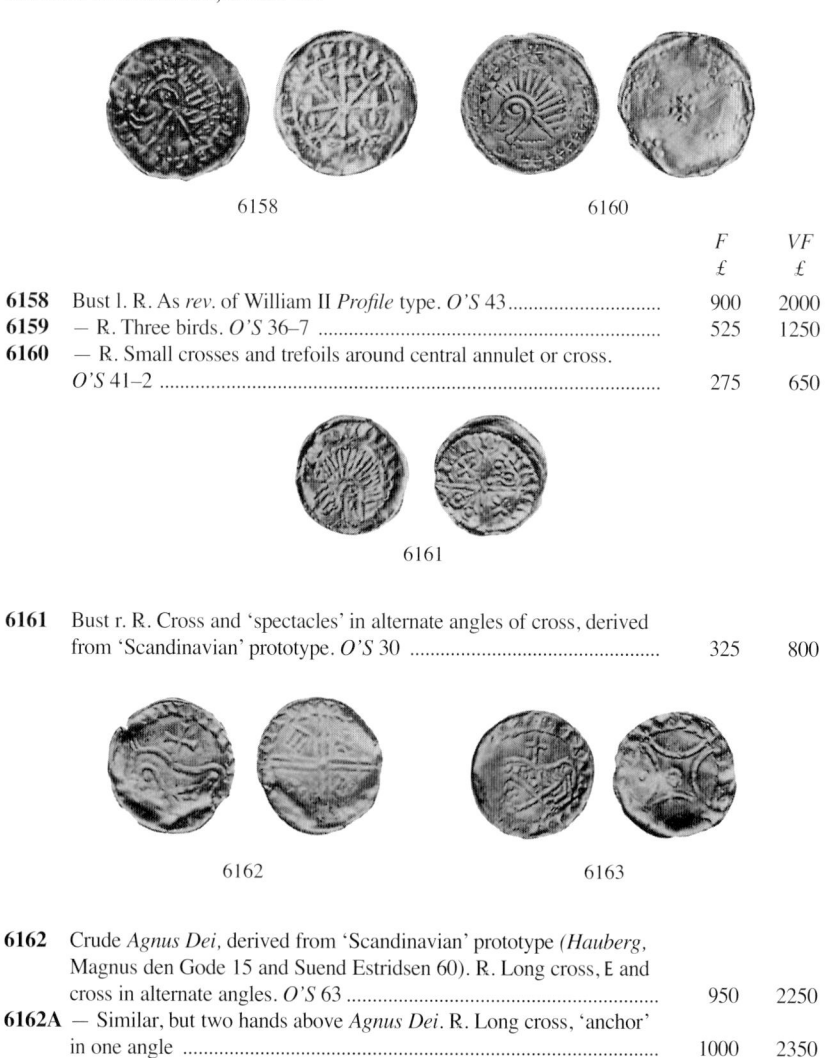

		F £	VF £
6158	Bust l. R. As *rev.* of William II *Profile* type. *O'S* 43	900	2000
6159	— R. Three birds. *O'S* 36–7	525	1250
6160	— R. Small crosses and trefoils around central annulet or cross. *O'S* 41–2	275	650

6161	Bust r. R. Cross and 'spectacles' in alternate angles of cross, derived from 'Scandinavian' prototype. *O'S* 30	325	800

6162	Crude *Agnus Dei*, derived from 'Scandinavian' prototype *(Hauberg, Magnus den Gode 15 and Suend Estridsen 60)*. R. Long cross, E and cross in alternate angles. *O'S* 63	950	2250
6162A	— Similar, but two hands above *Agnus Dei*. R. Long cross, 'anchor' in one angle	1000	2350
6163	— R. 'Bow' cross, annulet at centre. *O'S* 64	1000	2350

6164	Crude facing bust. R. Long cross with symbols in angles. *O'S* 44	1200	2750
6165	— Type as Edward the Confessor *Facing Bust/Small Cross*, but pellets in angles of cross. *BMI* 189–92	800	1750

		F	VF
		£	£
6166	— — R. Derived from Harold II **PAX** type. *BM* 184–5	900	2000
6167	— — R. Short cross. *BM* 183	800	1750
6168	Bareheaded facing bust, with sword (?) in r. hand, l. hand upraised. R. As *rev.* of William I *Bonnet* type. BM 187	1000	2500

6169   6178

6169	Facing bust derived from William I *Canopy* type. R. Three birds around central point. *O'S* 57	900	2000
6170	Facing bust, derived from William I *Two Sceptres* type. *O'S* 54	750	1750
6171	— —R. As *rev.* of William II *Cross in Quatrefoil* type. *O'S* 55	900	2000
6172	— —R. Crude bird, cross above. *O'S* 56	900	2000
6173	Facing bust derived from William I *Two Stars* type. R. Long cross with crude hand in one angle and/or other symbol. *O'S* 50	650	1500
6174	— — R. Derived from *rev.* of William I **PAX** type. *O'S* 51–2	900	2000
6175	Very crude facing head. R. Crude hand and bird in alternate angles, derived from Edward's *Sovereign* type. *O'S* 45	450	1000
6176	— — R. Similar, but hand and **S** (sometimes reversed) in angles. *O'S* 46	375	850
6177	— R. Similar, but reversed **S** and other symbol in angles of cross potent. *O'S* 48	400	900
6178	— R. Derived from *rev.* of William II *Cross in Quatrefoil* type. *O'S* 49	500	1250
6179	Crowned bust r., as William I *Profile right* type. *R.* 207	1000	2500
6180	Simple facing bust, two pellets either side, cross above. R. Two crosses and two scourges. *O'S* 53	425	950

6181

| 6181 | Cross with bar in two angles. R. Derived from Æthelred's **CRVX** type. *S. Supp.* 6 | 450 | 1000 |

		F £	VF £

6182 Annulet or cross at centre of four croziers in saltire; reversed **S** to l., scourge (?) to r. R. Long cross with symbols. *O'S* 58–9 .... 375 850
6183 — — R. As *rev.* of Cnut *Short Cross* type. *O'S* 60 .... 450 1000
6184 — — R. As *rev.* of Harthacnut *Jewel Cross* type. *BM* 199–201 .... 550 1200

6185

6185 — — R. As *rev.* of William I *Canopy* type. *O'S* 61–2 .... 600 1250
6186 Small flan coins. Types as 6168, 6153, 6161, etc. 350 800

VI. Very Late and Degraded Imitations of Long Cross Coins *c*.1095–*c*.1110

6187   6191

6187 Very crude bust l., crozier to l. R. Long cross with sceptres and pellets in alternate angles. *O'S* 22 .... 125 275
6188 — — R. Sceptres and crosses in alternate angles. *O'S* 23 .... 200 450
6189 As 6187, but bust to r. *R*. 179 .... 225 500

VII. Twelfth Century Semi-Bracteates and Bracteates *c*.1110–*c*.1150

A. *Semi-bracteates—probably the obverse and reverse types struck in separate stages.*

6190 Crude bust l. R. Voided long cross, sceptres in angles. *O'S* 67 .... 525 1250
6191 — — R. Long cross and quatrefoil. *O'S* 65 .... 425 950

6192

6192 — — R. Plain cross and cross botonee. *O'S* 66 .... 450 1000

Hiberno-Norse Issues, c.1110–c.1150

6193   6195   6197

B. *Bracteates—coins struck with design on one side only (the same design appearing incuse on the reverse).*

		F £	VF £
6193	Voided cross and sceptres. *O'S* 71–2	1250	3500
6194	Plain cross and quatrefoil. *O'S* 68	850	2500
6195	Plain cross with various symbols in angles. *O'S* 74	1000	3000
6196	Voided cross with various symbols in angles. *O'S* 79–80	1250	3500
6197	Cross pommee within quatrefoil. *O'S* 77	1000	3000
6198	Cross with trefoils in angles. *O'S* 78	1250	3500
6199	Cross with lis in each angle. *O'S* 73	1350	4000
6200	Cross potent with annulets in angles. *O'S* 82	1250	3500
6201	Hammer cross over quatrefoil. *O'S* 69	1250	3500
6202	Short cross pommee over long cross. *O'S* 70	1000	3000
6202A	Small cross pattee in inner circle, alternating sceptres and I's around	1350	4000
6202B	Cross pattee, pellet in each angle	1000	3000
6202C	Small cross pommee in inner circle	1100	3250
6202D	Cross fleury in inner circle, annulets alternating with crescents and pellets in angles	1250	3500
6202E	Double cross pommee, fleury sceptres in angles	1250	3500
6202F	Double cross pommee over hammer cross	1250	3500
6202G	Cross over quatrefoil, pellet in each angle	1350	4000
6202H	Cross fleury over long cross	1250	3500
6202J	Long cross, formalized head in each angle	1500	4250
6202K	— Similar, but heads alternating with crosses	1500	4250

ANGLO-IRISH COINS

JOHN

Lord of Ireland, 1172—Count of Mortain, 1189—King, 1199–1216

The Anglo-Norman conquest of Ireland began in 1169, in the reign of Henry II of England, when a powerful group of Norman Lords from South Wales invaded Leinster with an army of Normans, Flemings and Welsh. Dermot MacMurrough, King of Leinster, had lost his kingdom in a feud with Tiernan O'Ruairc, Lord of Brefni; and he unwisely went for assistance in recovering his territory, first to Henry II then to 'Strongbow', Richard FitzGilbert, Earl of Pembroke, to whom he promised the hand of his daughter, Eva, and the succession to his kingdom. The Norman invaders soon carved out new estates for themselves and Henry had to act quickly to set a limit to their power. He visited Ireland to secure the homage of his powerful subjects and was able to obtain papal recognition of his *de facto* suzerainty of the island. In 1172 the king's son, young Prince John, was given lordship of the new dominion and paid his first visit to the country in 1185. It is thought that this may have been the occasion when silver halfpence bearing a profile bust with name of John were struck by certain moneyers, probably in Dublin, but in any case the issue was a small one. Between 1190 and 1199 another series of silver halfpennies (and a few farthings) bearing a round moon-like face in the name of John as 'Lord of Ireland' were minted at Dublin, Carrickfergus, Kilkenny, Limerick and Waterford. In the north also, John de Courcy, who had secured considerable territory for himself in Ulster, issued halfpennies and farthings at his townships of Downpatrick and Carrickfergus.

About 1205 King John had minted in Dublin silver pennies bearing his bust set in a triangle. He ordered the weight and fineness of these coins to be of the English sterling standard (0.925 pure silver) at about 22½ grains weight. This coinage was initially under the sole control of a mintmaster named Roberd, probably Robert de Bedford who later became Bishop of Lismore. The coins, also minted at Limerick and Waterford, were mainly for use overseas and were largely for war service. However, a number of circular halfpennies and farthings were struck for purposes of normal trading within the colony and at the other two principal Anglo-Irish ports.

First (Profile) Coinage, *c*.1185
(has been also attributed to John de Curcy, Lord of Ulster)

6203

	F £	VF £
6203 Halfpenny. All *Dublin*? IOHANNES, head, r. R. Cross with lis and pellet in each angle. *Elis, Raul Blunt, Roger*	1250	3000

Second ('DOMinus') Coinage, c.1190–1199
Group I, c.1190–98. Group II, c.1198–99

6204   6205

		F £	VF £
6204	**Halfpenny.** *Dublin.* Ia. Facing diademed head, IOHANNES DOMIN YBER (or contraction). R. Voided cross potent, annulets in angles. Large flans. *Norman, Rodberd*	50	135
6205	— Ib. Similar, but smaller flan, obv. legend ends DOM, etc. *Adam, Nicolas, Norman, Rodberd, Tomas, Turgod*	30	80

6206

6206	— Ic. As above, but obv. legend ends DE MO, etc. (of Mortain?). *Rodberd*	75	200
6207	— IIa. As 6205. R. Voided cross pommée and annulets. *Adam, Huge, Tomas, Willelm*	40	100
6208	*Waterford.* Ib. As 6205, DOM, etc. *Davi, Gefrei, Marcus, Walter, Willmus, [Rob]ert*	50	125
6209	— Ic. As 6206, DE MO. *Gefrei*	100	225
6210	— Id. Similar, but legend ends COMI. *Willmus*	110	250
6211	— IIa. As 6205, but legend ends DOM, DNS, etc. *Gaifri, Willelmus*	80	200
6212	— IIb. Similar, but legend ends DE MO. *Willelm*	80	200
6213	*Kilkenny* ('KIL', 'KEN'). Ib. As 6205. *Andreh, Simund, Waltex*	350	850
6214	*Limerick.* Ib. As 6205, DOMI. *Siward*	425	1000
6215	— IIa. As 6207, DOM, *Siward*	450	1100

Second Coinage Halfpennies
| 6216 | *Carrickfergus* (CRAC). Ib. As 6205. *Roberd* | 500 | 1250 |
| 6217 | — (CRAG). IIa. As 6207. *Roberd* | 450 | 1000 |

6218   6220

6218	— (CFECIG, CRACFOR). IIc. Similar, but CAPVT IONIS PEGIS on obv. *Salmo, Thomas*	650	1500
6219	*Downpatrick* (DVNO). IIc. As 6218, CAPVT IOHANNIS, etc. *Thomas*	650	1500
6220	**Farthing** (Without name of prince or mint) *Dublin.* Mascle with trefoils at corners. R. Four letters of moneyer's name in angles of cross. *Adam, Nico, Norm, Robd, Toma*	250	525

			F £	*VF* £
6221	*Waterford*. Similar. *Marc*, *Walt* or *Gefr*		325	750
6222	*Limerick*. Similar. *Siwa*		500	1200

THE 'ST PATRICK' COINAGE OF JOHN DE CURCY, LORD OF ULSTER, *c*.1185–*c*.1205

John de Curcy took a private army into Ulster in 1177, seizing Downpatrick. Within five years he had subdued the whole kingdom of Uladh (Down and Antrim) which he ruled as an independent prince, marrying the daughter of Godred, the Norse king of Man. Refusing to pay homage to King John, he was outlawed and eventually taken prisoner by Hugh de Lacy who was granted the earldom of Ulster.

I. Issues with de Curcy's name. No mint name, but probably Downpatrick

6223 6224

6223	**Halfpenny**. As illustration, PATRICIVS. R. IOh's DE CVRCI	*Extremely rare*	
6224	**Farthing**. PATRICI, cross pattée. R. GOAN D CVRCI, voided cross potent	1000	2500

II. Anonymous 'St Patrick' issues, *c*.1195–1205

6225 6226 6227

6225	**Farthing**. *Downpatrick*. PATRICI, processional cross. R. Cross with crescents in angles	500	1250
6226	*Carrickfergus*. Obv. Similar. R. Voided cross pattée	550	1350
6227	— — R. Voided cross pommée	600	1450

KING JOHN

Third ('Rex') Coinage, *c.***1207–1211.** Wt. 22½ grains; 11 oz. 2 dwt. fineness (as English coinage)

6228

		F £	VF £
6228	**Penny.** *Dublin.* Crowned bust in triangle, hand holding sceptre. R. Sun, moon and three stars in triangle. *Roberd*	25	65
6228A	— — Similar, but moneyers, *Iohan, Willem, Wilelm P.*	50	135
6229	*Limerick.* Similar. *Willem, Wace*	125	175
6230	*Waterford.* Similar. *Willem*	250	550

6231   6234

6231	**Halfpenny.** *Dublin.* Similar bust but no sceptre. R. Cross, moon, and stars in triangle. *Roberd, Willem*	65	150
6232	*Limerick.* Similar. *Willem, Wace*	120	250
6233	*Waterford.* Similar. *Willem*	250	525
6234	**Farthing.** *Dublin* (but without mint name). Head in triangle. R. Whorled sun in triangle. *Roberd, Willem*	500	1250

HENRY III, 1216–1272

In 1247 Richard, Earl of Cornwall, King Henry's younger brother, was granted the right to strike new money for a period of twelve years in England, Wales and Ireland, in consideration of a substantial loan which he had made to the king. The agreement gave Richard half the profits of the minting and the exchange. Coins of new type, the *Long Cross* coins, were struck in England the same year, but it was not until the autumn of 1251 that coining operations recommenced at Dublin. Roger de Haverhull was put in charge of the mint in Ireland, but the moneyers *Ricard* and *Davi* whose names appear on the coins may have been the London moneyers Richard Bonaventure and David of Enfield, operating *in absentia*. The dies for the coinage were sent from London.

The coinage was of fairly short duration as the Dublin mint was closed again in January 1254, probably after all the older money in the island had been re-coined and it was no longer profitable to incur the expenses of maintaining a mint. No halfpennies or farthings were coined, but pennies are sometimes found cut into halves or quarters along the line of the voided cross for use as small change. It seems that a large proportion of the pence produced were exported to England and the continent; there were, for instance, over 1600 of these pieces amongst the huge hoard of sterling pence found in Brussels in 1908, and the types were even copied in Saxony.

6235   6239

		F £	VF £
6235	Penny. *Dublin*. Ia. Crowned facing head in double triangle, hand holding sceptre, cinquefoil to r. R. Voided long cross pommée, pellets in angles	25	70
	The letters ЄNR of the king's name are normally ligated.		
6236	— Ib. Head in single triangle	30	75
6237	— Ic. Sexfoil to r. of neck. Small triangle below central fleur of crown	40	100
6238	— Similar, but small star by head of sceptre	65	150
6239	— Id. Double band to crown	65	150

6240   6242   6243

6240	— IIa. Coarser work. Cinquefoil to r, of neck. Central pellets not joined to band of crown	30	75
6241	— IIb. Similar, but band of crown jewelled with pellets	75	175
6242	— IIc. Three curls either side of head instead of two	40	100
6243	— IId. Wide open shoulders	35	85

6243A   6243B

6243A	**Cut Halfpenny.** As illustration	10	25
6243B	**Cut Farthing.** As illustration	5	15

EDWARD I

Lord of Ireland, 1254 – King, 1272–1307

It seems that no coins were minted in Ireland after 1254 until Richard Olof was placed in charge of the Dublin mint between 1276 and 1279. The coins of this issue are of the same basic type as Henry III's *Long Cross* (*Double Cross*) coins and even continue the name HENRICVS; but, as on the English coins of the same period, a distinctive treatment of the king's hair distinguishes them from similar coins of the previous reign. Very few pieces of this issue have survived, which is not surprising as in 1280 there was a complete recoinage of earlier types.

Over the previous century there had been a gradual centralizing of control over the coinage and it was now considered unnecessary for a coin to bear the name of the moneyer or mintmaster. The 1280 issue retains the king's head in a triangle, now inverted, and the reverse has a plain cross and pellets with the name of the mint. A branch mint was opened at Waterford to help with the recoinage but it was closed by 1295, in which year a mint at Cork was opened for a short period. Minting was intermittent and probably ceased in the opening years of the 14th Century. Coins with a rose on the king's breast seem to coincide with a similar feature on English sterlings in 1294. Round halfpence and farthings were again coined for internal currency.

The normal obverse inscription is €DW'R' / ANGL'D / NS hYB (*Edwardus, Rex Angliae, Dominus Hiberniae–Edward,* King of England, Lord of Ireland) and on the reverse the name of the mint, CIVITAS DVBLIN, etc. Though many of the coins have three pellets on the king's breast, the top pellet is sometimes stamped into the drapery and is not easily visible on a worn coin.

As in earlier reigns, a large proportion of pence coined were exported and imitations of this type occur on the continental coins of Bar, Cologne and Lippe.

First ('hENRICVS') Coinage, 1276–79

6244/5

		F £	VF £
6244	**Penny.** *Dublin.* Facing crowned head in triangle, realistic hair. Roman V in hENRICVS and DIVE. *Ricard*	500	1400
6245	— — Similar, but Lombardic U in hENRICUS and DIUE. *Ricard*	650	1500

Second ('€DW') Coinage, 1279–1302. 11 oz. 2 dwt. fineness

The following classification has been retained in this edition on the grounds of simplicity. The actual sequence of the series, based on a close examination of the punches used is more complex and is set out in J.J. North, 'The Anglo-Irish Halfpence, Farthings and post-1290 Pence of Edward I and Edward III'. *BNJ 67,* 1997.

		F £	VF £
6246	**Penny.** *Dublin.* Ia. Crowned bust in triangle, trefoil of pellets on breast, no mark before ЄDW.R	20	50
6247	— Ib. Similar, but pellet before ЄDW.R	20	45
6248	— Ic. Similar, but small cross before ЄDW.R	30	75
6249	— II. Rosette on breast, ЄDW.R	225	500
6250	— III. Pellet in each angle of triangle	325	700
6251	— IVa. Single pellet below small bust, small lettering on *obv.*, large letters on *rev.*	20	45
6252	— IVb. Similar, but pellet before ЄDW.R	25	65
6253	— IVc. As 6251, but small lettering on both sides	30	75
6253A	— — Similar, oblong pellet below bust	125	300
6253B	— — Similar, but without pellet below bust	100	250
6254	*Waterford.* Ib. Trefoil of pellets on breast	20	50
6255	— II. Rosette on breast, irregular lettering	200	400
6256	*Cork* (CORGAGIЄ). III. Pellet in each angle of triangle	225	550
6256A	*Counterfeits.* Contemporary copy of Edward I penny	35	90
6256B	— Contemporary copy with English type *obv.*	65	150
6257	**Halfpenny.** *Dublin.* Ia. Early lettering, no pellet before ЄDW R	35	80
6258	— Ib. Pellet before ЄDW R	40	85
6259	— Ic. Pellet before ЄDW R	50	125
6260	— II. Rosette on breast	300	650
6261	— IVa. Late lettering, without pellet on breast	60	150
6262	— IVb. Similar, but pellet on breast	70	175

6263

		F £	VF £
6263	*Waterford.* Ia. Early lettering, no pellet before ЄDW R	45	90
6264	— Ib. Pellet before ЄDW R	40	85
6265	— III? Late lettering, bust as on Cork halfpenny	125	300
6266	*Cork.* III. Late lettering	650	1500
6267	*Farthing. Dublin.* I. ЄRA/NG/LIЄ	70	175

6267A 6268

| 6267A | — ЄDШ/ARDV/SRЄX | 250 | 600 |
| 6268 | — *Waterford.* I. ЄRA/NG/LIЄ | 100 | 250 |

EDWARD II TO HENRY VI 1307–1460

A great quantity of Irish silver had been drained out of the country by the export of 'sterlings' struck on the English standard by King John, Henry III and Edward I. To balance the shortage of native coinage some English money circulated, and Scottish coins also made their appearance, particularly in the North and West. An extremely rare coin, a Dublin halfpenny, is the only denomination to have survived of what must have been a very brief issue from the Dublin mint in 1339/40. Of similar type to the coins of Edward I, a star in the legends both sides links it to the base silver English coinage of 1335–43.

There was then a gap of many decades before another issue of coins was made in Ireland. Though the Norman conquest had been extensive, much of the country had been only thinly held. The descendants of the early settlers soon became largely assimilated in the South, West and North through intermarriage and the adoption by the conquerors of Irish customs and language. In the Eastern counties, in what became known as the 'Pale', closer links were maintained with England and the English crown, and the Anglo-Irish Parliament passed many restrictive ordinances which sought to keep the 'Irish enemy' under permanent subjection.

An ordinance of 1425 authorised a coinage at Dublin of the same weight and fineness as the English coinage and a moneyer was appointed the following year. Only two pennies are known of this issue, and the annulets in the inscriptions link the issue to the contemporary English 'Annulet Coinage' of 1422–26.

Complaints about the state of the currency are borne out by finds which show that clipped and false English coin were in common use. The notorious 'Oraylly' money has been shown to refer to ingenious counterfeits of clipped groats manufactured from thin surface plates of silver soldered to a base metal core (See M. Dolley and W.A. Seaby, 'Le Money del Oraylly (O'Reilly's Money)', *BNJ* 36 (1967). English coins were free to circulate in Ireland, but a full weight *groat* (4 pence) might pass for as much as sixpence.

Eventually, in 1460, Henry's Anglo-Irish Parliament meeting in Drogheda decided on a new coinage, but in order to prevent the coins being immediately exported it was planned to issue a groat containing only threepence worth of silver, and to prevent them getting into circulation in England the designs were to be quite distinctive. Before the coins could be issued the Yorkist Edward IV had ascended the throne.

Edward III, 1327–77

Coinage of 1339/40. 10 oz. fineness; wt. *c*.11 grs.

6269

	F £	VF £
6269 **Halfpenny.** *Dublin*. As Edw. I, but star before EDW / ARDV / SREX....	2250	6000

Henry VI

Coinage of 1425–6. Wt. *c*.15 grains.

6270

6270 **Penny.** *Dublin*. hENRICVS DNS hIBNIE, crowned bust in circle, star to r. Annulet at end of *obv.* legend and after CIVI	2500	6500

EDWARD IV, 1461–1483

The accession of Edward IV saw the issue of the coinage ordered in 1460. It was of distinctive type with a large crown on the obverse instead of a royal portrait, and to discourage the export of silver coin it was made to a specific Irish weight standard which was three-quarters that of the English coinage. In view of the events which led to the transfer of sovereignty from the Lancastrians to the Yorkists it is scarcely surprising that the first issue was anonymous. Another innovation was the minting of farthings made of billon (silver heavily debased with copper) in the name of St Patrick, followed in 1463 by a larger coin depicting the Saint's mitred head. A second silver coinage minted at Dublin and Waterford in 1463 was of somewhat similar type to the first except for the addition of the king's name and Irish title on the obverse, **EDWARDVS DEI GRA DNS HYBERN**, and an outer inscription on the reverse, **POSVI DEVM ADIVTOREM MEVM**, 'I have made the Lord my Helper'.

In 1465 the weights of the English silver coins were considerably reduced and it may be about this time that the Dublin mint followed suit by minting a new coinage only two-thirds the weight of the English issue, the earlier crown device being replaced by two Yorkist badges, a rose on one side with a cross superimposed and a sun in splendour on the other. Two years later the Irish money was again devalued, the Irish groat being rated half the English equivalent, but now an eightpenny coin was issued the same size as the English groat. A stylized royal portrait copied the English coin, but Edward's *rose en soleil* device supplied a distinctive type for the reverse, the coins being issued from the mints of Dublin and Drogheda and the great fortress at Trim. An interesting base metal farthing of this issue has for its obverse type a shield bearing the fifteenth-century arms of Ireland, three crowns.

No coins were minted in Ireland bearing the name of Henry VI during his brief restoration, 1470–1; the groats that at one time were attributed to this period are now clearly seen to be coins of Henry VII. In 1470 a new coinage giving nominal allegiance to King Edward was instituted which was the same type and almost the weight of his English issues, possibly made with the object of having them available, if necessary, for currency in England. They were minted at Dublin, Waterford, Drogheda and Trim and at temporary mints in the west and south-west at Galway, Limerick and Cork. Only two coins have survived of the Galway mint, and though it is possible that a mint was also opened at Carlingford no coins of this period are now known of that mint. Coins were also minted at Wexford but they are so crude that they are unlikely to be an official issue. About 1472 the coinage was again devalued by reducing the groat to 32 grains, though it is known that some of the 1470 'heavy' issue had been struck at weights below the proper standard. For this reason, and because heavy coins were frequently clipped down to the weights of the later issue, it is sometimes difficult to determine the proper issue of these coins. Some pence of this issue copy coins of York or Durham with a quatrefoil or D in the centre of the reverse.

On the coins of this English type, as well as other issues of Edward, an elaborate system of 'privy' marks (private or secret marks) were inserted into the design in order to discourage fraud at the mint and to detect counterfeits. In addition, initial marks or 'mintmarks' denoting the period of issue were usually inserted at the commencement of the inscription and were changed annually or at other intervals.

In 1476 in order to encourage the import of gold coin into Ireland the English noble of ten shillings was rated at 13s. 4d. Irish and the angel of 6s. 8d. at 8s. 4d., and at the same time foreign gold was made legal tender—ducats, riders, crowns, cruzados and salutes at five shillings and Burgundian nobles at ten shillings.

The last coinage of this reign was confined to the mints of Dublin and Drogheda, and the groats have roses and suns alternating by the king's neck and crown and a large rose in the centre of the reverse cross. The pence of this coinage are of two distinct types, the earlier with a small rose at the centre of the reverse cross and with roses and suns in the angles, the later with a large rose as on the groats.

SILVER

I. Anonymous 'Crown' Coinage, *c*.1460–63

6272   6276

		F £	VF £
6271	**Groat** (45 grs.). *Dublin*. Large crown in tressure of ten arcs with pellets at points, no legend. R. Mint name, cross and pellets	325	900
6272	— Similar, but tressure of nine arcs	225	650

		F £	VF £
6272A	— — Crosses in three top angles of tressure	250	750
6273	— Similar, but eight arcs to tressure, small suns in each angle	275	800
6274	— Similar, but arcs of tressured fleured, suns or rosettes in angles	325	900
6275	— — — Large rosette in each angle of tressure	350	950
6276	**Penny.** *Dublin.* As groat, 6272	725	1750
6277	— — Crosses in top angles of tressure	725	1750
6278	— — Saltire below crown	750	1800
6279	— Crown in tressure of 8 arcs	750	1800
6280	— No tressure	725	1750
6281	*Waterford.* Crown in tressure of fleured arcs	950	2250

II. Second 'Crown' Coinage, 1463–65

Mintmarks: rose *(Dublin)*, cross *(Waterford)*.

6282	**Groat.** *Dublin.* King's name and titles, large crown in tressure, small annulets in spandrels. R. POSVI, etc., cross and pellets. *Mm.* rose	1000	2500
6283	*Waterford.* Similar, but pellets in spandrels of tressure. *Mm.* cross	1100	2750
6284	— Annulets in spandrels of tressure, saltires by crown	1250	3000
6285	**Half-groat.** *Dublin.* Pellets in angles of tressure, two saltires over crown	1500	3500
6286	**Penny.** *Dublin.* Inscription around crown, no tressure	1000	2500
6287	*Waterford.* Similar	1100	2650

III. Small-Cross on Rose/Radiant Sun Coinage, *c*.1465–67?

6288	**Groat.** *Dublin.* Large rose, cross at centre, within tressure of five arcs. R. POSVI, etc., mint name, sun with face	1650	4000
6289	**Penny.** *Dublin.* Similar, but no tressure around rose. R. Mint name, sun with pellet in annulet at centre	750	1750

IV. Bust/Rose-on-Sun Coinage, 1467–70

6290

		F £	VF £
6290	**Double Groat** (45 grs.). *Dublin*. Crowned bust in fleured tressure. R. Rose at centre of large sun, suns and roses divide legend	1250	3000
6291	— Similar, but unfleured tressure	1250	3250
6292	*Drogheda*. As 6290	1350	3500
6293	*Trim*. Two pellets over crown and below bust	1750	4500

6294   6300

6294	**Groat**. *Dublin*. As 6291	1250	3000
6295	*Drogheda*. Similar	1500	3750
6296	*Trim*. Pellets over crown and below bust	1650	4250
6297	**Half Groat**. *Dublin*. As 6290	1000	2500
6298	— Similar, but crosses by neck	1100	2750
6299	*Trim*. As 6297	1250	3000
6300	— Similar, but two pellets over crown	1250	3000

6301

6301	**Penny.** *Dublin*. No tressure	950	2500
6302	*Drogheda*. Similar	950	2500

V. Heavy 'Cross and Pellets' Coinage, 1470?–73?

Basically the same type as the English coins of the period. The letter G on some coins is the initial of the mintmaster Germyn Lynch. Extra pellets, annulets, crosses or roses occur in one or more angles of the cross on some coins.

Mintmarks: rose, pierced cross double fitchy.

6303

		F £	VF £
6303	**Groat** *(c.41 grs.)*. *Dublin*. Bust in tressure, no marks	70	175
6304	— — Pellets in one or three lower spandrels of tressure	75	200
6305	— — — Pellet also to r. of crown	85	225
6306	— Stars by crown	125	350
6307	— G on breast	75	200
6308	*Drogheda*. Three pellets on some points of tressure, cross below bust	125	350
6309	— Fleured tressure, cross below bust	125	350
6310	— Nothing below bust	120	325
6310A	— — Pellet below bust	110	300
6311	*Limerick*. No letter on breast	225	525
6312	*Trim*. No letter on breast	125	300
6313	*Waterford*. No letter on breast	85	210
6314	— — Crosses by neck	90	250
6314A	— V on breast	90	250

6315   6316   6320

6315	— ⋜ on breast, crosses or saltires by neck	100	275
6316	*Cork*. Irregular issue. Rosettes by neck	850	2250
6317	— Crosses by neck	800	2000
6318	**Half Groat**. *Dublin*. Pellets over crown and below bust	300	800
6319	— — Similar, but pellets in each angle of tressure	325	850
6320	— Annulets by neck, no pellets	300	750
6321	*Galway*. Fleured tressure. R. **VILLA GALWEY**	1250	3500
6322	*Trim*. Two small pellets over crown	700	1750

EDWARD IV

		F £	VF £
6323	**Penny.** *Dublin.* No marks by bust	45	125
6324	— — Similar, but pellets over crown	50	135
6325	— Crosses by neck	65	175
6326	*Waterford.* Two crosses either side of neck, pellets by crown	100	300
6327	*Galway.* No marks by head	650	1750
6328	*Limerick.* No marks by head	175	525
6329	**Halfpenny.** *Dublin.* No marks by head	350	850

VI. Light 'Cross and Pellets' Coinage, 1473–78?

As last issue, but weight of groat reduced to *c*.32 grains in 1473.

It is possible that some of the coins listed below are clipped or light weight specimens of the 'heavy' coinage, but Dr E. Harris has noted that light coinage groats of Dublin and Drogheda have inner circles with a diameter of approx. 18 mm, compared with a diameter of 19 or 19.5 mm on the heavy coinage groats. Probably some heavy reverse dies were used with light obverse dies.

Mintmarks: pierced cross double fitchy, sun, rosette, plain cross, crown, trefoil.

		F	VF
6330	**Groat.** *Dublin.* G below bust (for Germyn Lynch)	65	165
6331	— — Similar, but annulets in two spandrels of tressure	75	185
6332	— — — As above, but with crosses by neck	100	250
6333	— — Annulets by neck	125	275
6334	— — Annulets by neck and in two spandrels of tressure	80	200
6335	— — Pellets in some spandrels of tressure	80	200
6336	— I on King's breast	175	450
6337	*Drogheda.* G below bust, annulets in two spandrels of tressure by crown	90	225
6338	— — Similar, but annulets by neck and in two spandrels of tressure	135	300
6339	— Trefoil on king's breast	150	350
6339A	— — No marks other than G. R Two extra pellets in one quarter	100	250
6340	*Limerick.* L on breast; quatrefoils, crosses or saltires by neck	135	350

		F £	VF £
6341	— Rosettes or cinque foils by neck	150	375
6342	*Trim*. No letter on breast	120	275
6343	— — Pellet in some spandrels of tressure and/or over crown	110	250
6344	— — Pellets by neck	135	350
6344A	— — B on breast	250	600
6345	*Waterford*. No letter on breast, rosettes by neck	135	300
6346	— — Crosses or saltires by neck	90	225
6347	— — Annulets by neck. R. Crowned leopard's head at end of legend (wt. 45 grs.)	250	600
6348	— V on breast	100	250
6349	— G on breast	75	185
6350	*Cork*. Crude work. No marks by neck	750	2000
6351	— — Pellets by neck	750	2000

6352	*Wexford*. Very crude. R. VILLA WEISFOR	1250	3000
6353	**Half Groat.** *Dublin*. No marks by neck	300	750
6354	— Annulets by neck	325	800
6355	*Drogheda*. No marks by neck	750	1750
6356	*Limerick*. L on king's breast, rosettes or cinquefoils by neck	650	1500
6357	— Similar but without letter on breast	600	1400
6358	*Waterford*. No marks on breast or neck	750	1750
6359	*Wexford*. Crude work. R. VILLA WEISFOR	1000	2500
6360	**Penny.** *Dublin*. Without marks by neck. R. Plain cross	25	80
6361	— — R. Quatrefoil in centre of cross	25	75
6361A	— — R. D in centre of cross	35	100
6362	— Crosses or saltires by neck. R. Plain cross	30	90
6363	— — Similar, but with saltire to r. of crown. R. Plain cross	30	90
6364	— Pellets by neck. R. Plain cross	25	80

6365

		F £	VF £
6365	— — R. Quatrefoil in centre of cross	20	75
6366	— Mullets by neck. R. Quatrefoil in centre of cross	30	85
6367	— Mullets by crown	30	85
6368	*Drogheda*. No marks by neck. R. Plain cross	30	85
6369	— —R. Quatrefoil in centre of cross	25	80
6370	— — Similar. R. Small rose at centre of cross	30	100
6371	— Crosses by neck. R. Plain cross	30	90
6372	— Pellets by neck. R. Plain cross	30	90
6373	— Pellets by neck and/or crown. R. Quatrefoil in centre of cross	30	90
6374	— Pellets and rosettes by neck. R. Plain cross	50	150
6375	— Pellet and rosette by neck, saltire by crown. R. Small rose at centre of cross	65	225
6376	*Limerick*. Rosettes or cinquefoils by neck	125	400
6377	— Crosses by neck	135	425
6378	*Waterford*. No marks on *obv*.	75	250
6379	— Annulets by neck. R. Plain cross	85	275
6379A	— — Similar. R. Quatrefoil in centre of cross	75	250
6380	— Pellets by neck. R. Plain cross	85	275
6381	— Crosses by neck and crown	100	300
6382	— Crosses by neck. R. Quatrefoil at centre of cross	75	250
6383	*Trim*. No marks. R. Plain cross	90	300
6384	— Similar. R. Quatrefoil in centre of cross	100	325
6385	— Pellets by bust. R. Plain cross	90	300
6386	— — Similar. R. Quatrefoil in centre of cross	90	300
6387	*Cork*. Pellets by crown	300	750
6387A	— Unusually large head	350	850

Note: These pennies rarely turn up on a full round flan and are usually clipped as the illustration above. A full flan coin is worth considerably more.

Bust with Suns and Roses/Rose-on-Cross Coinage, *c*.1478–83.

Mintm*ark:* rose.

6388	**Groat.** *Dublin*. Sun and rose alternating at crown and neck. R. POSVI, etc., mint name, large rose at centre of cross	325	750
6389	— Similar, but rose and sun alternating at crown and neck	350	800

6390   6391

6390	— — Larger symbols by crown and neck	400	950
6391	*Drogheda*. As 6388	325	750

		F £	VF £
6392	— As 6389	350	850
6393	**Penny.** *Dublin.* I. Sun and rose alternating at crown and neck. R. *Small* rose at centre of cross, rose and 2 suns and sun and 2 roses alternating in angles	100	250

6394

6394	— — Similar, but rose and sun alternating at crown and neck	90	225
6395	— — — Similar, but larger symbols on *obv.*	125	300
6396	— II. Sun and rose, alternating at crown and neck. R. *Large* rose at centre of cross, no marks in angles	165	450

6397

| 6397 | — — Rose and sun alternating at crown and neck .... | 150 | 425 |
| 6398 | — — — Similar, but without symbols by crown .... | 200 | 550 |

Issues of *c*.1460–61

6399   6400

6399	**Half Farthing,** or 'Patrick' (Æ). PA branch TRIK branch, crown in centre. R. Large cross no legend	500	1250
6399A	—Similar, but retrograde inscription	525	1350
6400	— — R. P in one angle of cross	600	1500

Issue of 1462

6401

| 6401 | **Farthing** (billon). Large crown, sun and roses in place of legend. R. Mint name, cross .... | 625 | 1500 |

Issue of 1463–65

6402   6404

		F £	VF £
6402	**Farthing** (Æ). PATRICIVS, mitred Saint's head facing, sun and rose. R. SALVATOR, cross with rose and sun in alternate angles. Several varieties	600	1500
6403	**Half Farthing** (Æ). Crown, no legend. R. Cross and pellets, no legend	650	1650

Issue of 1467–70?

6404	**Farthing** (Æ). Shield bearing three crowns. R. Cross with rose over sun at centre	750	1750

A 'farthing' of brass in the Nat. Mus. of Ireland with a facing bust and cross and pellets on the reverse, with strokes for legend, is probably a counterfeit of an English halfpenny of Henry VII or VIII.

RICHARD III, 1483–1485 & HENRY VII, 1485–1509

A new coinage was ordered in 1483, but before it came into production transitional coins were minted at Drogheda of the last type of Edward IV, but with Richard's name. It seems likely that the rare coins of Dublin and Waterford of the type of Edward's fifth coinage were also struck at this time.

The new coinage had the royal arms on the obverse and on the reverse the arms of Ireland, three crowns in pale, set over a cross with triple pellet ends, hence the coinage is known as the 'Three Crowns' issue. At one time it was thought that the coinage commenced in the reign of Edward IV, but it is now certain that it was first issued under Richard III and that rare coins with the name EDWARDVS were struck for Lambert Simnel, the Pretender 'Edward VI', who was crowned at Christchurch Cathedral, Dublin, on 24 May 1487.

The earliest Three Crowns coins struck in Henry's reign omit the sovereign's name, merely reading REX ANGLIE FRANCIE on one side and DOMINVS HYBERNIE or the Waterford mint name on the other. At Dublin, Gerald, Earl of Kildare, who had been deputy for Richard, Duke of York, and his son, Prince Edward, held what was virtually a royal court and it is noteworthy that the early coins bear no reference to King Henry. In contrast, at Waterford, which was a Butler (and anti-Yorkist) stronghold, the coins display the city's allegiance to Henry by having an initial 'H' below the lowest crown. After Simnel left Dublin on his abortive attempt to win the crown of England, the Three Crowns issue was continued but with the arms of the 'Great Earl' (the Fitzgerald saltire cross) inserted on small shields either side of the royal arms.

Simnel was defeated at the Battle of Stoke, and Henry then sent an envoy to Ireland to secure oaths of allegiance to the King and to grant a royal pardon to Kildare. It must be from this time that the later Three Crowns coins omit the Geraldine arms. The issue continued until about 1490 with Dublin the sole mint. The half-groat normally had the DOMINVS VBERNIE legend or the mint name on the reverse, but there is an interesting variant which reads DOMINE KERIE and it has been postulated that this was a rendering of *Domine Kyrie* 'O Lord, O Lord'—a Latin-Greek mule.

There exist Irish portrait coins of Henry VII which may have been issued early in his reign, but the first regular portrait coinage was probably not issued before Kildare was allowed to return to Ireland in 1496 after his imprisonment at London for complicity in the Perkin Warbeck affair. The earliest groats of this issue are of English type and have an open crown, some are made from double-struck obverse dies and on some the normal POSVI DEVM legend is transformed to PROVIDEBO ADIVTORIVM, IVTOREVM, etc. These are superseded by arched-crown groats which become progressively cruder and on the latest coins the king's head appears in a plain circle without a tressure, often with grossly blundered inscriptions. The portrait halfgroats and most of the pennies are of comparatively good style and must come early in the series. A rare, but interesting penny has a large crowned H instead of a portrait, perhaps derived from the lower part of the Three Crowns type.

RICHARD III

Bust with Suns and Roses/Rose-on-cross coinage

6406

		F £	VF £
6406	**Groat.** *Drogheda*. Sun and rose alternating at crown and neck. R. Rose at centre of cross	900	2000
6407	— — Similar, but RIC altered from EDW	1000	2250
6408	**Penny.** *Drogheda*. As 6406. R. Large rose at centre of cross	1250	3000

Cross and Pellets Coinage

6410

| 6410 | **Penny.** *Dublin*. Annulets by neck. R. Quatrefoil in centre of cross | 950 | 2250 |
| 6411 | — *Waterford*. Annulets by neck. R. Quatrefoil in centre of cross | 1000 | 2500 |

The cross-and-pellets half-groat listed by Coffey is probably a coin of Edward IV's fifth coinage.

RICHARD III AND HENRY VII

'THREE CROWNS' COINAGE, 1483–c.1490

Issued by Richard III, Henry VII, Lambert Simnel ('Edward VI') and Gerald, Earl of Kildare

Note: The earlier coins have the cross-ends terminating in triple pellets (pellet crosses); the later coins have triple annulets at the ends of the cross arms (annulet crosses). The change takes place at Waterford appreciably earlier than at Dublin and there are a number of pellet-annulet and annulet-pellet mules.

I. Richard III, 1483–85

6412   6413

		F £	VF £
6412	**Groat.** No mint name (*Dublin*). RICARD, etc., arms over cross with pellet ends. R. DOMINVS hYBERNIE, three crowns in pale over cross	325	700
6413	*Waterford.* Arms within tressure of four arcs. R. CIVITAS WATERFOORD, three flat crowns in tressure of eight arcs	900	2000

II. Henry VII, Early 'Three-Crowns' Issues, 1485–87

6414

6414	**Groat.** No mint name (*Dublin*). As Ric. III, but REX ANGLIE FRANCIE. R. DOMINVS hYBERNIE. Pellet crosses	70	200
6415	— — Similar, but DOMINVS hYBERNIE legend both sides. Pellet crosses	85	225
6416	— — As 6414, but ET REX hYBERNIE on *rev.*	100	275

Early 'Three Crowns' Coinage

6417	*Waterford.* hENRICVS, etc., arms in quatrefoil. R. Mint name, three crowns with h below, two lis by central crown, trefoils on points and angles of tressure. Pellet crosses	125	300

6418

		F £	VF £
6418	— — No lis by centre crown, trefoils on points of rev. tressure but not in angles	125	300
6419	— Arms with no quatrefoil. R. Three crowns with no tressure. Annulet crosses	200	550
6420	— Arms in quatrefoil. R. Three crowns in tressure, h below. Annulet crosses	85	225
6421	— — Similar, but crosses or mullets in lower angles of quatrefoil	95	250
6422	— — — Similar. R. Stars by lower crown	150	400

6423

6423	**Half Groat.** No mint name (*Dublin*). As 6415, pellet crosses. REX ANGLIE FRANCIE. R. DOMINVS HIBERNIE	125	300
6423A	— — Similar, but lis below lower crown	175	475

6424   6425

6424	**Penny.** No mint name (*Dublin*). Similar	325	850
6425	**Halfpenny.** No mint name (*Dublin*). Similar	600	1500

'Three Crowns' Coinage
III. Lambert Simnel, as 'Edward VI', May?–July? 1487

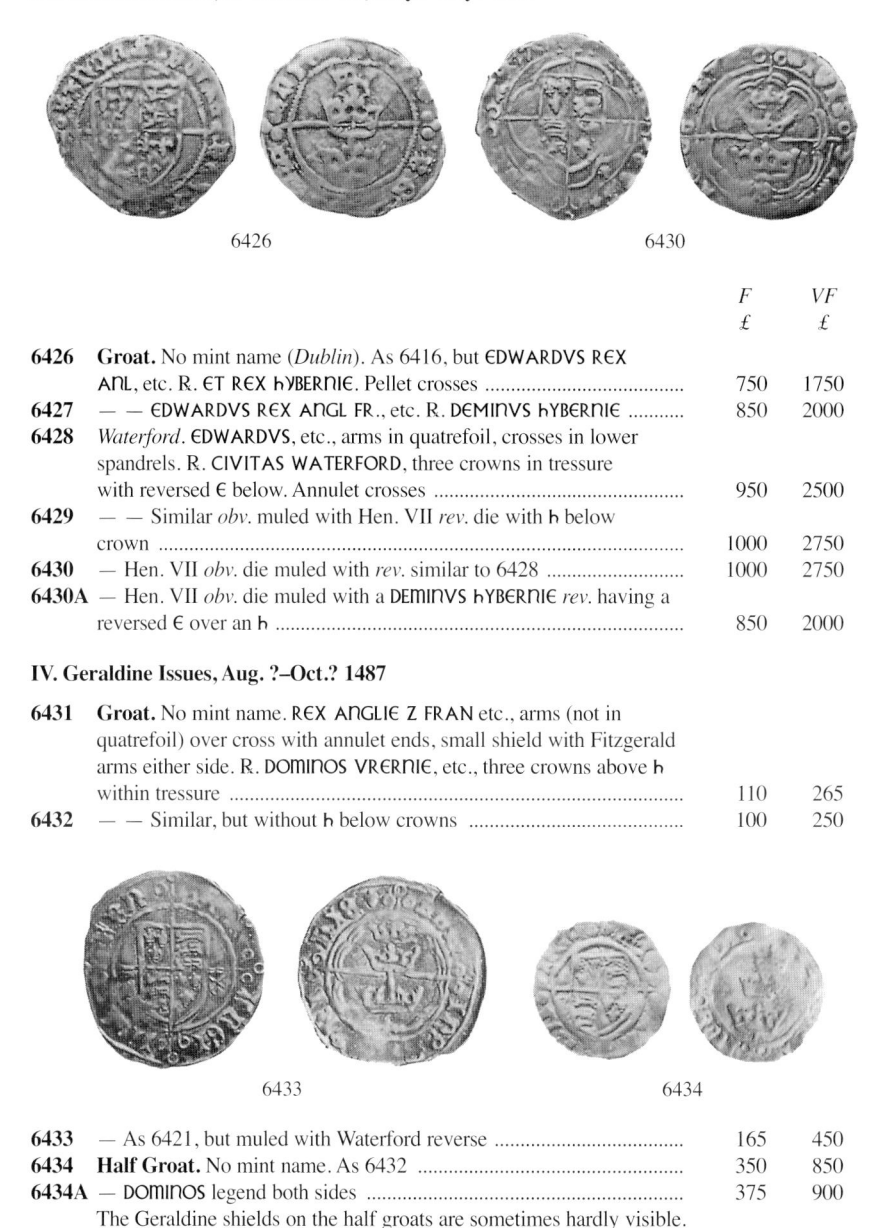

6426   6430

		F £	VF £
6426	**Groat.** No mint name (*Dublin*). As 6416, but ЄDWARDVS RЄX ANL, etc. R. ЄT RЄX hYBЄRNIЄ. Pellet crosses	750	1750
6427	— — ЄDWARDVS RЄX ANGL FR., etc. R. DЄMINVS hYBЄRNIЄ	850	2000
6428	*Waterford.* ЄDWARDVS, etc., arms in quatrefoil, crosses in lower spandrels. R. CIVITAS WATERFORD, three crowns in tressure with reversed Є below. Annulet crosses	950	2500
6429	— — Similar *obv.* muled with Hen. VII *rev.* die with h below crown	1000	2750
6430	— Hen. VII *obv.* die muled with *rev.* similar to 6428	1000	2750
6430A	— Hen. VII *obv.* die muled with a DЄMINVS hYBЄRNIЄ *rev.* having a reversed Є over an h	850	2000

IV. Geraldine Issues, Aug. ?–Oct.? 1487

6431	**Groat.** No mint name. RЄX ANGLIЄ Z FRAN etc., arms (not in quatrefoil) over cross with annulet ends, small shield with Fitzgerald arms either side. R. DOMINOS VRЄRNIЄ, etc., three crowns above h within tressure	110	265
6432	— — Similar, but without h below crowns	100	250

6433   6434

6433	— As 6421, but muled with Waterford reverse	165	450
6434	**Half Groat.** No mint name. As 6432	350	850
6434A	— DOMINOS legend both sides	375	900

The Geraldine shields on the half groats are sometimes hardly visible.

		F £	VF £

V. Henry VII, Late 'Three Crowns' Issues, 1488–c.1490

6435	**Groat.** No mint name (*Dublin*). hENRICVS, etc. R. DOMINOS VBERNIE, etc., h below crowns. Crosses with annulet ends	125	350
6436	— — Similar, but *obv.* legend REX ANGLIE Z FRANC, etc.	110	300

6437   6438

6437	— — Similar, but DOMINOS VBERNIE both sides, h below crowns	125	325
6438	*Dublin.* hENRICVS, etc. R. Mint name, upper crown arched and surmounted by cross, h below lower crown. Crosses with annulet ends	135	375
6439	**Half Groat.** No mint name (*Dublin*). REX ANGLIE Z FRANCIE, cross with pellet ends. R. DOMINOS VBERNIE, h below crowns, cross with annulet ends	150	375
6440	— — Similar, but no h below crowns	150	375
6441	— Crosses with annulet ends both sides, no h	165	400
6442	— DOMINOS legends both sides, h below crowns. Annulet crosses	175	450

6442A   6446

6442A	— — — Similar, but variant *obv.* reading DOMINE KERIE	200	525
6443	— — As 6442, but no h	175	450
6444	*Dublin.* As 6441, REX ANGLIE. R. Mint name, no h. Annulet crosses	225	600
6445	— hENRIC, etc. R. As above, but h below crowns	250	650
6446	**Penny.** No mint name (*Dublin*). REX ANG, etc., arms over cross fourchée. R. DOMINOS VRERNIE, etc., h below crowns, no cross	450	950
6447	— — DOMINOS legend both sides, h below crowns	475	1000
6448	*Dublin.* hENRICVS, etc. R. Mint name, no h below crowns	425	900

HENRY VII

Portrait Coinage

Early Portrait Issue?

It is not apparent at present exactly where this issue fits into the series.

6450

		F £	VF £
6450	**Penny.** *Dublin?* Facing bust with open crown. R. Large rose on cross	650	1750

The Waterford groat listed by Coffey as a Henry VII portrait issue coin is a piece of rather poor style, the name is indistinct and it is possibly of Edward IV's fifth coinage.

Late Portrait Issues, *c.*1496–1505

The standard weight of the groats of Groups I and IA is about 32 grains, but later groups seem to have been struck to a standard of 28 grains.

6451	**Groat.** *Dublin.* I (at one time given to Hen. VI). Broad facing head (often from double-struck dies), open crown with straight band, fleured tressure. R. POSVI DEVM, etc., long cross pattée	95	225
6452	— — Similar, but rev. reads PROVIDEBO, etc.	125	300

6453   6455

6453	— — Smaller head, usually plain tressure. R. POSVI etc.	80	175
6454	— — — R. Legend reads PROVIDEBO, etc.	100	250
6455	— IA. Arched crown, bust breaks plain tressure. R. Long cross pattée	120	275
6456	— — Similar, but reverse legend begins PROVIDEBO	135	325

6457

6457	— IIA. Arched crown, triple-pellets on some points of tressure. R. ꝯ in centre of indented cross	140	350

		F £	VF £
6458	— — Similar, but annulets by crown and neck	175	450
6459	— IIB. Open crown with curved bands, plain tressure, saltires by neck. R. Indented cross	125	300

6460   6461

6460	— IIc. Similar, but saltires on points of tressures	125	300
6461	— IID. Open crown, no tressure, crosses by crown. R. Legends usually blundered	140	350
6462	— — Rosettes by crown	185	500
6463	— — No marks by crown. R. Rosette in centre of cross	185	500

6464

6464	— III. Open flat crown, no tressure. R. Indented cross	85	225
6464A	— — Similar but reads 'SIVITAS'	95	250

6465   6467

6465	**Half Groat.** *Dublin.* II. Arched crown, bust breaking tressure	675	1500
6466	— — Arched crown, bust within fleured tressure, V (?) below bust	725	1650
6467	— — Similar, but V below bust inverted	675	1500

Note: A half groat similar to 6460 (groats of class IIc) but with very blundered legends, is in Ulster Museum. It may be a contemporary forgery.

Silver

		F £	VF £
6468	**Penny.** Dublin. II. Large crown with jewelled arches over large **h**. R. Indented cross and pellets	750	2000
6469	— — Facing bust with arched crown. R. Mint name, cross with wavy end	700	1500
6470	— — — Similar, but pellets by bust	650	1450

| **6471** | — — III. Bust with flat open crown. R. Mint name, indented cross and pellets .... | 525 | 1250 |

HENRY VIII, 1509–1547

No coinage was produced specifically for Ireland during the first twenty-six years of the reign of Henry VIII. A Tudor who believed in the central control of all the organs of state, particularly with regard to its fund-raising aspects, it was in keeping with Henry's policies that when a decision was taken to mint Irish money again it was to be coined at London rather than in Ireland.

The new coins, known as 'Harp' groats, together with half-groats, were made of silver debased slightly below the sterling standard and, after a second debasement in 1540, were forbidden to be re-imported into England. As on the Three Crowns coinage of the previous reign, the obverse type was the royal arms of England, though now the shield was crowned, and on the reverse a large crowned Irish harp appears for the first time on the Irish coinage. The earlier issues are of particular interest for, as on Henry's gold crowns, the initials of the royal consorts are inserted on the reverse: 'H A' for Henry and Anne Boleyn, 'H I' for Jane Seymour and 'H K' for Katherine Howard. As queen succeeded queen perhaps it was to discourage ribald gibes that the consorts' initials were eventually replaced with 'R' for *Rex*.

Following the king's clash with Rome an Anglo-Irish parliament was prevailed upon to recognise Henry as the supreme head of the Church in Ireland and in June 1541, in order to dispose of the belief widely held amongst the Irish that the kings of England only held the temporal lordship of Ireland from the Pope, an Act was passed declaring Henry to be 'King of Ireland'. It is from 1541 that the title *Hiberniae Rex* replaces *Dominus Hiberniae* on the Harp coins.

Early in 1544 the silver content of the coins was reduced to two-thirds with one-third alloy and, at the same time, the current value of the groat was 'called up' to sixpence. Later the same year the fineness was decreased again to 50% silver. The Harp coins issued during the last year of the reign were minted at the Bristol mint and these bear the **WS** monogram of William Sharrington, the Bristol mintmaster. They rival in baseness the most debased of Henry's English coins, being struck in silver of only 0.250 fineness. Late Harp groats are the first Irish coins to be dated, having the regnal year '37' or '38' at the end of the reverse inscription. Harp groats are sometimes found with a small countermark of four pellets, possibly a mark of value stamped on them in a later reign to indicate a reduction in value from 6d. to 4d.

The Dublin coins which bear Henry's portrait were, in fact, minted after his death and are listed under the coins of Edward VI.

HARP COINAGE

1st Harp issue, 1534–40. Silver of 10 oz. 2 dwt. fineness (0.842). *Mm.* crown.

		F £	VF £
6472	**Groat.** With title *Dominus*. Crowned arms. R. Crowned harp dividing crowned **hA** (Henry and Anne Boleyn, 1534–5)	45	110

6473   6476

6473	— — Similar, but initials **h** and **I** (Jane Seymour, 1536–7)	40	100
6474	— — Similar, but **h** and **K** (Katherine Howard, 1540)	60	125
6475	— — Similar, but **h** and **R** (*Henricus Rex*) (1540)	50	110
6476	**Half groat.** As 6462, **hA** (Anne Boleyn)	425	900
6477	— — As 6473, **hI** (Jane Seymour)	725	1650
6478	— — As 6474, **hK** (Katherine Howard)	650	1500

2nd Harp issue, 1540–42. Silver of 9 oz. 2 dwt. fineness (0.758). *Mm.* trefoil.

6479	**Groat.** With title *Dominus*. As 6475, except for mintmark	40	90
6479A	— — Similar, but omits VIII after king's name	60	150

6480

| 6480 | — With new title 'hIBERNIE REX' on *rev.* .... | 40 | 95 |

	F £	VF £

3rd Harp issue, 1543. Silver of 10 oz. fineness (0.833). *Mm.* rose

6481	Groat. As 6480, except for *mm.*	45	110

4th Harp issue, 1544. Silver of 8 oz. fineness (0.666). *Mm.* lis

6482	Sixpenny Groat. As above, except for *mm.*	50	125

5th Harp issue, 1544–46. Silver of 6 oz. fineness (0.500). *Mm.* lis

6483

6483	Sixpenny Groat. As above, but *rev.* legend ends 'REX S'	70	175
6483A	— — Similar, but regnal year '37' after REX	100	250

6th Harp issue, 1546–47. Silver of 3 oz. fineness (0.250). Made at Bristol under William Sharrington. *Mm.* lis

6484   6484B

6484	Sixpenny Groat. Different style, hENRIC 8. R. Legend commences with 'WS' monogram and ends with regnal year '38'	100	250
6484A	— — Similar, but omits regnal year (issued posthumously)	135	350
6484B	Harp Groat. Countermarked with four pellets	200	450

EDWARD VI, 1547–1553

The first coins issued in this reign were Harp groats which differ from the last issue of the previous reign only by the omission of the regnal year. Edward's ministers in England planned to finance the restoration of sound currency there by a continued but temporary issue of debased money. To conceal the means of reform from the general public the coins were minted with the name and portrait of Henry VIII, and when the Dublin mint was reopened in 1548 base groats, halfgroats, pence and halfpence of English type, and of marginally better alloy than the worst of Henry's Harp coins, were made current for 6 pence, 3 pence, 3 halfpence and 3 farthings. However in 1552 there was a reversion to the baser 0.250 fineness. Some of the dies are of English workmanship, though others of cruder style are obviously of local manufacture.

It seems likely that base English shillings, with a portrait of the young King Edward and with the harp mintmark, may have been struck expressly for Ireland in 1552 though there is no surviving documentary evidence for the issue. It is known that in Elizabeth's reign base Edward VI shillings were shipped to Ireland to pass first at sixpence and later at twopence, and brass imitations known as 'bungals' continued to circulate in Connacht at a penny each. English base 'Rose' pennies of the York mint may also have been exported to Ireland. England's coinage was virtually restored to its old standards in 1551, but it was to be another ten years before an issue in 'fine' silver was made for Ireland.

For the first coins of this reign see No. 6484A of the 'Harp' coinage, listed above.

'Posthumous' Old Head Coinage, Henry VIII, 1547–c.1550

These have the name and portrait of Henry VIII, as do the English coins of the same period, the *sixpence* being the same size as the English *groat*. The earliest coins appear to be from dies made in England, others being from locally made dies.

Mintmarks: boar's head, harp, P.

6485

		F £	VF £
6485	**Sixpence.** I. Bust of early London 'Tower' style. R. Arms over cross	100	325

6486   6487   6488

6486	— II. Large facing bust of local style. Several varieties	95	300
6487	— III. Smaller bust of local style	95	300
6488	— IV. Small bust facing half-right, style of late 'Tower' coins ...	60	185

EDWARD VI

		F	VF
		£	£
6489	**Threepence.** I. Early 'Tower' bust	85	250
6490	— II. Bust of local style	100	300
6491	— IV. Late 'Tower' bust	75	225

6492	**Three Halfpence.** I. Early 'Tower' bust	275	750
6492A	— IV. Late 'Tower' bust	175	450
6493	**Three Farthings.** I. Full Face 'Tower' bust	425	1250

Coinage of 1552. *Mm.* harp

6494	**Shilling.** Young crowned bust r. R. Arms in oval garnished shield, legend ends MDLII	450	1500
6494A	— Contemporary brass imitation of above	75	185

MARY TUDOR, 1553–1558

It was in this reign that the Pale and the power of the English crown was extended by the shiring and plantation of English settlers in Leix and Offaly and other areas. The quality of the silver used for the earliest of Mary's coins was an improvement on that of the previous reigns, but after Mary's marriage to Philip of Spain base shillings and groats were issued with the heads of the two monarchs face to face and these were of the base 0.250 fineness metal. To provide small change base 'rose' pennies from the London mint were also sent to Ireland.

Pre-Marriage Coinage, 1553–54. Base silver, 0.583 fineness, with groat of about 32 grains. *Mintmark*: fleur-de-lis.

Note: Counterfeits exist of most of these coins.

	F £	VF £

6495

		F	VF
6495	**Shilling.** Crowned bust l. R. Crowned harp, legend ends MDLIII (1553)	525	1750
6496	— Similar, but *rev.* legend ends MDLIIII (1554)	850	3000

6497 6499

6497	**Groat,** undated. Similar type	1000	3250
6497A	— Similar, but local dies dated MDLIII	*Extremely rare*	
6497B	— Similar, but local dies dated MDLIV	*Extremely rare*	
	Doubt has been expressed about the authenticity of the two latter coins.		
6498	**Half Groat,** undated. Similar. R. Harp uncrowned	1250	4000
6499	**Penny,** undated. As 6497, crowned harp	1000	3500

MARY AND PHILIP OF SPAIN, 1554-8

Base silver 0.250 fineness, with groat of about 48 grains. *Mintmarks:* portcullis, rose

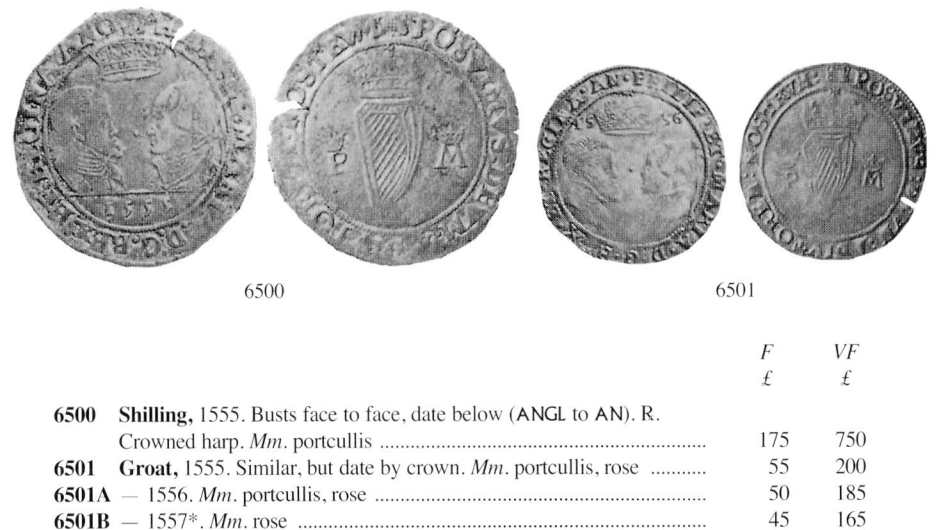

6500

6501

		F £	VF £
6500	**Shilling**, 1555. Busts face to face, date below (**ANGL** to **AN**). R. Crowned harp. *Mm.* portcullis	175	750
6501	**Groat**, 1555. Similar, but date by crown. *Mm.* portcullis, rose	55	200
6501A	— 1556. *Mm.* portcullis, rose	50	185
6501B	— 1557*. *Mm.* rose	45	165
	*The figure 7 on some of these coins looks like a 3.		
6501C	— — Similar, but 'Z' for 'ET'	50	175
6501D	— 1558. *Mm.* rose	50	185
6502	**Penny** of English type (made for currency in Ireland) (*York*). P . Z . M . D . G . etc., Royal Arms. R. Rose, **CIVITAS EBORACI**	75	225

ELIZABETH I, 1558-1603

The initial Irish coinage of Elizabeth was a continuation of the base issue of the previous reign, but in 1561 an issue of 'fine' silver shillings and groats almost restored the sterling standard to Ireland; the old base money was devalued and later called in. For the better part of the reign English money circulated in Ireland, as is evident from coin hoards and many single finds.

The shiring of Irish land and the extension of English law and land tenure proceeded apace; in the closing years of the century the final reduction of the independent and warlike Irish of the North who were led by O'Neill was conducted at first unsuccessfully by the Earl of Essex, until he was recalled to London to his execution, and later by Mountjoy. Large numbers of troops were involved in the campaign, and it was doubtless to help finance the war and pay the troops that an emergency Irish coinage of base silver money was ordered in 1601, with regal copper pence and halfpence also being coined.

152   ELIZABETH I

Base Coinage of 1558. Silver 3 oz. fine (0.250). *Mintmark:* rose

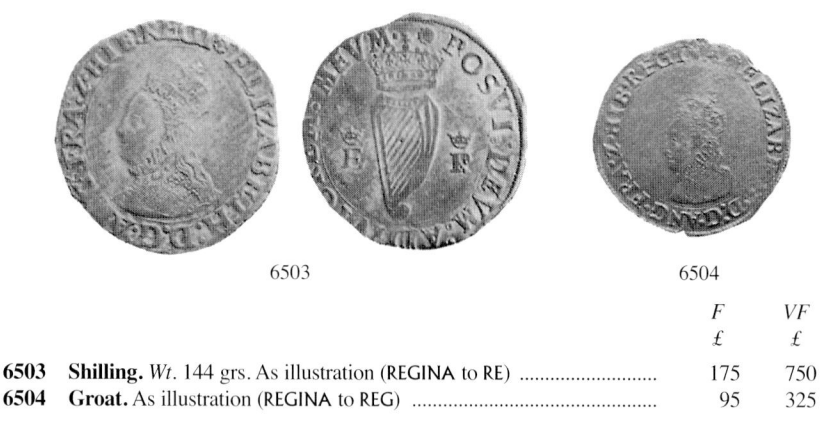

6503   6504

	F £	VF £
6503 Shilling. *Wt.* 144 grs. As illustration (REGINA to RE)	175	750
6504 Groat. As illustration (REGINA to REG)	95	325

'Fine' Coinage of 1561. Silver 11 oz. fine (0.916). *Mintmark:* harp

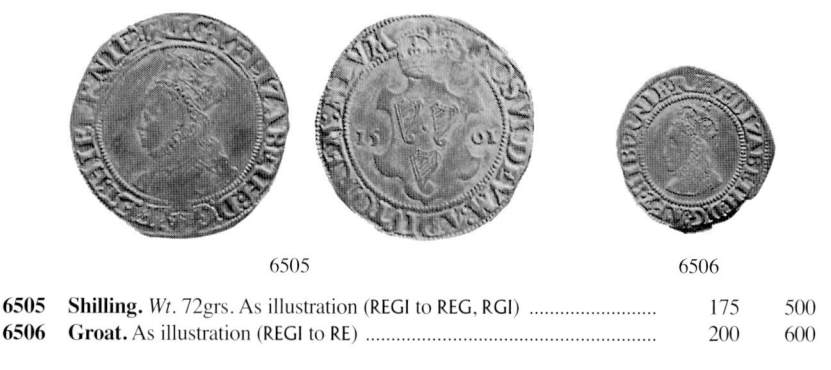

6505   6506

6505 Shilling. *Wt.* 72grs. As illustration (REGI to REG, RGI)	175	500
6506 Groat. As illustration (REGI to RE)	200	600

Third (Base) Coinage, 1601–1602. Silver 3 oz. fine. *Mintmarks:* trefoil, star, martlet

BASE SILVER

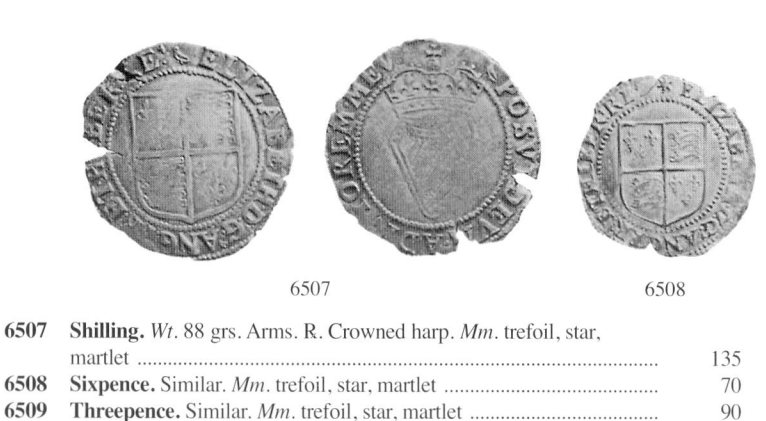

6507   6508

6507 Shilling. *Wt.* 88 grs. Arms. R. Crowned harp. *Mm.* trefoil, star, martlet	135	450
6508 Sixpence. Similar. *Mm.* trefoil, star, martlet	70	250
6509 Threepence. Similar. *Mm.* trefoil, star, martlet	90	350

COPPER

6510   6511

		F £	VF £
6510	**Penny,** 1601. As illustration. *Mm.* trefoil, star	25	80
6510A	— 1602. *Mm.* martlet	25	85
6510B	— Undated. *Mm.* star	275	650
6511	**Halfpenny,** 1601. Similar. *Mm.* trefoil, star	35	125
6511A	— 1602. *Mm.* martlet	60	225

JAMES I, 1603–1626

The war in the North had ended in defeat and famine for the native Irish, and though with the accession of a Scottish monarch a general amnesty was declared, once the power of the Northern chiefs had been drastically curtailed it was only a matter of time before confiscation of great tracts of land and the establishment of new plantations of Scots and English led to the final subjection of Ulster. In order to replace Elizabeth's war-time base money James issued a new coinage in 'fine' silver between 1603 and 1607 which was minted in London; but his objective was a uniform currency throughout his realm of 'Great Britain and Ireland' and thenceforward only the standard silver coins of the Tower mint were made for use in Ireland. The smaller Irish shilling was then tariffed at ninepence sterling, the groat at threepence.

In 1613 the farthing tokens manufactured under royal licence by Lord Harrington were authorized as legal tender for use in Ireland as well as England (though this was not con- firmed by the Irish Parliament until 1622). Though these coins were made for circulation in both islands they are included in this catalogue owing to the prominence given to the Irish harp used as the reverse type, and because it has been suggested that the coins struck on oval flans were originally intended for use in Ireland only. These farthings were stamped in strips before being punched out, and sometimes can still be found in strips of various length.

Mintmarks: Bell 1603–4   Rose (large and small) 1605–6
              Martlet 1604–5   Escallop 1606–7
Latin legends: EXVRGAT DEVS DISSIPENTVR INIMICI
              HENRICVS ROSAS REGNA IACOBVS
              TVEATVR VNITA DEVS

SILVER

First Coinage, 1603–4. With title 'ANG · SCO · FRA · ET HIB · REX'

6512   6513

		F £	VF £
6512	**Shilling.** First bust r., short square-cut beard, with title ANG · SCO. R. EXVRGAT, etc., crowned harp. *Mm.* bell	60	175
6513	— Second bust r., pointed beard. *Mm.* bell, martlet	65	200

6514

| 6514 | **Sixpence.** First bust. R. TUEATUR, etc., crowned harp. *Mm.* bell, martlet .... | 45 | 150 |

Second Coinage, 1604–7. With title 'MAG · BRIT · FRA · ET HIB · REX'

6515   6516

| 6515 | **Shilling.** Third bust r., longer square-cut beard, MAG · BRIT, etc. R. HENRICVS, etc. *Mm.* martlet, rose, escallop .... | 60 | 175 |
| 6516 | — Fourth bust, long beard, less ornate cuirass. *Mm.* rose, escallop .... | 65 | 185 |

JAMES I 155

6517

	F £	VF £

6517 Sixpence. First bust, as 6514, but MAG BRIT. R. TVEATVR, etc. *Mm.* martlet, rose, escallop 50 160

COPPER, ETC.

Farthing Tokens, issued under royal licence, from 1613

6520   6521

6520 Farthing. I. Small size 'Harrington' issued with tinned surface. Crown over crossed sceptres. R. Crowned harp. *Mintmarks* (sometimes between sceptres or on band of crown): **A, B, C, D, F, S,** ermine, millrind, pellet, **:L**, trefoil, crescent, mullet or none 35 125
6520A — As last, but with untinned surface 30 60
6521 — II. Normal size, untinned, 'Harrington' issue. Similar, *obv.* inscription starts at 11 o'clock. *Mintmarks:* cinquefoil, saltire, lis, martlet, mullet, trefoil 20 40

From 1616

6522

6522 — III. 'Lennox' issue. Similar type, but slightly larger flan and *obv.* inscription starts at 1 o'clock. *Mintmarks:* annulet, ball, bell, coronet, crescent, cross fleury, cross fourchée, dagger, eagle's head, flower, fusil, grapes, key, lion-passant or rampant, 3 lis, mascle, quatrefoil, rose, star, stirrup, thistle, trefoil, triangle, tun, woolpack 8 20
6523 — IV. Similar, but oval flan, *obv.* legend starts at 7 o'clock. *Mintmark:* cross pattée 50 100

CHARLES I AND THE GREAT REBELLION

English silver and the 'royal farthings' made privately under licence circulated in Ireland during the first fifteen years of the reign of King Charles, supplemented by some foreign coin, principally silver and a little gold from Scotland, the Low Countries, Spain or Spanish-America and from Portugal and even copper *tournois* from France and *turners* from Scotland.

Racial and religious discrimination and the dispossession of large numbers of the native Irish population earlier in the century had assured a permanently discontented majority of the population, and tension exploded into open rebellion in October 1641. Two Protestant Lords Justices had prevented the Irish parliament passing a Royal bill to alleviate Catholic grievances. This precipitated an attempt to seize Dublin Castle which failed, but the Irish rose in Ulster under Sir Felim O'Neill and slaughtered many thousands of the new 'planters'. The insurrection spread throughout Leinster and Munster and English troops and Protestant settlers fell back on fortified towns such as Londonderry and Drogheda in the North and Bandon, Kinsale and Cork in the South. An army raised in Scotland under General Munro landed in Ulster to suppress the insurrection, and when in 1642 civil war broke out in England between King Charles and the English parliament, Lord Inchiquin was appointed to command the Protestant forces in Munster.

Additional coin was urgently needed and the Lords Justices in Dublin issued an emergency currency consisting of pieces of silver plate cut to specified weights which were to circulate at their bullion value. The first issue of 1642 showed only the weights in pennyweights and grains, though later the lower denominations had the number of pence indicated by annulets.

The Irish Catholics set up their own Council, the Catholic Confederacy, at Kilkenny in 1642, where they proclaimed their loyalty to the king. They, too, issued their own coinage of silver halfcrowns, the so-called 'Blacksmiths' Money', copying the type of the king's English coins; and they also struck large copper halfpence and farthings of the type of the small and unpopular 'royal' farthing. The following year the Confederacy issued crowns and halfcrowns with a large cross on one side.

In the meantime, the Lords Justices at Dublin followed their first 'weight money' issues with a new coinage, the first type of which had the sterling denomination stamped on both sides though later coins acknowledged allegiance to King Charles with a crowned 'CR' on the obverse. This latter coinage is usually known as 'Ormonde Money' after the Earl of Ormonde who was appointed Lieutenant of Ireland in 1643. In 1646 another issue of 'weight money' was struck, this time in gold to the equivalent weights of the French pistole (*Louis d'or*) and double pistole which were legal tender in Ireland. These gold coins are now extremely rare.

Dissension amongst the Catholics prevented the capture of Dublin and in 1646 the arrival of the Papal Nuncio, Rinuccini, with financial aid from France, put an end to secret negotiations for a peace settlement between the Confederates and the King. After the Battle of Naseby the King's cause seemed to be lost in England and Ormonde, a Protestant royalist, preferred to surrender the capital to a Cromwellian expedition rather than risk a Catholic victory.

Counterstamped or crudely struck copper money, sometimes even stamped on foreign coins, had been issued by the Parliamentary forces besieged at Bandon, Cork, Kinsale and Youghal; and the Cork garrison had also made crude silver shillings and sixpences from cut plate. The final coinage of the Rebellion period was issued by Ormonde after he returned to Ireland in 1648 to lead a more united royalist alliance. After the execution of Charles I he struck crowns and halfcrowns in the name of Charles II, 'Defender of the Faith'.

CHARLES I, 1625–1649

Farthing Tokens, issued under Royal Licence, 1625–1644

COPPER

6524

	F £	VF £

6524 Farthing. I. 'Richmond' issue. As 'Lennox' coins. Single arched crown, no inner circles. *Mintmarks*: A, annulet, bell, book, cinquefoil, crescent, cross with pellets, cross pattée[P], cross fitchy, cross patonce, cross saltire, dagger, ermine, estoile, eye, fish-hook, fleece, fusil, two fusils, gauntlet, halberd, harp, heart, horseshoe, leaf, lion-passant, lion rampant, lis, demi-lis, three lis, martlet, mascle, nautilus, rose, shield, spearhead, tower, trefoil, woolpack 6 18

P6524 Charles I. 'Richmond' proof farthing, *mm*. cross pattee .... Æ EF £1000

6525 — II. Transitional issue. Similar, but double-arched crown. *Mintmarks*: harp, quatrefoil 18 45

6526

6526 — III. 'Maltravers' issue. Similar, but inner circles. *Mintmarks*: bell, billet, cross pattée, cross fitchy, harp, lis, martlet, portcullis, rose, woolpack 6 18

6527 — IV. As 6524, but on oval flan and legend commences at bottom left. *Mintmarks*: crescent, cross pattée, demi-lis, martlet, millrind, rose, scroll, 9 .... 30 50

6528 — V. Similar, but double-arched crown. *Mintmark*: lis 45 80

6529 — VI. 'Rose' farthing. Smaller thicker flan, usually with brass wedge inserted. Crown over sceptre. R. Crowned single rose. *Mintmarks*: lis, martlet, cross pattée, mullet, crescent 10 20

P6529 — Proof 'rose' farthing, *mm*. lis .... Æ EF £1000

6530 — VII. Similar, but with single-arched crown. R. Crowned single rose. *Mintmarks*: mullet, crescent[P] 4 12

P6530 — Proof *mm*. crescent .... Æ EF £1000

6531 — VIII. Similar, but sceptres below crown. *Mintmark*: mullet 30 50

THE GREAT REBELLION

Coinages of the Lords Justices

Issue of 1642. Sometimes referred to as 'Inchiquin Money', stamped from cut pieces of flattened plate.

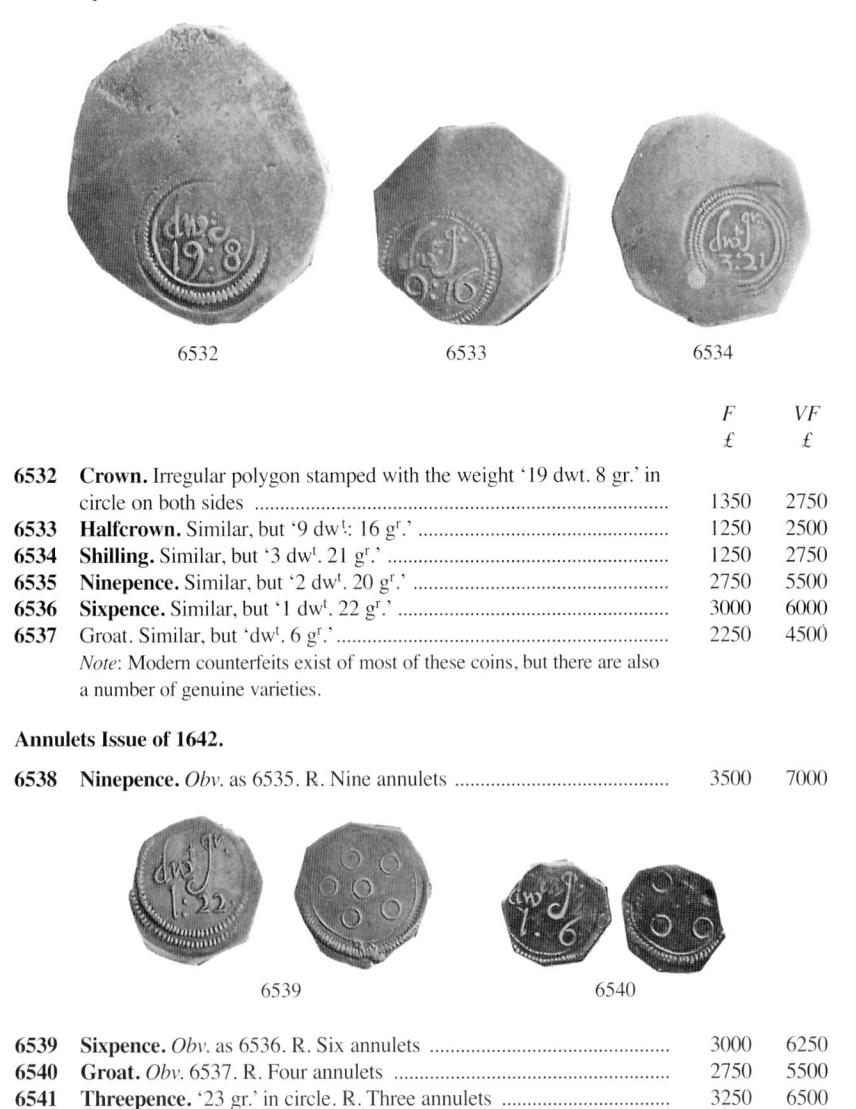

6532   6533   6534

		F £	VF £
6532	**Crown.** Irregular polygon stamped with the weight '19 dwt. 8 gr.' in circle on both sides	1350	2750
6533	**Halfcrown.** Similar, but '9 dw^t: 16 g^r.'	1250	2500
6534	**Shilling.** Similar, but '3 dw^t. 21 g^r.'	1250	2750
6535	**Ninepence.** Similar, but '2 dw^t. 20 g^r.'	2750	5500
6536	**Sixpence.** Similar, but '1 dw^t. 22 g^r.'	3000	6000
6537	Groat. Similar, but 'dw^t. 6 g^r.'	2250	4500

Note: Modern counterfeits exist of most of these coins, but there are also a number of genuine varieties.

Annulets Issue of 1642.

| 6538 | **Ninepence.** *Obv.* as 6535. R. Nine annulets .... | 3500 | 7000 |

6539   6540

6539	**Sixpence.** *Obv.* as 6536. R. Six annulets	3000	6250
6540	**Groat.** *Obv.* 6537. R. Four annulets	2750	5500
6541	**Threepence.** '23 gr.' in circle. R. Three annulets	3250	6500

CHARLES I

Issue of 1643 sometimes called 'Dublin Money'

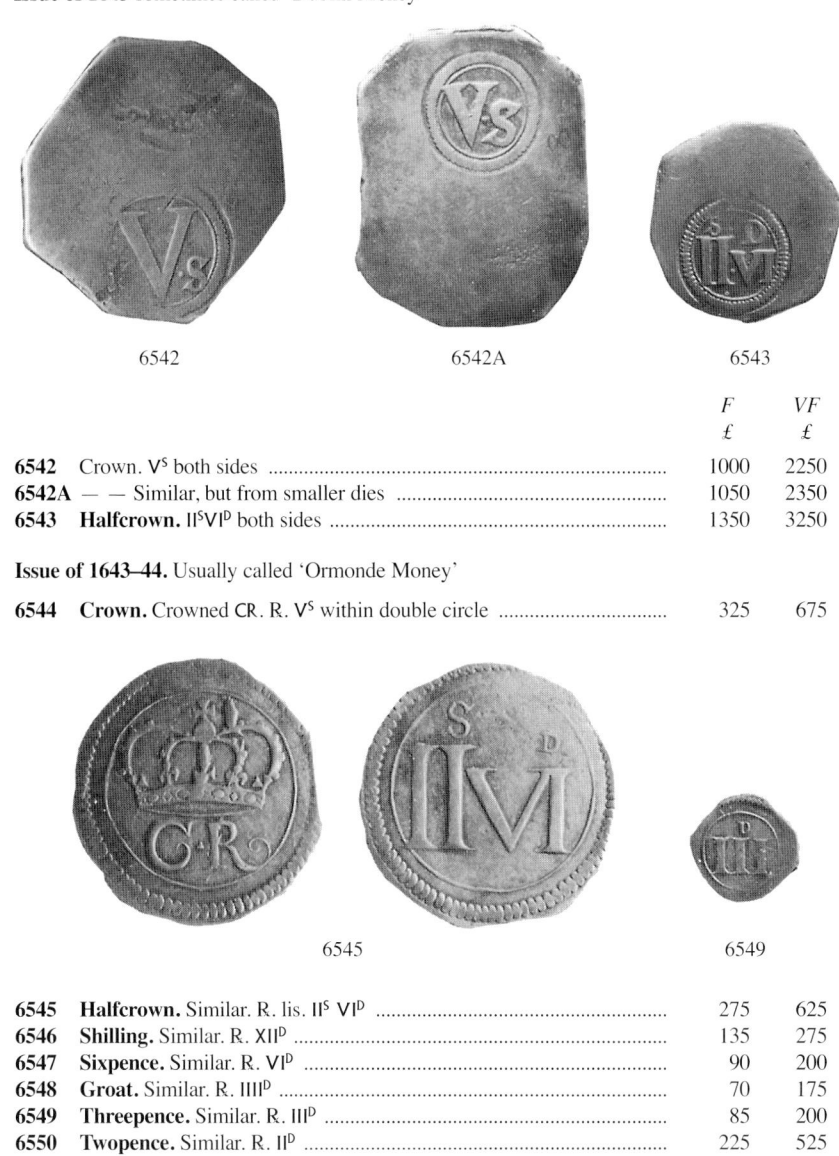

			F £	VF £
6542	Crown. V^S both sides		1000	2250
6542A	— — Similar, but from smaller dies		1050	2350
6543	Halfcrown. II^{S}VI^D both sides		1350	3250

Issue of 1643–44. Usually called 'Ormonde Money'

6544	Crown. Crowned CR. R. V^S within double circle	325	675

6545	Halfcrown. Similar. R. lis. II^S VI^D	275	625
6546	Shilling. Similar. R. XII^D	135	275
6547	Sixpence. Similar. R. VI^D	90	200
6548	Groat. Similar. R. IIII^D	70	175
6549	Threepence. Similar. R. III^D	85	200
6550	Twopence. Similar. R. II^D	225	525

For varieties see Aquilla Smith, 'On the Ormonde Money', *PRSAI* (1854).

Ormonde's Gold Coinage of 1646

	F	VF
	£	£

6551 Double pistole. Irregular polygon stamped with '8 dw^{tt}. 14 g^r.' on both sides 37500 85000

6552 Pistole. Similar, but stamped '4 dw^{tt}. 7 g^r.' each side 24500 52500

Ormonde's Silver Coinage of 1649. Issued after the death of Charles I
Mintmark: lis

6553 **Crown.** CAR · II · D · G · MAG · BRIT around large crown.
R. FRA · ET · HIB · REX · F · D. & around V^s 2500 6000

6554 **Halfcrown.** Similar, but II^s.VI^D on *rev.* 2000 4750

ISSUES OF THE CONFEDERATE CATHOLICS

Kilkenny Issues of 1642–43

6555

		F £	VF £
6555	**Halfpenny,** Æ. Crown and two sceptres. R. Crowned harp. *Mm.* harp	125	550

6556

| **6556** | **Farthing,** Æ. Similar .... | 175 | 700 |

Contemporary forgeries of the last two are common.

| **6557** | **'Blacksmith's' Halfcrown** (*date uncertain*). Crude copy of London issue. King on horse l., cross on housings. R. Oval shield between CR. *Mm.* cross (*obv.*), harp (*rev.*) .... | 425 | 1050 |

6557A

| **6557A** | — Similar, but without cross on horse's housings .... | 475 | 1250 |

CHARLES I

Issues of 1643–4. Sometimes called 'Rebel Money'

		F £	VF £
6558	**Crown.** Large cross, pellet or star in margin. R. V^s	1350	3250

6559

| 6559 | **Halfcrown.** Similar, small star in margin. R. II^{s}VI^D .... | 1500 | 3500 |

LOCAL ISSUES OF THE SOUTHERN 'CITIES OF REFUGE'

6560   6561

6560	**Bandon (Bridge).** Æ **Farthing.** BB. R. Three Castles	350	850
6561	**Cork.** AR **Shilling.** Octagonal. CORK/1647. R. X.II	1000	2750
6561A	— AR **Sixpence.** Similar. R. VI	450	1250
	Modern forgeries of the last two are not uncommon		
6562	— Æ **Halfpenny.** CORK in double circle. R. Castle	625	2000

6562A   6562B

| 6562A | — Æ **Farthing.** CORK or CORKE in circle of pellets R. Castle .... | 425 | 1350 |
| 6562B | — — CORK countermarked on copper coin .... | 325 | 975 |

The coin illustrated is a 4 *maravedi* of Carlos and Johanna of Spain (1515–1566). The brass pieces countermarked with **CORKE** and a lion's head are struck over the 1677 tokens of William Ballard and may be of the period of the Civil War, 1689–91. This cmk. also appears on worn English shillings of Elizabeth I.

CHARLES I AND THE COMMONWEALTH

6563

	F £	VF £
6563 Kinsale. Æ Farthing. K · S in circle of pellets R. Chequered shield	350	1350

6563A   6563B

6563A Kilkenny. Æ Halfpenny. Castle with K below countermarked on copper coin	325	1200
6563B — — Five small castles (in form of a rosette) countermarked on copper coin (possibly New Ross?)	300	1000
6564 Youghal. Æ Farthing. YT R. Ship (yawl)	400	1250

6565

6565 — Bird over YT, 1646 below. R. As above	300	950
6565A — Circular farthing. YT. R. Fish or Whale?	575	1450

THE COMMONWEALTH, 1649–1660

The conquest of Ireland by Cromwell and his Puritan army continued until Galway finally surrendered in 1652. Over 30,000 Irish Catholic soldiers were allowed to leave Ireland for France and Spain, Catholic landowners were transported to the West of Ireland and nine counties were confiscated to grant land to Cromwell's army or sold to pay his troops.

No coinage was minted especially for Ireland, but from 1649 the Commonwealth gold and silver coins had a shield bearing the Irish harp set alongside the republican arms of England, the cross of St George. However, a large number of copper tokens, mostly pennies, were issued by the merchants of the old cities and the new towns. Ireland was formally declared part of the Protectorate in 1653, and the granting of free trade with England and Scotland helped to raise the prosperity of the new merchant classes.

CHARLES II 1645–1685

In 1660 Charles II granted a patent to Sir Thomas Armstrong for a term of twenty-one years for coining farthings and at the same time prohibited the use of all other tokens. The Irish authorities were, however, opposed to the circulation of these farthings in Ireland, though they were considerably heavier than the 'Royal' farthings of the previous reign and, as a result, comparatively few were issued. In consequence, during the ten years 1663 to 1673, further large numbers of private merchant's tokens were put into circulation. It was probably about 1674 that the curious coins known as 'St Patrick's' money were made, though little is known of the circumstances of the issue. These halfpennies and farthings have a figure of the Saint on one side and a kneeling figure of King David playing the harp on the reverse, and most have a milled edge and a plug of brass impressed into the flan to discourage counterfeiting. As the obverse of the farthing closely copies the type of the Dublin farthing token of Richard Grenwood this coinage should, perhaps, be more properly treated as a token issue. After they were called in about 1680/1 a large quantity were taken by an emigrant named Mark Newby to the State of New Jersey, where they were allowed to circulate officially as currency. They also circulated in the Isle of Man.

More traders' tokens were issued between 1676 and 1679, and the City of Dublin issued its own halfpenny in that year, but the following year Irish regal halfpennies were minted under a new patent granted to Sir Thomas Armstrong and Col. George Legge for a term of twenty-one years. These coins were considerably larger and heavier than most of the traders' tokens and successfully drove them out of circulation.

Armstrong's Coinage of 1660-1

6566

		F £	VF £	EF £
6566	**Farthing.** Crown and two sceptres. R. Crowned harp. *Mm.* plumes			
	Undated inverted die axis	50	150	250
	— Struck with an upright die axis, en medaille	75	200	300
	— — Proof struck in silver	200	750	1250

'St Patrick's' Coinage. Usually with milled edge and brass spot on the *rev.*

6567	**Halfpenny.** King David playing harp, crown above, FLOREAT REX. R St. Patrick holding cross and crozier preaching to multitude, arms of Dublin to r., ECCE GREX	100	250	750
	— — Proof struck in silver	500	1500	—
	— Similar, with FLORE AT T REX instead	200	400	1000

CHARLES II

6568

	F	VF	EF
	£	£	£

		F	VF	EF
6568	**Halfpenny.** Similar, but star in *obv.* legend	200	400	1000
	— Similar, — with plain edge	250	500	1250
	— — Proof struck in silver	750	2000	—

6569

		F	VF	EF
6569	**Farthing.** As above. R. St Patrick with patriarchal cross driving away reptiles, cathedral to r., QVIESCAT PLEBS	75	200	600
6570	— Stars in *rev.* legend	100	250	750
	— — Similar, Proof struck in silver	400	1250	—
	— — Similar, Proof struck in gold	*Extremely rare*		
6571	— Martlet below king	200	500	1250
6572	— Annulet below king	150	400	1000
6572A	— Nimbus around St Patrick	200	500	1250
	— — Similar, Proof struck in silver	*Extremely rare*		
6572B	— Annulets and martlet below King	175	450	1100

Armstrong and Legge's Regal Coinage, 1680–84

6574

		F	VF	EF
6574	**Halfpenny.** Laur. and draped bust r., as illustrated. R. Crowned harp. Large lettering			
	1680 pellets in legend	50	150	400
	1680 Similar, proof struck in silver	750	1750	—
	1680 Similar, — GARTIA error	150	350	750
	1680 crosses in legend on obv	125	250	600
	1681	45	125	350
	1682	50	150	400

6575

		F £	VF £	EF £
6575	**Halfpenny.** Similar, but small lettering			
	1681	175	400	900
	1681 Similar, proof struck in silver	250	750	2000
	1682	35	100	300
	1683	35	100	300
	1683 MAG BR FRA larger than rest of legend	45	125	350
	1684	100	300	700

JAMES II, 1685–1691

In 1685 James II transferred the unexpired patent for minting halfpence to Sir John Knox, the Lord Mayor of Dublin, and these were issued until 1688. James fled from England to France in that year and the crown was offered to his daughter, Mary and her husband, William of Orange. After drumming up Catholic support on the Continent James landed in Ireland in March 1689 to continue the struggle. Having insufficient funds to prosecute the war a plan was devised to issue official base metal token coins which would be exchanged for sterling silver after the war was won, and a nominal month as well as the year of issue was inscribed on them so that they could be redeemed in stages over a period of time. The coins were made of brass or latten from old cannon, bells and other scrap metal and were called 'Brass Money', though they later became known as 'Gunmoney' coins.

Minted at Dublin and Limerick, the first issue consisted of halfcrowns, shillings and sixpences, but in 1690, as stocks of metal ran down, the sizes of halfcrowns and shillings were reduced and the old halfcrowns were restruck as crowns. Later that year, crowns, groats, pence and halfpence were also struck in pewter and most had a plug of brass through them to distinguish the genuine pieces from counterfeits which might be cast in lead. The Gunmoney coins became increasingly unpopular and as soon as William III seized the Dublin mint, after the Battle of the Boyne, the coins were reduced to their proper value; in 1691 they were demonetized. It is for this reason they are relatively common today. Limerick continued to hold out for James well into 1691 and the mint there recoined the large Gunmoney shillings into halfpence and the small shillings into farthings.

JAMES II

Regular Coinage

6576

	F £	VF £	EF £
6576 **Halfpenny.** Laur. bust l., as illustrated. R. Crowned harp			
1685	40	125	350
1685 Similar, proof struck in pewter	*Extremely rare*		
1686	40	125	350
1686 Similar, proof struck in silver	*Extremely rare*		
1687	500	—	—
1688	75	175	400

CIVIL WAR COINAGE, 1689–91

'Gunmoney' Coinage, 1689–90

6577

6577 **Crown** (overstruck on large size Gunmoney halfcrown), 1690. King on horse l., legend commences to r. of head	150	300	600

6578

6578 — Similar, but legend commences to l. of head, with smaller lettering and bust of different style	60	120	250
6578A — Similar, *rev.* reads VICTO/RE	100	200	400

		F £	VF £	EF £
6578B	**Crown.** Similar, but also reads RIX for REX	200	400	800
6578BB	— Similar, RIX and cinquefoil stop after CHRISTO	\multicolumn{3}{c}{Extremely rare}		
6578C	— Similar, struck with inverted die axis	125	250	450
6578D	— Similar, struck with 90° die axis to left	150	300	500
6578E	— — same axis but no lines above ANO DOM	200	400	800
6578F	— Similar, inverted die axis no lines ANO DOM	250	450	850
6578G	— Similar, struck on a thick flan	500	1000	—
6578H	— Similar, TRIUMPHO reverse (U for V)	200	400	800

Note: *The following coins are unusual in that they bear the* **month** *as well as the year of issue. At this period the New Year commenced on March 25th, hence January 1689 followed December 1689, and coins marked March 1689 and March 1690 were issued in the same month. The abbreviation used is shown in parentheses.*

6579N

6579	**Halfcrown.** Large size. Laur. and draped bust l. R. Crown over sceptres dividing *JR,* XXX above, month of issue below			
A	1689 July (*July*)	60	125	300
AA	— — smaller and less garnished J R	120	250	600
B	— August (*Aug. Aug: Augt Augt:*)	40	100	250
BB	— (*Aug*) proof struck in silver	\multicolumn{3}{c}{Extremely rare}		
C	— Crown and sceptres reversed (*Augt:*)	120	250	600
D	— September (*Sepr. Sepr: Sepr Sept: Septr.*)	40	100	250
DD	— — (*Sep*) proof struck in silver	\multicolumn{3}{c}{Extremely rare}		
DDD	— — (*Sepr*) no stops on obverse	80	200	250
E	— October (*Oct: Octr. OCT (. or :) OCTr OCTr.*)	40	100	250
F	— — (8r 8 BER 8BER)	80	200	400
G	— November (*Nov. Nov: Novr.*)	40	100	250
GG	— — (*Nov*) proof struck in silver	\multicolumn{3}{c}{Extremely rare}		
H	— December (*Dec. Dec: Decr.*)	40	100	250
I	— — (10r 10r.)	80	200	400
J	— January (*Jan Jan. Jan: Jay*)	40	100	250
JJ	— — (*Jan*) proof struck in silver	\multicolumn{3}{c}{Extremely rare}		
JJJ	— — (*Jan – note italic J*) plain edge	60	125	300
K	— February (*Feb Feb. Feb:*)	40	100	250
KK	— — (*Feb:*) proof struck in silver	\multicolumn{3}{c}{Extremely rare}		
L	— March (*Mar Mar. Mar: Mar Mar:*)	40	100	250
LL	— — (*Mar:*) proof struck in silver	\multicolumn{3}{c}{Extremely rare}		
M	— 1690 March, large O in date (*Mar: Mar*)	50	120	275

		F	VF	EF
		£	£	£
MM	**Halfcrown.** — (*Mar*) proof struck in silver	*Extremely rare*		
MMM	— — (*Mar:*) ... MAO error for MAG	100	200	500
N	— April (*Apr. Apr: Apr. Apr:*)	40	100	250
NN	— — (*Apr.*) proof struck in silver	*Extremely rare*		
NNN	— — (*Apr.*) proof struck in gold	*Extremely rare*		
O	— May (*May May: also tailed with y*)	30	85	200
OO	— — (*May:*) struck with inverted reverse	40	100	250

6580G

6580	Small size. Laur. head l., otherwise similar			
A	1690 April (*Apr*)	100	250	600
B	— May (*May May May. may MAY* date large O)	30	85	200
BB	— — (*May*) variety FR.A for FRA (stops vary)	50	120	300
BBB	— — (*May*) proof struck in pewter	*Extremely rare*		
b	— — (*May.*) proof struck in silver	*Extremely rare*		
bb	— — (*May*) proof struck in gold	*Extremely rare*		
C	— — (*May*) Variety with cinquefoil stops	100	250	600
CC	— — (*May.*) struck on a thick flan	75	175	400
D	— June (*Jun June June.*)	40	100	250
E	— — (error *Jnue*)	75	250	600
F	— July (*July Iuly*)	50	120	300
FF	— — (*July*) struck with 90° die axis	75	250	600
G	— August (*Aug:*) struck in Limerick	75	250	600
H	— September – all speciments seen have been contemporary forgeries			
I	— October (*Oct:*) struck in Limerick	200	500	—

6581A

6581	**Shilling.** Large size. Similar, but XII over crown			
A	1689 July (*July July.*)	30	60	150
AA	— — (*July.*) half of milling absent	50	100	200

		F £	VF £	EF £
AAA	**Shilling.** — (*July*) proof struck in silver	*Extremely rare*		
B	— — (*July*) No stops on *obv*.	60	125	250
C	— August (*Aug. Aug: Augt Augt. Augt:*)	30	60	150
CC	— — (*Augt*) proof struck in silver	*Extremely rare*		
D	— September (*Sep: SEPR. Sepr (. or :) Sept (. or :) Septr.*)	25	50	120
DD	— — (*Sept*) proof struck in silver	*Extremely rare*		
E	— October (*Oct, (. or :) OCT OCT. OCTR. OCTr.*)	25	50	120
EE	— — (OCT.) FI instead of ET on reverse	100	200	500
F	— — (8 *br.* 8BR, 8BER, 8Ber)	80	175	400
G	— — (OCT.) No stops on *obv*.	50	100	200
H	— November (*Nov Nov Nov: NOV novr: Nov (. or :)*)	30	60	150
I	— — (9, 9r)	50	100	250
J	— (9r) small castle under bust between pellets	400	1000	—
JJ	— Similar, but no pellets by castle	350	900	—
K	— December (*Dec Dec. Dec: Decr.*)	25	50	120
L	— — (10 or 10r)	35	85	175
LL	— (10r) struck with inverted reverse	50	120	250
M	— January (*Jan Jan. Jan:*)	25	50	120
MM	— — (*Jan.*) ERA instead of FRA error	60	120	300
MMM	— — (*Jan*) struck with 90° die axis	35	85	175
m	— (*Jan:*) reversed 'a' in Jan	125	250	600
mm	— — (*Jan:*) reversed 'a' proof struck in silver	*Extremely rare*		
mmm	— — (*Jan*) no stops on *rev*. ERA EI for FRA ET	60	150	300
Mm	— — (*Jan*) edge perpendicularly milled	50	100	200
Mmm	— — (*Jan:*) proof struck in silver	*Extremely rare*		
N	— February (*Feb Feb. Feb:*)	25	50	120
NN	— — (*Feb Feb:*) with 90° die axis or inverted	35	85	175
NNN	— — — Similar, no I in HIB	50	100	120
n	— (*Feb:*) proof struck in silver	*Extremely rare*		
O	— March (*Mar Mar: Mar Mar.*)	30	70	150
OO	— — (*Mar*) struck with inverted reverse	35	85	175
OOO	— — (*Mar:*) struck on a thick flan	60	150	300
o	— — (*Mar. Mar:*) proof struck in silver	*Extremely rare*		
P	1690 March (*Mar Mar. Mar:*)	30	70	150
PP	— — (*Mar*) no stops on reverse	35	85	175
PPP	— — (*Mar. Mar:*) proof struck in silver	*Extremely rare*		
p	— — (*Mar.*) proof struck in gold	*Extremely rare*		
Q	— April (*Apr Apr:*)	40	100	200
QQ	— — (*Apr*) proof struck in silver	*Extremely rare*		
QQQ	— — (*Apr*) proof struck in gold	*Extremely rare*		

6582G

		F £	VF £	EF £
6582	**Shilling.** Small size. Similar – stops can vary – either cinquefoils or pellets			
A	1690 April (*apr Apr*), pellet stops	40	100	200
B	— — Variety with cinquefoil stops on *obv.*	40	100	200
C	— — — Cinquefoil stops both sides	40	100	200
D	— May (*May,* **MAY**), pellet stops	30	70	150
DD	— — (*May*) struck with inverted die axis	50	125	250
DDD	— — (*May*) proof struck in silver	*Extremely rare*		
D	— — (*May May.*) proof struck in gold	*Extremely rare*		
E	— — — Variety with cinquefoil stops on *obv*	30	70	150
F	— — (*May.*) Var. reading **GRATA**	75	175	400
FF	— — (*MAY*) Variety reading **ERA** for **FRA**	75	175	400
G	— June (*June June.*)	35	85	175
GG	— (*June*) struck on a thin flan	100	250	500
GGG	— (*June.*) with a pewter plug	*Extremely rare*		
g	— (*June*) proof struck in silver	*Extremely rare*		
gg	— (*June*) proof struck in gold	*Extremely rare*		
H	— July – all specimens seen have been contemporary forgeries			
I	— August (*Augt:*) if genuinely dated 1690	1000	—	—
J	— September (*Sep:*) struck in Limerick	250	650	—

6583A

		F	VF	EF
6583	**Sixpence.** Laur and draped bust l. R. **VI** over crowned sceptres			
A	1689 June (*June June. Jvne Jvne.*)	35	85	175
B	— July (*July July.*)	35	85	175
BB	— — (*July*) struck with a wide date	40	100	200
BBB	— — (*July*) proof struck in silver	*Extremely rare*		
C	— August (*Aug Augt Augt.*)	35	85	175
CC	— — (*Aug:*) struck with a plain edge	65	150	300
CCC	— — (*Aug*) proof struck in silver	*Extremely rare*		
D	— —(*Aug*) **FR**, instead of **FRA**	75	175	400
E	— September (*Sep Sepr Sepr:*)	35	85	175
EE	— — (*Sep*) struck in copper with plain edge	150	350	—
EEE	— — (*Sept*) proof struck in silver	*Extremely rare*		
F	— — (*7 ber*)	100	250	600

JAMES II

		F £	VF £	EF £
G	**Sixpence.**— October (*Oct:*) all speciments seen have been spurious			
H	— November (*Nov Nov. Nov:*)	35	85	175
I	— December (*Dec. Dec:*)	35	85	175
J	— January (*Jan Jan. Jan:*)	35	85	175
JJ	— — — Similar, ERA for FRA error	50	125	250
JJJ	— — — Similar, RE.X error and I over O in date	75	175	400
j	— — (*Jan*) no stops on reverse	50	125	250
jj	— — (*Jan*) no stops on obverse	50	125	250
jjj	— — (*Jan Jan:*) proof struck in silver	*Extremely rare*		
jjj	— — (*Jan*) proof struck in gold	*Extremely rare*		
jjj	— — (*Jan*) proof struck over James II Half-Guinea	*Extremely rare*		
K	— February (*Feb Feb:*)	40	100	200
KK	— — (*Feb. Feb:*) proof struck in silver	*Extremely rare*		
KKK	— — (*Feb. Feb:*) proof struck in gold	*Extremely rare*		
L	— March (*Mar:*) all specimens seen have been spurious			
M	1690 March (*Mar:*) all specimens seen have been spurious			
N	— April (*Apr apr:*) all specimens seen have been spurious			
O	— May (*May May.*)	60	150	300
OO	— — (*May:*) struck on a thich flan with plain edge	120	250	—
OOO	— — (*May*) proof struck in gold	*Extremely rare*		
P	— June (*June*) proof struck in gold	*Extremely rare*		

Emergency 'Pewter Money' of 1689–90

6584

6584	**Crown.** Type as 'Gunmoney' crown but finer work. Edge inscribed: MELIORIS TESSERA FATI ANNO REGNI SEXTO. Brass plug stamped into flan	600	1500	3500
	Similar, proof struck in copper	*Extremely rare*		
	Similar, proof struck in silver mis-spelt edge	*Extremely rare*		
	Similar, proof struck in gold mis-spelt edge	*Extremely rare*		
6585	— Similar, but plain edge	*Extremely rare*		
	— — proof struck in copper	*Extremely rare*		
	— — proof struck in silver	*Extremely rare*		
	— — proof struck in pewter	*Extremely rare*		
	— — proof struck in gold	*Extremely rare*		

6586

		F £	VF £	EF £
6586	**Groat.** As 'Gunmoney' sixpence. R. II either side of crowned harp, 1689	500	1250	3000
6587	**Penny.** Type I. As large 'Gunmoney' shilling. R. Crowned harp, date 1689 above	500	100	2500

6588

6588	— — 1690	350	750	2000

6589

6589	**Penny.** Type II. Smaller laur. head l., I^D behind. R. Harp dividing date 1690	300	600	1500
6590	**Halfpenny.** Type I. Bust with short hair l. R. Date over crowned harp, 1689	300	600	1500

6591   6592

6591	— — 1690	125	250	600
6591A	— — 1690 struck with inverted reverse	200	400	900
	— — 1690 similar, proof struck in silver	250	500	1000
	— — 1690 — — silver proof, thin flan	300	600	1250
	— — 1690 proof over France Louis XIV 5 sols	400	1000	—

		F £	VF £	EF £
6592	**Halfpenny** Type II. Smaller laur. head l., leaf below. R. Crown divides date, 1690. Brass plug through flan	150	300	750

Limerick besieged 1690–91. The halfpence struck over large gunmoney shillings and the farthings on small gunmoney shillings

6594

| 6594 | **Halfpenny.** Laur. and draped bust l. R. Hibernia seated l., holding cross, reversed N in HIBERИIA 1691 | 50 | 100 | 250 |

6595

6595	**Farthing.** Similar	80	175	400
6595A	— — Variety reading GRAVTIA		*Extremely rare*	
6596	— Normal N in HIBERNIA	120	250	600

WILLIAM AND MARY, 1689–1694
WILLIAM III (alone), 1694–1702

The regular issue of Dublin halfpence was continued between 1692 and 1694 for the two rulers, and both their heads are displayed on the coinage. After Mary's death halfpence for William alone were struck in 1696.

William and Mary, 1689–94

6597

	F £	VF £	EF £
6597 **Halfpenny.** Conjoined busts. R. Crowned harp			
1692, GRATIA	35	125	300
1692, error unbarred A's in GRATIA	50	200	450
1692, GVLIELMVS error	100	275	650
1693	25	85	200
1693 struck with plain edge	35	125	300
1693, similar, proof struck in silver		*Extremely rare*	
1694	35	125	300

William III, 1694–1702

6598

6598 **Halfpenny.** Laur. and draped bust r., GRA. R. Crowned harp, BR legend 1696	50	200	450
1696 GWLIELMVS error	100	300	700
1696 proof in silver	500	1250	—
6598A — Similar, R. BRI type legend	65	250	550
— — Similar, proof in silver	650	1500	—
6599 — Similar, but cruder undraped bust, GRATIA, 1696	200	500	—
1696 proof in silver		*Extremely rare*	

GEORGE I, 1714–1727

No copper coins had been struck for Ireland since 1696 so that by 1720 the dearth of small change had become acute. In 1722 a patent for minting copper coins for Ireland and for the American Colonies was granted to William Wood, a London merchant, who had the coins struck at his Bristol foundry. The coins were to be struck at the rate of 2s. 6d. worth to the pound, though this was substantially lighter than the contemporary English coppers. The Irish

Parliament was aggrieved at the circumstances under which the patent was granted and government officials were instructed not to accept them; and a general boycott of the coins was urged by Dean Swift in his scathing 'Drapier's Letters' which alleged that Wood was attempting to defraud the public. It became obvious that the coins were unacceptable in Ireland so that in 1724 Wood was forced to stop production, and he surrendered his patent the following year in exchange for a pension of £3,000 a year. The coins were recalled from Ireland and shipped out to America where they circulated alongside Wood's *Rosa Americana* coins. No official coinage was undertaken to replace Wood's Irish coinage as the London mint ceased production of copper coin between 1724 and 1729.

William Wood's Coinage, 1722–24

6600

	F £	VF £	EF £
6600 **Halfpenny.** Type I. Laur. bust r. R. Hibernia seated facing, looking l., holding harp l., 1722	50	150	400
1722 proof		Extremely rare	
1722 proof in silver		Extremely rare	

6601

	F	VF	EF
6601 — Type II. R. Hibernia seated l., leaning on harp and holding branch 1722	45	135	375
1722 proof		Extremely rare	
1722 with second 2 inverted	100	250	650
1723	30	75	250
1723 proof		Extremely rare	
1723 proof in silver		Extremely rare	
— 3 over 2	40	100	300
— *Obv*. R's altered from B's	40	100	300
— Star after HIBERNIA		Extremely rare	
— No stop after date	35	90	275
1724 *Rev.* legend divided	40	100	300
— Legend continuous	50	150	400
1724 Similar proof in silver		Extremely rare	

		F	VF	EF
		£	£	£
6602	**Farthing.** Type I. Laur. bust r., D : G : REX. R. As 6600, 1722	200	750	1750
6603	— Type II. Similar. R. As 6601, 1723	60	250	1000
6603A	— — — 1723 no colon before REX	100	350	1500

6604

6604	— Type III. Similar, but read DEI · GRATIA · REX			
	1723	23	90	350
	1723 proof		*Extremely rare*	
	1723 proof in silver		*Extremely rare*	
	1724	40	100	400
	1724 proof in silver		*Extremely rare*	
	1724 no stop after date	60	150	500

GEORGE II, 1727–1760

Owing to the shortage of small change, tokens again appeared in Dublin in 1728 and substantial numbers were issued in Ulster between 1734 and 1736. In 1736 a new coinage of halfpence was put in hand at the London mint which continued in most years until 1755, and to allay further public outcry it was directed that any profit accruing from the coinage should be credited to the public revenue of Ireland. Farthings were also coined in 1737–38 and 1744. In 1760 another issue of George II halfpence and farthings was minted for Ireland but owing to the king's death they were not sent to Ireland. They finally arrived in 1762.

Young Head Coinage, 1736–55

6605

6605	**Halfpenny.** Type I. Laur. bust l., GEORGIUS. R. Crowned harp. Small lettering			
	1736	15	60	150
	1736 proof		FDC	350
	1736 proof in silver		*Extremely rare*	
	1737	10	50	120
	1737 proof		FDC	350
	1738	10	50	120

6606

		F £	VF £	EF £
6606	**Halfpenny.** Type II. Similar, but large lettering			
	1741	10	50	120
	1742	10	50	120
	1743	15	60	150
	1744	15	60	150
	1744, 4 over 3	10	50	120
	1746	15	60	150
6607	— Type III. Similar, but GEORGIVS			
	1747	10	50	120
	1748	10	50	120
	1749	10	50	120
	1750	10	50	120
	1751	10	50	120
	1752	10	50	120
	1752 proof		*FDC*	350
	1753	15	60	150
	1755 Royal Mint records show **no** issue for this date			

6608

6608	**Farthing.** Type I. As 6605, small lettering			
	1737	20	75	200
	1737 proof		*FDC*	350
	1737 proof in silver		*Extremely rare*	
	1738	15	60	150
6609	— Type II. As 6606, large lettering.			
	1744	15	60	150

Old Head Coinage, 1760. Not issued in Ireland until 1762

6610

		F	VF	EF
		£	£	£
6610	**Halfpenny.** As 6609, but older features	10	50	120
	— 1760 proof		FDC	350

6611

| 6611 | **Farthing.** Similar. 1760 | 10 | 40 | 90 |

GEORGE III, 1760–1820

Probably as a result of the delay in sending the 1760 copper coins to Ireland a brief issue of tokens, the 'Voce Populi' series, was produced in Dublin to supply the need for small change, and in the North others following the pattern of the earlier promissory tokens, were made for McMinn, McCully and others. New Irish coppers were minted at London in 1766 and 1769 and again in 1775–6 and 1781–2, but supplementing these were large quantities of light-weight counterfeits, manufactured mainly in Birmingham.

The scarce 'Northumberland shillings' of 1763, named after the Earl of Northumberland who had £100 worth for distributing to the populace of Dublin on his appointment as Lord Lieutenant, were not a specifically Irish coin and many more than 2,000 must have been struck at London. Otherwise, virtually no silver coin was struck at London between 1758 and 1804 (apart from an issue of shillings and sixpences in 1787). Gold had become the standard of currency and silver coin became progressively scarcer and what was in circulation was badly worn. In Ireland these worn coins continued to circulate as a token currency, the thin discs being stamped with the names or initials of traders through whose hands they passed.

In 1804 the Bank of Ireland had quantities of Spanish and Spanish-American 8 *reales* or 'dollars' restruck as Six Shilling Bank Tokens (the Bank of England had similar coins struck into Five Shilling tokens, for in Ireland silver coin was still at a premium). These were produced by revolutionary steam-powered coining-presses at Matthew Boulton's private mint at Soho, near Birmingham. In the following years 10 pence and 5 pence Bank Tokens were also minted for Ireland, and 30 pence tokens were struck in 1808. In 1813 another issue of 10 pence tokens were struck at the London Mint's new premises on Tower Hill which had been fitted up with Boulton and Watt's steam-powered minting presses.

A great many new copper and some lead tokens were circulating in Ireland between 1789 and 1804, mainly issued by the mining companies and Dublin traders, but in 1805 the Soho mint struck large quantities of heavy-weight copper pennies, halfpennies and farthings and today these are perhaps the commonest of the older Irish coins still surviving. The precision striking and the engrailed edges made them difficult to counterfeit; they were the last official copper issue until 1822 but further tokens made their appearance in order to satisfy the public demand.

After the attempted French expeditions of 1796 and 1797 had failed and the Wolfe Tone rising of '98 was crushed, the establishments agreed on a merger of the two realms and the English and Irish parliaments approved the Act of Union in May 1800. This is reflected in the changed inscriptions on the gold coinage of 1801 and the new silver coinage of 1816 when M . B . ET H . REX ('King of Great Britain and Ireland') became BRITANNIARUM REX ('King of the Britains').

'London Coinage', 1766–82

6612

	F £	VF £	EF £
6612 **Halfpenny.** Type I. Laur. bust with short hair. R. Crowned harp			
1766	10	50	120
1766 proof		FDC	350
1769	10	50	120

6613   6614

6613 — Type II. Similar, but taller head of better style, 1769	15	60	150
6614 — Type III. Laur. bust r. with long hair			
1774 (proof only)		FDC	350
1775	20	70	200
1775 proof		FDC	350
1775 proof on thick flan struck en medaille		FDC	1000
1776	25	85	400
1781	10	50	120
1781 proof		FDC	350
1782	10	50	120
1782 struck with an upright die axis, en medaille	20	100	250
1782 proof		FDC	350

Note: Counterfeits exist of most dates, including 1783, some being of quite good workmanship.

Bank of Ireland Coinage, 1804–13

6615

		F £	VF £	EF £
6615	**Six Shillings.** Laur. and draped bust r. R. Hibernia seated l., with harp,			
	1804 *obv.* top leaf to upright of E in legend	100	250	600
	1804 Similar, proof in copper		*FDC*	650
	1804 Similar, proof in copper gilt		*FDC*	750
	1804 Similar, proof in gilt silver		*FDC*	1500
	1804 — — no stops in CHK on truncation	125	300	700
	1804 *obv.* top leaf points to centre of E in DEI.....................................	100	*250*	600
	1804 Similar, proof in copper		*FDC*	650
	1804 — — no stop after REX	125	300	700
	1804 Similar, proof in copper		*FDC*	650
	1804 *obv.* top leaf points to right side of E in DEI	100	250	700
	1804 Similar, proof		*FDC*	950
	1804 Similar, proof in copper		*FDC*	650
	1804 Similar, proof in copper gilt		*FDC*	750
	1804 Similar, proof in gilt silver		*FDC*	1500

6616

6616	**Thirty Pence.** Laur., draped and cuirassed bust, 1808. R. Hibernia, as above. **XXX PENCE IRISH** below	35	75	200
6616A	— — Top of harp points to O in TOKEN	60	125	300

6617 6618

		F £	VF £	EF £
6617	**Ten Pence.** Type I. *Obv.* similar. R. Inscription across field			
	1805 *obv.* front leaf of wreath under **E** of **DEI**	10	25	50
	1806 *obv.* front leaf of wreath under **D** of **DEI**	5	20	40
	1806	15	30	75
6618	— Type II. Laur. head r. R. Inscription in wreath, 1813	5	20	50
	1813 proof		*FDC*	300

6619

6619	**Five Pence.** As 6617			
	1805	5	20	50
	1806	10	25	60

Note: The Bank tokens were much counterfeited, probably mostly in Birmingham. They were copied in base metal and silvered over.

'Soho' (Birmingham) Coinage, 1805–6

6620

6620	**Penny.** Laur. and draped bust r. R. Crowned harp,			
	1805	10	40	150
	1805 proof		*FDC*	200
	1805 proof in bronzed copper		*FDC*	200
	1805 proof in gilt copper		*FDC*	300
	1805 proof in silver		*FDC*	2000
	1805 proof in gold		*FDC*	10000
	1805 reverse muled with English Penny reverse		*FDC*	2000

6621

		F £	VF £	EF £
6621	**Halfpenny.** Similar, 1805	3	15	50
	1805		*FDC*	175
	1805 proof in bronzed copper		*FDC*	175
	1805 proof in bronzed copper plain edge		*FDC*	150
	1805 proof in gilt copper		*FDC*	275
	1805 proof in gilt copper on a thick flan		*Extremely rare*	
	1805 proof in silver		*FDC*	1500
	1805 proof in gold		*Extremely rare*	
	1805 proof in gold plain edge		*Extremely rare*	

6622

		F	VF	EF
6622	**Farthing.** Similar, 1806	2	10	30
	1806 proof		*FDC*	125
	1806 proof in bronzed copper		*FDC*	125
	1806 proof in bronzed copper no stop after date		*FDC*	100
	1806 proof in gilt copper		*FDC*	200
	1806 proof in gilt copper, thin flan no stop after date		*FDC*	200
	1806 proof in gilt copper plain edge		*FDC*	175
	1806 proof in silver plain edge		*FDC*	850
	1805 proof in gold		*Extremely rare*	

GEORGE IV, 1820–1830

Although formal union of the two countries took place in 1800, the two exchequers were not merged until 1817. In 1821 the two currencies were amalgamated, which meant that the shilling in Ireland was exactly the same value as the same coin in England. One further issue of copper was made specifically for Ireland in 1822 and 1823 but Irish coinage was formally withdrawn in 1826; thenceforth the imperial coinage was the only regal one current in Ireland for more than a century.

6623

	F £	VF £	EF £
6623 **Penny.** Laur. and draped bust l. R. Crowned harp			
1822	10	50	150
1822 proof		FDC	350
1822 proof in bronzed copper		FDC	350
1822 proof on a thick flan		*extremely rare*	
1823	10	55	175
1823 proof		FDC	350
1823 proof in bronzed copper		FDC	350

6624

6624 **Halfpenny.** Similar			
1822	5	25	50
1822 proof		FDC	200
1822 proof in bronzed copper		FDC	200
1823	5	25	50
1823 proof		FDC	200
6624A **Farthing.** Similar, 1822, proof only		FDC	2500
6625B **Farthing.** — — proof only thin flan struck en medaille		FDC	5000

MODERN IRISH COINAGE FROM 1928

The struggle to have the Act of Union repealed, so valiantly conducted by Daniel O'Connell and others who followed him, was carried on for over a century. The Home Rule Bill which was placed on the statute book in 1914 was suspended during the Great War and was then superseded by the Government of Ireland Act of 1920. This led to the setting up of the Irish Free State, *Saorstát Éireann*, but in the North six of the nine counties of Ulster retained their links with the British crown and became a constituent part of the 'United Kingdom of Great Britain and Northern Ireland'.

The new Irish government decided to institute a coinage quite distinct from the United Kingdom coinage, which continued to circulate throughout Ireland, and in 1926 an advisory committee was appointed under the chairmanship of W.B. Yeats, the poet. The committee invited a number of artists to submit designs and those who competed were three Irishmen, Jerome Connor, Albert Power and Oliver Sheppard, and Paul Manship from America, Percy Metcalfe from England, Carl Milles of Sweden and Publio Morbiducci of Italy. The harp was chosen for the obverse type, the symbol used on all Irish coins since its introduction under Henry VIII. The reverse designs were to represent the fauna of the Irish countryside, the animals chosen being the horse, salmon, bull, wolfhound, hare, chicken, pig and the woodcock. Many masterpieces were produced but Metcalfe's set was outstanding artistically and his designs were also technically suited to modern coin production processes. The new Irish coinage set an extremely high standard for coinage design and how successful it was is evidenced by the fact that the designs were retained virtually unchanged for forty years.

The new coins were made at the Royal Mint in London in 1928. The three highest denominations, the halfcrown, florin and shilling, were made of 0.750 silver alloyed with 0.250 copper. This produced a whiter metal that discoloured less with wear than the 0.500 silver-copper alloy used for the UK coinage, though it was more expensive to produce. The sixpence and threepence were made a larger size proportionally by striking them in pure nickel, a metal that stands up well to wear. The penny, halfpenny and farthing were made of bronze, an alloy of 0.955 copper, 0.030 tin and 0.015 zinc. Six thousand specimen sets of the coinage were specially prepared with 'proof' surfaces and about 4,000 of these were sold to the general public in presentation cases.

In June 1937 a new constitution declared the Free State a sovereign republic with the name 'Eire' and this name appeared on the next coins to be issued in 1939. For technical reasons minor modifications were made to the design of the harp and also to the reverses of the halfcrown and the penny. In 1942 pure nickel for the sixpence and threepence was abandoned in favour of cupro-nickel alloy, 0.750 copper and 0.250 nickel. By 1943 the rising price of silver made it uneconomic to mint coins of 0.725 silver, so no shillings were minted that year and of the halfcrowns and florins minted very few went into circulation. No further coins of these denominations were produced until after the 1950 Coinage Act which specified the same cupro-nickel alloy for these coins as was being used for the sixpence and threepences.

The fiftieth anniversary of the 'Easter Rising' of 1916 was commemorated with a special issue of 0.833 silver ten shilling pieces. These bear the bust of Pádraig H. Pearse on one side and on the reverse a copy of the statue by Oliver Sheppart of Cúchulainn, the legendary hero of the *Táin Bó Cúailnge*, which now stands in the Post Office at Dublin. The coin did not prove popular with the public as an additional high denomination, and over half the issue has been recalled and melted down.

IRISH FREE STATE

SILVER

6625

		F £	VF £	EF £	Unc. £
6625	**Halfcrown.** R. Horse standing l.				
	1928 Mintage 2,160,000	5	8	15	30
	1928 Proof Mintage 6,001 *FDC* £35				
	1930 Mintage 352,000	6	15	125	300
	1930 Proof *FDC* £1000				
	1931 Mintage 160,000	8	20	150	350
	1931 Proof *FDC* £1000				
	1933 Mintage 336,000	6	15	125	300
	1933 Proof *FDC* £1000				
	1934 Mintage 480,000	5	8	50	125
	1934 Proof *FDC* £1000				
	1937 Mintage 40,000	40	100	450	1250
	1937 Proof *FDC* £1000				

6626

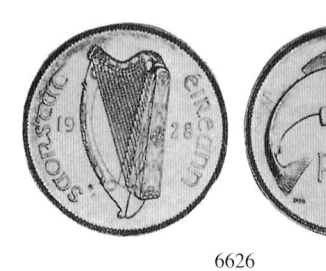

6626	**Florin.** Harp. R. Salmon r.				
	1928 Mintage 2,025,000	3	6	15	25
	1928 Proof Mintage 6,001 *FDC* £30				
	1930 Mintage 330,000	4	10	125	300
	1930 Proof *FDC* £1,500				
	1931 Mintage 200,000	5	30	200	450
	1931 Proof *FDC* £1,000				
	1933 Mintage 300,000	4	10	125	300
	1933 Proof *FDC* £1,000				

IRISH FREE STATE 187

	F £	VF £	EF £	Unc. £
6626 1934 Mintage 150,000	5	40	300	550
1934 Proof *FDC* £1,000				
1935 Mintage 390,000	4	10	125	300
1935 Proof *FDC* £1,000				
1937 Mintage 150,000	5	30	200	450
1937 Proof *FDC* £1,000				

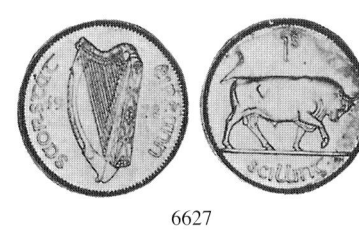

6627

6627 Shilling. Harp. R. Bull butting r.

	F	VF	EF	Unc.
1928 Mintage 2,700,000	2	4	8	20
1928 Proof Mintage 6,001 *FDC* £25				
1930 Mintage 460,000	3	15	120	300
1930 Proof *FDC* £750				
1931 Mintage 400,000	3	7	50	125
1931 Proof *FDC* £750				
1933 Mintage 300,000	3	15	75	175
1933 Proof *FDC* £750				
1935 Mintage 400,000	2	6	40	90
1935 Proof *FDC* £750				
1937 Mintage 100,000	6	30	250	650
1937 Proof *FDC* £750				

NICKEL

6628   6629

6628 Sixpence. Harp. R. Wolfhound standing l.

	F	VF	EF	Unc.
1928 Mintage 3,201,480	1	2	5	15
1928 Proof Mintage 6,001 *FDC* £20				
1934 Mintage 600,000	2	4	10	40
1934 Proof *FDC* £650				
1935 Mintage 520,000	3	5	15	75
1935 Proof *FDC* £650				

IRISH FREE STATE

	F £	VF £	EF £	Unc. £

6629 Threepence. Harp. R. Hare seated l.
1928 Mintage 1,500,000 1   2   4   12
1928 Proof Mintage 6,001 *FDC* £15
1933 Mintage 320,000 4   8   50 150
1933 Proof *FDC* £700
1934 Mintage 800,000 2   4   10   40
1934 Proof *FDC* £600
1935 Mintage 240,000 3   6   25 100
1935 Proof *FDC* £600

BRONZE

6630

6630 Penny. Harp. R. Chicken and chicks l.
1928 Mintage 9,000,000 1   2   4   15
1928 Proof Mintage 6,001 *FDC* £20
1931 Mintage 2,400,000 2   4   12   30
1931 Proof *FDC* £500
1933 Mintage 1,680,000 3   5   15   75
1933 Proof *FDC* £500
1935 Mintage 5,472,000 2   4   10   25
1935 Proof *FDC* £500
1937 Mintage 5,400,000 2   4   12   30
1937 Proof *FDC* £400

6631

6631 Halfpenny. Harp. R. Pig and piglets l.
1928 Mintage 2,880,000 1   2   4   12
1928 Proof Mintage 6,001 *FDC* £15
1933 Mintage 720,000 4   8   50 300
1933 Proof *FDC* £500

IRISH FREE STATE AND EIRE

	F £	VF £	EF £	Unc. £

6631 1935 Mintage 960,000 .... 3 5 25 175
1935 Proof *FDC* £500
1937 Mintage 960,000 .... 1 3 8 25
1937 Proof *FDC* £400

6632

6632 Farthing. Harp. R. Woodcock flying l.
1928 Mintage 300,000 .... 1 2 4 10
1928 Proof Mintage 6,001 *FDC* £15
1930 Mintage 288,000 .... 1 2 5 15
1930 Proof *FDC* £300
1931 Mintage 192,000 .... 1 3 8 20
1931 Proof *FDC* £300
1932 Mintage 192,000 .... 1 4 10 25
1932 Proof *FDC* £300
1933 Mintage 480,000 .... 1 2 5 15
1933 Proof *FDC* £300
1935 Mintage 192,000 .... 1 5 15 30
1935 Proof *FDC* £300
1936 Mintage 192,000 .... 2 6 18 35
1936 Proof *FDC* £300
1937 Mintage 480,000 .... 1 2 5 15
1937 Proof *FDC* £250

EIRE

SILVER

6633

6633 Halfcrown. Type as 6625, but reading EIRE and minor alterations to design and lettering
1938 .... *unique*
1939 Mintage 888,000 .... 3 6 15 50

	F £	VF £	EF £	Unc. £

6633 1939 Proof *FDC* £650
1940 Mintage 752,000 .... 3 6 20 60
1940 Proof *FDC* £750
1941 Mintage 320,000 .... 4 8 25 70
1941 Proof *FDC* £750
1942 Mintage 285,600 .... 3 6 15 40
1943 ....100 300 1000 2500

6634

6634 Florin. Type as 6626, but EIRE
1939 Mintage 1,080,000 .... 3 6 12 35
1939 Proof *FDC* £500
1940 Mintage 670,000 .... 4 8 16 45
1940 Proof *FDC* £600
1941 Mintage 400,000 .... 6 12 25 60
1941 Proof *FDC* £600
1942 Mintage 109,000 .... 4 8 16 40
1942 Proof *FDC* £600
1943 .... 2500 5000 10000 20000

6635

6635 Shilling. Type as 6627, but EIRE
1939 Mintage 1,140,000 .... 2 4 10 25
1939 Proof *FDC* £450
1940 Mintage 580,000 .... 3 6 15 30
1940 Proof *FDC* £500
1941 Mintage 300,000 .... 4 8 20 45
1941 Proof *FDC* £500
1942 Mintage 286,000 .... 3 6 15 30
1942 Proof *FDC* £450

EIRE

NICKEL

6636   6637

		F £	VF £	EF £	Unc. £
6636	**Sixpence.** Type as 6628, but EIRE				
	1939 Mintage 876,000	2	4	10	30
	1939 Proof *FDC* £400				
	1940 Mintage 1,120,000	2	4	10	30
	1940 Proof *FDC* £500				
6637	**Threepence.** Type as 6629, but EIRE				
	1939 Mintage 64,000	5	10	60	200
	1939 Proof *FDC* £350				
	1940 Mintage 720,000	2	4	10	35
	1940 Proof *FDC* £400				

CUPRO-NICKEL

6638

		F	VF	EF	Unc.
6638	**Halfcrown.** Type as 6633, except for change of metal				
	1951 Mintage 800,000	1	2	10	25
	1951 Proof *FDC* £700				
	1954 Mintage 400,000	1	3	14	30
	1954 Proof *FDC* £750				
	1955 Mintage 1,080,000	1	2	6	15
	1955 Proof *FDC* £750				
	1959 Mintage 1,600,000	1	2	5	12
	1959 Proof *FDC* £750				
	1961 Mintage 1,600,000	1	2	6	15
	1961 Proof *FDC* £500				
	1962 Mintage 3,200,000	1	2	5	12

		F £	VF £	EF £	Unc. £
6638	1962 Proof *FDC* £500				
	1963 Mintage 2,400,000	1	2	5	12
	1963 Proof *FDC* £500				
	1964 Mintage 3,200,000	—	1	2	5
	1964 Proof *FDC* £500				
	1966 Mintage 700,000	—	2	6	15
	1966 Proof *FDC* £500				
	1967 Mintage 2,000,000	—	1	2	5
	1967 Proof *FDC* £500				
6638A	— — 1961. Similar, but muled with *rev.* of 6625	10	30	250	650
6639	**Florin.** Type as 6634, except for change of metal				
	1951 Mintage 1,000,000	1	2	6	18
	1951 Proof *FDC* £550				
	1954 Mintage 1,000,000	1	2	5	15
	1954 Proof *FDC* £600				
	1955 Mintage 1,000,000	1	2	4	14
	1955 Proof *FDC* £600				
	1959 Mintage 2,000,000	1	2	3	12
	1959 Proof *FDC* £600				
	1961 Mintage 2,000,000	1	3	10	35
	1961 Proof *FDC* £350				
	1962 Mintage 2,400,000	1	2	3	12
	1962 Proof *FDC* £350				
	1963 Mintage 3,000,000	—	1	2	10
	1963 Proof *FDC* £300				
	1964 Mintage 4,000,000	—	—	1	8
	1964 Proof *FDC* £300				
	1965 Mintage 2,000,000	—	—	1	6
	1965 Proof *FDC* £300				
	1966 Mintage 3,625,000	—	—	—	3
	1966 Proof *FDC* £250				
	1968 Mintage 1,000,000	—	—	—	2
	1968 Proof *FDC* £250				
6640	**Shilling.** Type as 6635, but cupro-nickel				
	1951 Mintage 2,000,000	—	2	4	15
	1951 Proof *FDC* £400				
	1954 Mintage 3,000,000	—	1	3	10
	1954 Proof *FDC* £400				
	1955 Mintage 1,000,000	—	2	4	15
	1955 Proof *FDC* £400				
	1959 Mintage 2,000,000	—	3	6	30
	1962 Mintage 4,000,000	—	1	2	8
	1962 Proof *FDC* £300				
	1963 Mintage 4,000,000	—	—	2	5
	1963 Proof *FDC* £300				
	1964 Mintage 4,000,000	—	—	1	3
	1964 Proof *FDC* £300				
	1966 Mintage 3,000,000	—	—	1	2
	1966 Proof *FDC* £250				
	1968 Mintage 4,000,000	—	—	—	2
	1968 Proof *FDC* £250				

		F £	VF £	EF £	Unc. £
6641	**Sixpence.** Type as 6636, but cupro-nickel				
	1942 Mintage 1,320,000	1	2	8	35
	1942 Proof *FDC* £400				
	1945 Mintage 400,000	3	10	40	125
	1945 Proof *FDC* £400				
	1946 Mintage 720,000	5	15	75	350
	1946 Proof *FDC* £400				
	1947 Mintage 800,000	2	8	30	100
	1947 Proof *FDC* £400				
	1948 Mintage 800,000	1	2	6	30
	1948 Proof *FDC* £400				
	1949 Mintage 600,000	1	3	10	45
	1949 Proof *FDC* £400				
	1950 Mintage 800,000	2	20	35	120
	1950 Proof *FDC* £400				
	1952 Mintage 800,000	1	2	5	20
	1952 Proof *FDC* £400				
	1953 Mintage 800,000	1	2	6	25
	1953 Proof *FDC* £400				
	1955 Mintage 600,000	—	1	4	18
	1955 Proof *FDC* £400				
	1956 Mintage 600,000	—	1	3	15
	1956 Proof *FDC* £400				
	1958 Mintage 600,000	1	2	8	40
	1958 Proof *FDC* £400				
	1959 Mintage 2,000,000	—	1	3	16
	1959 Proof *FDC* £400				
	1960 Mintage 2,020,000	—	—	2	10
	1960 Proof *FDC* £400				
	1961 Mintage 3,000,000	—	—	2	8
	1961 Proof *FDC* £300				
	1962 Mintage 4,000,000	1	2	8	35
	1962 Proof *FDC* £300				
	1963 Mintage 4,000,000	—	—	1	3
	1963 Proof *FDC* £300				
	1964 Mintage 4,000,000	—	—	1	2
	1964 Proof *FDC* £250				
	1966 Mintage 2,000,000	—	—	1	2
	1966 Proof *FDC* £250				
	1967 Mintage 4,000,000	—	—	—	1
	1967 Proof *FDC* £250				
	1968 Mintage 4,000,000	—	—	—	1
	1968 Proof *FDC* £250				
	1969 Mintage 2,000,000	—	—	—	1
	1969 Proof *FDC* £200				
6642	**Threepence.** Type as 6637, but cupro-nickel				
	1942 Mintage 4,000,000	—	1	5	25
	1942 Proof *FDC* £450				
	1943 Mintage 1,360,000	—	1	10	70

		F	VF	EF	Unc.
		£	£	£	£
6642	1943 Proof *FDC* £450				
	1946 Mintage 800,000	—	2	8	30
	1946 Proof *FDC* £450				
	1948 Mintage 1,600,000	1	3	18	85
	1948 Proof *FDC* £450				
	1949 Mintage 1,200,000	—	1	6	20
	1949 Proof *FDC* £450				
	1950 Mintage 1,600,000	—	1	6	15
	1950 Proof *FDC* £450				
	1953 Mintage 1,600,000	—	1	5	12
	1953 Proof *FDC* £450				
	1956 Mintage 1,200,000	—	—	2	8
	1956 Proof *FDC* £450				
	1961 Mintage 2,400,000	—	—	1	5
	1961 Proof *FDC* £350				
	1962 Mintage 3,200,000	—	—	2	10
	1962 Proof *FDC* £350				
	1963 Mintage 4,000,000	—	—	1	2
	1963 Proof *FDC* £250				
	1964 Mintage 6,000,000	—	—	—	1
	1964 Proof *FDC* £250				
	1965 Mintage 3,600,000	—	—	—	1
	1965 Proof *FDC* £250				
	1966 Mintage 4,000,000	—	—	—	1
	1966 Proof *FDC* £250				
	1967 Mintage 2,400,000	—	—	—	1
	1967 Proof *FDC* £250				
	1968 Mintage 4,000,000	—	—	—	1
	1968 Proof *FDC* £250				

BRONZE

6643

6643 **Penny.** Type as 6630, but EIRE
1938 only two specimens known *FDC* £30,000
1940 Mintage 312,000 .... 1 5 100 400
1940 Proof *FDC* £1250
1941 Mintage 4,680,000 .... — 1 10 35

		F £	VF £	EF £	Unc. £
6643	1941 Proof *FDC* £350				
	1942 Mintage 17,580,000	—	1	4	12
	1942 Proof *FDC* £350				
	1943 Mintage 3,360,000	—	1	6	30
	1943 Proof *FDC* £350				
	1946 Mintage 4,800,000	—	1	5	15
	1946 Proof *FDC* £350				
	1948 Mintage 4,800,000	—	1	4	12
	1948 Proof *FDC* £350				
	1949 Mintage 4,080,000	—	1	5	15
	1949 Proof *FDC* £250				
	1950 Mintage 2,400,000	—	—	3	10
	1950 Proof *FDC* £300				
	1952 Mintage 2,400,000	—	—	1	4
	1952 Proof *FDC* £300				
	1962 Mintage 1,200,000	—	—	2	8
	1962 Proof *FDC* £200				
	1963 Mintage 9,600,000	—	—	1	3
	1963 Proof *FDC* £200				
	1964 Mintage 6,000,000	—	—	1	2
	1964 Proof *FDC* £200				
	1965 Mintage 11,160,000	—	—	—	1
	1965 Proof *FDC* £200				
	1966 Mintage 6,000,000	—	—	—	1
	1966 Proof *FDC* £150				
	1967 Mintage 2,400,000	—	—	—	1
	1967 Proof *FDC* £150				
	1968 Mintage 9,000,000	—	—	—	1

6644   6645

6644	**Halfpenny.** Types as 6631, but EIRE				
	1939 Mintage 240,000	1	10	35	125
	1939 Proof *FDC* £300				
	1940 Mintage 1,680,000	1	8	40	175
	1940 Proof *FDC* £350				
	1941 Mintage 2,400,000	—	2	5	25
	1941 Proof *FDC* £300				
	1942 Mintage 6,931,200	—	—	3	10
	1943 Mintage 2,668,800	—	1	4	20
	1943 Proof *FDC* £300				
	1946 Mintage 720,000	1	3	15	60

	F £	VF £	EF £	Unc. £
6644 1946 Proof *FDC* £300				
1949 Mintage 1,344,000	—	1	3	15
1949 Proof *FDC* £275				
1953 Mintage 2,400,000	—	—	1	3
1953 Proof *FDC* £250				
1964 Mintage 2,160,000	—	—	—	1
1964 Proof *FDC* £250				
1965 Mintage 1,440,000	—	—	1	2
1965 Proof *FDC* £250				
1966 Mintage 1,680,000	—	—	—	1
1966 Proof *FDC* £250				
1967 Mintage 1,200,000	—	—	—	1
1967 Proof *FDC* £250				
6645 Farthing. Type as 6632, but EIRE				
1939 Mintage 768,000	—	1	3	10
1939 Proof *FDC* £200				
1940 Mintage 192,000	—	2	8	25
1940 Proof *FDC* £200				
1941 Mintage 480,000	—	1	3	10
1941 Proof *FDC* £200				
1943 Mintage 480,000	—	1	2	8
1943 Proof *FDC* £200				
1944 Mintage 480,000	—	1	4	15
1944 Proof *FDC* £200				
1946 Mintage 480,000	—	—	1	5
1946 Proof *FDC* £200				
1949 Mintage 192,000	—	1	3	14
1949 Proof *FDC* £200				
1953 Mintage 192,000	—	—	—	1
1953 Proof *FDC* £200				
1959 Mintage 192,000	—	—	—	1
1959 Proof *FDC* £200				
1966 Mintage 96,000	—	—	1	4

Easter Rising Commemorative Issue, 1966 (Sterling silver 0.925)

6457

6646 Ten Shillings. Bust r. of Patrick Pearse. R. The statue of Cúchulainn by Oliver Sheppard. *Edge:* ÉIRÍ AMAC NA CASCA 1916 ('The Easter Rising 1916') Mintage 2,000,000 .... — 1 5 10
— — Similar, Proof Mintage 20,000 *FDC* £15
— — Similar, edge error NACASCA or NASCA .... — 20 40 75

THE ISLANDS

Jersey
Guernsey
Man
Lundy

INTRODUCTION TO COINS OF THE ISLANDS

The coinages of smaller islands of the British Isles and the Channel Islands add an interesting dimension to those of Great Britain and Ireland. The Channel Islands were at one time part of the dukedom of Normandy and their allegiance to the English crown dates to the time of William the Conqueror. Due to their short distance from the coast of France their small change was reckoned in French 'doubles' or 'sous'. Man, with its own variant Celtic tongue, Manx, came within the orbit of the Norsemen, then the lords of the Western Isles, was disputed by the kings of Scotland and England, was granted to the earls of Derby and eventually sold back to the British crown in the eighteenth century. Today its coinage contributes to the revenue from its tourist trade.

LATIN AND OTHER LEGENDS

QVOCVNQVE JECERIS (or GESSERIS) STABIT (However you throw it stands). Earl of Derby copper coins of Man.
SANS CHANGER (Changeless). Earl of Derby coppers of Man.
S BALLIVIE INSVLE DE GERNEREVE (Seal of the Bailiwick of the Island of Guernsey). Appears on 7221, 7225 and 7226.

SELECT BIBLIOGRAPHY

CHANNEL ISLANDS

LOWSLEY, LT.-COL. B. *The Coinages of the Channel Islands*. 1897.
MARSHAL-FRASER, LT.-COL. W. *The Coinages of the Channel Islands*. 1949.
PRIDMORE, F. *The Coins of the British Commonwealth of Nations,* Part 1 European Territories, 1960.

ISLE OF MAN

DOLLEY, M. 'Hiberno-Manx Coinage, *c*.1025–35'. *NC*, 1976.
NELSON, P. 'Coinage of the Isle of Man'. *NC*, 1899.
— 'Contemporary Forgeries of the Isle of Man Coinage of 1733'. *SNC*, 1901.
LISTER, MAUD. *Manx Money*, 1947.
CLAY, C. 'On the Brass, Copper and other Currency of the Isle of Man'. *Proc. Manchester Num. Soc.*, Pts. I–V, 1864–7.
PRIDMORE, F. *The Coins of the British Commonwealth of Nations,* Part 1 European Territories, 1960.

LUNDY

MORRIESON, LT.-COL. H.W. 'The Coinage of Lundy 1645–6'. *BNJ* XIX, 1927/8.

JERSEY

The Channel Islands off the French coast have been in the possession of the British Crown since the English kings held the Dukedom of Normandy. Jersey, the largest island in the Channel Island group, changed from French to English currency in 1834. As the pound was then equivalent to 26 French *livres* of 20 *sous* each, and a *sous* was equal to one halfpenny, it followed that the 'Jersey' penny or *pièce de deux sous,* should be one thirteenth of a shilling. The first copper coinage did not appear until 1841, and was struck at the Royal Mint in London. A change to a bronze coinage was made in 1866, and in 1877 the values were altered to the more convenient one twelfth, one twenty-fourth, and one forty-eighth of a shilling. Unlike the neighbouring coins of Guernsey, the Jersey coins have always borne the portrait of the reigning monarch.

After the War, in 1949, an issue of pennies commemorating the liberation of the island from German occupation carry the inscription LIBERATED 1945. The name STATES OF JERSEY was replaced by ISLAND OF JERSEY on the Liberation issue, and was changed to BAILIWICK OF JERSEY on the 1957 pennies.

In 1960 a penny was issued commemorating the Tercentenary of the Restoration, and a crown, threepence and penny dated 1066–1966 commemorates the accession of William, Duke of Normandy, to the throne of England. Decimal coinage was introduced in 1968.

VICTORIA 1837–1901

COPPER

7001

	F £	VF £	EF £	Unc. £
7001 **One thirteenth of a shilling.** Young head, date below. R. Arms of Jersey				
1841 Mintage 116,480	10	30	75	125
1841 Proof *FDC* £250				
1844 Mintage 27,040	15	40	90	150
1844 Proof *FDC* £275				
1851 Mintage 160,000	20	50	100	175
1851 Proof *FDC* £300				
1858 Mintage 173,333	15	40	90	150
1858 Proof *FDC* £275				
1861 Mintage 173,333	20	50	100	175
1861 Proof *FDC* £300				
1865 Proof only *FDC* £750				

		F £	VF £	EF £	Unc. £
7002	**One twenty-sixth of a shilling**				
	1841 Mintage 232,960	5	15	60	100
	1841 Proof *FDC* £175				
	1844 Mintage 232,960	5	15	60	100
	1851 Mintage 160,000	5	15	55	90
	1858 Mintage 173,333	5	15	55	90
	1858 Proof *FDC* £150				
	1861 Mintage 173,333	5	15	50	85
	1861 Proof *FDC* £150				
7003	**One fifty-second of a shilling**				
	1841 Mintage 116,480	15	60	150	300
	1841 Proof *FDC* £600				
	1861 Proof in copper *FDC* £750				
	1861 Proof in bronze. *Extremely rare*				

BRONZE

First issue, with 'square' shield. Type as before

7004

7004	**One thirteenth of a shilling**				
	1866 Mintage 173,333	5	15	35	65
	1866 Proof *FDC* £200				
	1866 no L.C.W. on truncation, Pr.9B proof only *FDC* £400				
	1870 Mintage 160,000	5	15	35	65
	1870 Proof *FDC* £200				
	1871 Mintage 160,000	5	15	35	65
	1871 Proof *FDC* £200				
7005	**One twenty-sixth of a shilling**				
	1866 Mintage 173,333	5	10	25	45
	1866 Proof *FDC* £150				
	1870 Mintage 160,000	5	10	25	45
	1870 Proof *FDC* £150				
	1871 Mintage 160,000	5	10	25	45
	1871 Proof *FDC* £150				

Second issue, with 'spade' shield, new diameter and increased weight

7006

		F £	VF £	EF £	Unc. £
7006	**One twelfth of a shilling**				
	1877 Proof only *FDC* £200				
	1877 Proof in nickel *FDC Extremely rare*				
	1877H Mintage 240,000	5	10	20	30
	1877H Proof *FDC* £150				
	1877H Proof in nickel *FDC Extremely rare*				
	1881 Mintage 75,153	5	15	30	45
	1888 Mintage 180,000	5	15	25	40
	1894 Mintage 180,000	5	15	25	40
	1894 Proof *FDC* £175				
7007	**One twenty-fourth of a shilling**				
	1877 Proof only *FDC* £200				
	1877H Mintage 336,000	1	5	10	15
	1877H Proof *FDC* £100				
	1888 Mintage 120,000	3	10	15	25
	1894 Mintage 120,000	3	10	15	25
	1894 Proof *FDC* £200				
7008	**One forty-eighth of a shilling**				
	1877 Proof only *FDC* £250				
	1877H Mintage 288,000	10	30	75	150
	1877H Proof *FDC* £200				

EDWARD VII 1901–1910

BRONZE

7009

7009	**One twelfth of a shilling.**				
	1909 Mintage 180,000	5	10	25	35
7010	**One twenty-fourth of a shilling,**				
	1909 Mintage 120,000	5	15	30	40

GEORGE V 1910–1936

BRONZE

First issue, 'spade' shield as before

7011

		F £	VF £	EF £	Unc. £
7011	**One twelfth of a shilling**				
	1911 Mintage 204,000	5	10	20	30
	1913 Mintage 204,000	5	10	20	30
	1923 Mintage 204,000	5	10	20	30
7012	**One twenty-fourth of a shilling**				
	1911 Mintage 72,000	5	15	25	40
	1913 Mintage 72,000	5	15	25	40
	1923 Mintage 72,000	5	15	30	45

Second issue, 'square' shield, scrolls above and below

7013

7013	**One twelfth of a shilling**				
	1923 Mintage 301,200	5	10	20	30
	1926 Mintage 82,800	5	15	25	35
7014	**One twenty-fourth of a shilling**				
	1923 Mintage 72,000	5	15	25	35
	1923 Proof *FDC* £85				
	1926 Mintage 120,000	5	10	20	30
	1926 Proof *FDC* £85				

Third issue, type as before, but scrolls omitted

7015

	F £	VF £	EF £	Unc. £
7015 One twelfth of a shilling				
1931 Mintage 204,000		5	10	15
1931 Proof *FDC* £350				
1933 Mintage 204,000		5	10	15
1933 Proof *FDC* £350				
1935 Mintage 204,000		5	10	15
1935 Proof *FDC* £350				
7016 One twenty-fourth of a shilling				
1931 Mintage 72,000		5	15	25
1931 Proof *FDC* £250				
1933 Mintage 72,000		5	15	25
1933 Proof *FDC* £250				
1935 Mintage 72,000		5	15	25
1935 Proof *FDC* £250				

GEORGE VI 1936–1952

First issue

7017

	F £	VF £	EF £	Unc. £
7017 One twelfth of a shilling.				
1937 Mintage 204,000		5	10	15
1937 Proof *FDC* £200				
1946 Mintage 204,000		1	5	10
1946 Proof *FDC* £200				
1947 Mintage 444,000		1	5	10
1947 Proof *FDC* £200				

JERSEY – GEORGE VI AND ELIZABETH II

	F £	VF £	EF £	Unc. £
7018 One twenty-fourth of a shilling.				
1937 Mintage 72,000	5	10	20	30
1937 Proof *FDC* £250				
1946 Mintage 72,000	5	10	20	30
1946 Proof *FDC* £200				
1947 Mintage 72,000	5	10	20	30
1947 Proof *FDC* £200				

Second ('Liberation') issue.

7019

7019 One twelfth of a shilling. Dated 1945. Issued in 1949, 1950 and 1952
1945 Mintage 1,200,000 1   5   10
1945 Proof *FDC* £100

ELIZABETH II 1952–present

CUPRO-NICKEL

7020

7020 Five shillings, 1966. William I commemorative, 1066–1966
1966 5   10
1966 Proof *FDC* £15 ....

JERSEY – ELIZABETH II

		F £	VF £	EF £	Unc. £
7021	**Fourth of a shilling** (threepence). Round flan, 1957			5	10
	1957 Proof *FDC* £15				
	1960 Proof only, *FDC* £100				
7021A	— Dodecagonal flan, 1964			5	10
	1964 Proof *FDC*				
7022	— William I commemorative, 1066–1966			5	10
	1966 Proof *FDC* £10				

BRONZE

7023	**One twelfth of a shilling.** 'Liberation' issue dated 1945 (issued in 1954) 1945			5	10
7024	— Normal issue, without 'LIBERATED 1945' 1957			5	10
	1957 Proof *FDC* £20				
	1964			5	10
	1964 Proof *FDC* £10				
7025	**Restoration Tercentenary commemorative,** with dates 1660–1960 1960			5	10
	1960 Proof *FDC* £10				
7025A	— Mule with obv. as 7023, Proof only *FDC* £250				

7026

	F	VF	EF	Unc.
	£	£	£	£
7026 William I Commemorative, 1066–1966			5	10
1966 Proof *FDC* £10				

PROOF AND SPECIMEN SETS

		No. of coins in set	FDC £
7160	1957 Double set, ¼ & 1/12 sh.	(4)	10
7161	1960 Double set, ¼ & 1/12 sh.	(4)	10
7162	1964 Double set, ¼ & 1/12 sh.	(4)	10
7163	1966 Double set, ¼ & 1/12 sh.	(4)	10
7164	1966 Double set of two crowns	(2)	10

GUERNSEY

Guernsey, the other large island in the Channel Islands group, officially retained French denominations as its legal money of account until 1921. The unit of local coinage was the Double, derived from the French *double tournois*; a small seventeenth century copper coin. Prior to 1921 twelve eight-doubles went to the 'Guernsey shilling', but twenty-one of these were equated with the pound sterling. It can be said that the double was worth approximately half a farthing—8 doubles being of equivalent value to the old British penny.

The first Guernsey coins were copper four doubles and one doubles made in 1830 at Boulton and Watt's Soho Mint; an eight doubles was issued in 1834 and a two doubles in 1858. A change to a lighter bronze coinage was made in 1864. The designs were maintained practically unchanged until 1956, when a Guernsey Lily was used as an emblem on the eight and four doubles, and a new threepenny denomination was introduced depicting the Guernsey cow. The two doubles was last minted in 1929, and the one double in 1938.

In 1935 500 proof-like eight doubles, dated 1934 were issued to commemorate both the Silver Jubilee of George V and the centenary of the institution of the coinage.

A square ten shilling piece was issued in 1966 to celebrate the 9th Centenary of the Battle of Hastings. It depicts William the Conqueror on the reverse. Decimal coinage was introduced in 1971.

Pre-Decimal Coinage

WILLIAM IV 1830–1837

COPPER

7200

		F £	VF £	EF £	UNC £	Proof FDC £
7200	**Eight doubles.** Arms of Guernsey etc. R. Inscription and date 1834 Mintage 221,760	5	15	65	150	250
7201	**Four doubles.** Similar, smaller denomination 1830 Mintage 655,200	4	15	50	100	125
7202	**Double.** Similar, smaller denomination 1830 Mintage 1,648,640 total	2	10	30	65	85
	1830 Stop before date	10	30	100	200	—

VICTORIA 1837–1901

COPPER

		F	VF	EF	UNC	*Proof* FDC
		£	£	£	£	£
7203	**Eight doubles.** Type as before Mintage 111,469					
	1858 five berries on l. branch	20	50	125	250	300
	1858 four berries on l. branch	30	75	150	300	—
7204	**Four doubles,** 1858 Mintage 114,060	20	50	125	250	—
7205	**Two doubles,** 1858 Mintage 56,128	30	75	150	300	—

BRONZE

H = Struck by R. Heaton & Sons, Birmingham, later, The Mint, Birmingham, Ltd.

7206

		F	VF	EF	UNC	FDC
7206	**Eight doubles**					
	1864 (5 *obv.*, 2 *rev.* dies) Mintage 184,736	5	20	60	100	—
	1864 three stalks to spray	10	30	75	125	—
	1868 (5 *obv.* dies) Mintage 54,720	10	35	85	150	—
	1874 (4 *obv.*, 2 *rev.* dies) Mintage 73,248	10	30	75	125	—
	1885H Mintage 69,696	3	10	35	70	200
	1889H Mintage 215,620	2	5	30	60	—
	1893H large or small lettering on rev. Mintage 117,600	2	5	30	60	—
7207	**Four doubles**					
	1864 Single stalk Mintage 212,976	2	10	30	50	—
	1864 Three stalks	3	15	35	60	—
	1868 Mintage 57,696	5	20	40	70	—
	1874 Mintage 69,216	2	10	30	50	—
	1885H Mintage 69,696	1	5	25	40	125
	1889H Mintage 103,744	1	5	20	35	500
	1893H Mintage 52,224	1	5	20	35	—
7208	**Two doubles**					
	1868 Single stalk Mintage 35,136	30	75	150	300	—
	1868 three stalks	40	100	175	350	—
	1874 wide & narrow dates Mintage 45,216	25	60	125	250	—
	1885H Mintage 76,800	1	4	20	35	100
	1889H Mintage 35,616	1	4	20	35	—
	1899H Mintage 35,636	1	5	25	40	—

GUERNSEY – VICTORIA, EDWARD VIII AND GEORGE V

		F	VF	EF	UNC	*Proof* FDC
		£	£	£	£	£
7209	**Double**					
	1868 Four leaves Mintage 64,368	25	60	125	250	—
	1868 Date altered from 1830	20	50	100	200	—
	1885H Three leaves Mintage 76,800		1	5	10	75
	1889H Mintage 112,016		1	5	10	—
	1893H Mintage 56,016		2	8	15	—
	1899H Mintage 56,000		2	8	15	—

EDWARD VII 1901–1910

BRONZE

		F	VF	EF	UNC	FDC
7210	**Eight doubles**					
	1902H Mintage 235,200	1	5	10	20	—
	1903H Mintage 117,600	1	5	12	25	—
	1910H Mintage 91,467	1	5	15	30	—
7211	**Four doubles**					
	1902H Mintage 104,534	1	5	10	18	—
	1903H Mintage 52,267	1	5	10	20	—
	1906H Mintage 52,266	1	5	10	20	—
	1908H Mintage 25,760	5	10	20	40	—
	1910H Mintage 52,267		5	10	20	—
7212	**Two doubles**					
	1902H Mintage 17,818	5	10	20	40	—
	1903H Mintage 17,818	5	10	20	40	—
	1906H Mintage 17,820	5	15	25	45	—
	1908H Mintage 17,780	5	15	25	45	—
7213	**Double**					
	1902H Mintage 84,000		2	8	15	—
	1903H Mintage 112,000		1	6	12	—

GEORGE V 1910–1936

BRONZE

7214

7214	**Eight doubles.** Mintage for 1911 is 78,400					
	1911H Three leaves above shield	5	20	60	100	—

7214A

	F £	VF £	EF £	UNC £	Proof FDC £
7214A — Redesigned shield					
1914H Mintage 156,800		3	8	15	—
1918H Mintage 156,800		3	8	15	—
1920H Mintage 156,800		2	7	14	—
1934H Mintage 123,600		2	7	14	125
7215 Four doubles. Mintage for 1911 is 52,267					
1911H Three leaves above shield	5	20	60	100	—
7215A 1914H Redesigned shield					
1914H Mintage 209,067		3	8	15	—
1918H Mintage 156,800		3	8	15	—
1920H Mintage 156,800		2	7	14	—
7216 Two doubles. Mintage for 1911 is 28,509					
1911H Three leaves above shield	8	25	70	125	—
7216A — Redesigned shield					
1914H Mintage 28,509	8	25	70	125	—
1917H Mintage 14,524	50	100	200	400	—
1918H Mintage 57,018	2	10	30	50	—
1920H Mintage 57,018	1	10	30	50	—
1929H Mintage 79,100		3	8	15	—
7217 Double. Mintage for 1911 is 67,200					
1911H Three leaves above shield		3	10	20	—
7217A — Redesigned shield		2	9	18	—
1914H Mintage 44,800	1	5	15	30	—
1929H Mintage 79,100		2	8	16	—
1933H Mintage 96,000		1	5	10	—

GEORGE VI 1936–1952

BRONZE

Bronze. Types as before

7218 Eight doubles

1938H Mintage 120,000	1	5	10	20	—
1945H Mintage 192,000		1	5	15	—
1947H Mintage 240,000		1	5	15	—
1949H Mintage 230,000		1	5	15	—

		F £	VF £	EF £	UNC £	Proof FDC £
7219	**Four doubles**					
	1945H Mintage 96,000	5	10	15	25	—
	1949H Mintage 19,200	5	10	20	30	—
7220	**Double,** 1938 Mintage 96,000		1	5	15	—

ELIZABETH II 1952–present

CUPRO-NICKEL

7221

7221	**Threepence.** R Guernsey cow				
	1956 Mintage over 500,000	1	5	15	25
	1959 increased weight Mintage 480,000		2	10	15
	1966 Proof only Mintage 10,000				10

Battle of Hastings Commemorative

7223

7223	**Ten shillings,** Bust of William the Conqueror			
	1966 Mintage 300,000	1	5	15

BRONZE

	F	VF	EF	UNC	Proof FDC
	£	£	£	£	£

7225 **Eight doubles.** Guernsey Lily
　　　1956 Mintage 480,000 .... 1　5　10　15
　　　1959 Mintage 480,000 .... 1　5　10　—
　　　1966 Proof only Mintage 10,000 ....　　　　　　　　10

7226

7226 **Four doubles**
　　　1956 Mintage 240,000 .... 1　4　8　15
　　　1966 Proof only Mintage 10,000 ....　　　　　　　　10

PROOF SETS
Issued in official case

	No. of coins in set	FDC £
7320 1956 Double set; Threepence, 8 and 4 doubles	(6)	25
7321 1966 Ten shillings, Threepence, 8 and 4 doubles	(4)	15

ISLE OF MAN

Man is situated in the Irish Sea, and was at one time an independent Viking kingdom, although suzerainty of the island has been claimed at various periods by the kings of Norway, Scotland, and England. In 1406 the island was granted with sovereigns rights to Sir John Stanley, and the Earls of Derby held the island, first as 'Kings' and later as 'Lords' of Man. The island was inherited by James Murray, the second Duke of Atholl in 1736, who sold it to the British Crown in 1765 for the sum of £70,000. Man still has its own parliament, the Tynwald, and passes its own laws.

Irish, Scottish, and English coins circulated freely in the island and although coins from an early 11th century Hiberno-Manx mint are now known, a distinct Manx minor coinage was not introduced until 1709. These pennies and halfpennies were cast in moulds, and have the Earl's motto, SANS CHANGER, together with the Stanley crest; an eagle clutching a child upon the Cap of Maintenance. The reverse of most Manx coins bears the Triune, or 'three legs' with the motto QVOCVNQUE JECERIS STABIT (Whichever way you throw it, it will stand). In 1733 a second issue of coins appeared which were die-struck, and not cast.

The first coins issued under the British Crown were made at the Mint in London in 1786, but the 1798 and 1813 issues were made by Matthew Boulton at the Soho mint, Birmingham, and in style resemble the English 'cartwheels'. In 1840 the older Manx coins were demonetized as until the 1839 coinage, fourteen Manx pennies were equal to the English shilling. The new shilling of twelve pence caused serious rioting. The island's coinage was allowed to lapse until the 200th anniversary of the Revestment of the Manx crown rights to the British Crown which was marked in 1965 by a gold coin set issue. This was followed by the issue of a Crown piece depicting a Manx cat in 1970. A year later, decimal currency was introduced.

HIBERNO-MANX ISSUE c.1025

7400 Penny. Blundered copy of Æthelred II. Legend mostly upright strokes, quatrefoil at beginning of legend and behind head. F. Pellet in each quarter of cross copying Irish coins of the moneyer Feremin of Dublin .... *Extremely rare*

JAMES STANLEY, TENTH EARL OF DERBY

First issue

7401

	F £	VF £	EF £
7401 Penny, 1709, cast. The Stanley crest; eagle and child on cap of maintenance. R. Triskelis (triune)	25	75	250
a — — Struck in brass	45	100	300
b — — Proof in Æ	200	500	750
7402 Halfpenny, 1709, cast. As 7401	40	125	600
a — — — Annulet stops on *rev.*	60	200	1000

Second issue

A. Copper issue

		F £	VF £	EF £
7403	**Penny**, 1733. IDJ between legs	60	150	250
	a — — Proof *EF* £350			
7404	— — IDJ, O's instead of Q's in QVOCVNQVE	75	200	300
7405	**Halfpenny**, 1733. As 7404 (various dies)	60	150	200
	a — — Proof *EF* £350			

B. Bath metal (bronze) issue

		F £	VF £	EF £
7406	**Penny**, 1733. IDJ between legs. Inside of cap plain	75	200	300
	a — — Piedfort	*Extremely rare*		
	b — — Proof in Æ *EF* £350			
7407	— —Pellets replaced by annulets on the legs	75	200	300

7408

		F £	VF £	EF £
7408	— — Similar to 7406, but inside of cap frosted	100	250	400
	a — — Proof *EF* £350			
	b — — Struck in brass	100	250	400
	c — — Proof in Æ *EF* £500			
	d — — Proof in Æ on thin flan *EF* £750			
7409	**Halfpenny**, 1733. As 7406	40	100	200
	a — — Proof in Æ *EF* £300			
7410	— — As 7408	40	100	200
	a — — Struck on thin flan	75	150	300
	b — — Struck in brass	40	100	200
	c — — Proof *EF* £300			
	d — — Proof in Æ *EF* £600			

Note: The copper issue, consisting of £300 in pence and £200 in halfpence were struck by William Wood's successors in either London or Bristol. The Bath metal coins were made at Castletown in 1733/4 from old bronze cannon from Castle Rushen.

JAMES MURRAY, SECOND DUKE OF ATHOLL

7411

		F £	VF £	EF £
7411	**Penny,** 1758. AD monogram surmounted by a ducal coronet	20	75	200
	a — — Proof *EF* £300			
	b — — Proof in silver (two edges) *EF* £800			
	c — — Struck on small flan	100	250	400
7412	**Halfpenny,** 1758. Similar	10	50	150
	a — — Proof *EF* £300			
	b — — Piedfort	100	250	300
	c — — Struck on thin flan	75	200	300

GEORGE III 1760–1820

First issue. London

7413

		F	VF	EF
7413	**Penny,** 1786. Laur. bust r., milled edge	25	100	200
	a — — Similar, pellet below bust	35	175	300
	b — — Proof *FDC* £350			
	c — — Bronzed proof *FDC* £350			
	d — — Plain edge		*Extremely rare*	
	e — — Proof on smaller and thicker flan, high relief *FDC* £500			
7414	**Halfpenny,** 1786. Similar	15	90	200
	a — — Proof *FDC* £300			
	b — — Plain edge, struck on large flan		*Extremely rare*	
	c — — — Proof *FDC* £300			
	d — — — Bronzed proof *FDC* £300			

Second issue. Soho 'Cartwheel' coinage

7415

		F	VF	EF
		£	£	£
7415	**Penny.** Laureate and draped bust r. Milled edge			
	1798	15	75	200
	a — Proof *FDC* £250			
	b — Bronzed proof *FDC* £250			
	c — Gilt proof *FDC* £500			
	d — Proof in Æ £2000			
	1813	15	75	200
	e — Proof *FDC* £250			
	f — Bronzed proof *FDC* £250			
	g — Gilt proof £500			
7416	**Halfpenny.** Similar			
	1798	10	50	125
	a — Proof *FDC* £200			
	b — Bronzed proof *FDC* £200			
	c — Gilt proof £450			
	d — Proof in Æ £2000			
	1813	10	50	125
	e — Proof *FDC* £200			
	f — Bronzed proof *FDC* £200			
	g — Gilt proof £450			

VICTORIA 1837–1901

7417	**Penny,** 1839. Bust l., edge plain	5	30	100
	2839 in error	200		
	a — 1839 Bronzed proof *FDC* £500			
	b — 1841 Bronzed proof *FDC* £1500			
	c — 1859 Bronzed proof *FDC* £3500			

ISLE OF MAN – ELIZABETH II

7418

		F £	VF £	EF £
7418	**Halfpenny,** 1839. Similar	5	20	75
	1839 9 over 8	10	40	125
	a — 1839 Bronzed proof *FDC* £350			
	b — 1841 Bronzed proof *FDC* £1250			
	c — 1860 Bronzed proof *FDC* £2000			
	d — 1860 Bronzed proof with streak of gold *FDC* £3500			
7419	**Farthing,** 1839. Similar	1	15	60
	1839 raised rim	10	25	100
	a — — Bronzed proof *FDC* £300			
	b — — Gilt proof, milled edge		*Extremely rare*	
	c — 1841 Bronzed proof *FDC* £1000			
	d — 1860 Bronzed proof *FDC* £2500			
	e — 1860 Bronzed proof with streak of gold *FDC* £3500			
	f — 1864 with I ww on truncation *FDC* £5000			

ELIZABETH II 1952–present
ROYAL MINT ISSUES
GOLD

Bicentenary issue

7422

		Unc. £	Proof
7420	**Five pounds,** 1965. Legs of Man on shield within wreath	300	400
7421	**One pound,** 1965. Similar	50	60
7422	**Half pound,** 1965. Similar	30	40

CUPRO NICKEL

First Cat crown

7423

		Unc. £
7423	**Crown.** R. Manx cat l., 1970	3
	a — — (*R* Proof in case) *FDC* £4	

SPECIMEN SETS IN OFFICIAL CASES

		No. of coins	*FDC* £
7770	1965 A/ £5, £1, £$\frac{1}{2}$	(3)	500

LUNDY ISLAND

Lundy, an impregnable cliff-girt island in the Bristol Channel, was once noted as a pirate stronghold; today it is a favourite day sea excursion for summer visitors to North Devon. The island has had some celebrated owners, the most recent being Martin Coles Harman, who issued his own stamps and coins in 1929. On being prosecuted for contravention of the 1870 Coinage Act Mr Harman defended his sovereign right to do so before the Devonshire Quarter Sessions on the grounds that Lundy was outside the Realm of England. His appeal to the King's Bench against a fine of £5 was dismissed.

The coins, called 'puffins' and 'half puffins', depict the seabird for which Lundy is famous, and they have around the edge the inscription LUNDY LIGHTS AND LEADS.

MARTIN COLES HARMAN
BRONZE

		EF	Unc.
7850	**Puffin,** 1929	3	10
7851	**Half puffin,** 1929	3	10

Note: Sets of Lundy Island 'coins' manufactured in 1965 are not listed as they were a purely private speculative issue of no numismatic significance.